EMPTINESS

EMPTINESS

A PRACTICAL
GUIDE
for
MEDITATORS

GUY ARMSTRONG

Foreword by JOSEPH GOLDSTEIN

Wisdom

Wisdom Publications
199 Elm Street
Somerville, MA 02144 USA
wisdompubs.org

Library of Congress Cataloging-in-Publication Data
Names: Armstrong, Guy, author.
Title: Emptiness: a practical guide for meditators / Guy Armstrong.
Description: Somerville, MA: Wisdom Publications, 2016. | Includes bibliographical references and index.
Identifiers: LCCN 2016023033 (print) | LCCN 2016025665 (ebook) | ISBN 9781614293637 (hardcover: alk. paper) | ISBN 1614293635 (hardcover: alk. paper) | ISBN 9781614293798 () | ISBN 1614293791 ()
Subjects: LCSH: Sunyata. | Buddhism—Doctrines. | Meditation—Buddhism.
Classification: LCC BQ4275 .A76 2016 (print) | LCC BQ4275 (ebook) | DDC 294.3/42—dc23
LC record available at https://lccn.loc.gov/2016023033

ISBN 978-1-61429-363-7   ebook ISBN 978-1-61429-379-8

21 20 19 18 17   5 4 3 2 1

Cover design by Phil Pascuzzo.
Interior design by Jordan Wannemacher. Set in Diacritical Garamond Pro 10.75/15.

To the teachers who kindly pointed me toward emptiness:
Joseph Goldstein, Tsoknyi Rinpoche, Christopher Titmuss,
and of course Gotama Buddha

You should train yourselves thus: "When those discourses spoken by the Tathāgata that are deep, deep in meaning, supramundane, dealing with emptiness, are being recited, we will be eager to listen to them, will lend an ear to them, will apply our minds to understand them; and we will think those teachings should be studied and mastered." Thus should you train yourselves.

—The Buddha, Samyutta Nikāya 20:7

CONTENTS

FOREWORD

IN THIS REMARKABLE BOOK, Guy Armstrong guides the reader through the foundational realizations necessary to explore the profound truth of emptiness and the increasingly subtle understandings of its deeper meanings.

For thousands of years, different Buddhist schools have highlighted aspects of the path to freedom, each reflecting the liberating insights of its own particular tradition—and from time to time, there have been great masters who have seen what is held in common by many of these schools and woven together paths of practice that integrate elements from each of them. Guy's eminently practical and deeply investigative work follows in this nonsectarian tradition, weaving together teachings from the Pali Canon, the writings of Chinese and Japanese Zen masters, and the great Tibetan lineage-holders. He does this so skillfully that in the very reading of the book we are led to a more comprehensive understanding of the path and the various skillful means needed for its fruition.

What makes this book so user-friendly is its nondogmatic presentation of views. While referencing different points of controversy among the various Buddhist schools, Guy's approach remains pragmatic: How do these teachings help to liberate the mind? With this wonderfully clear book he invites us to consider and practice different approaches, all of which lead to our own deepening and freeing realization of the nature of awareness and its intrinsic emptiness—and to the manifestation of compassion in our lives.

Joseph Goldstein

PREFACE

I'VE ALWAYS LIKED A GOOD MYSTERY. From Sherlock Holmes to John le Carré, I've been fascinated by the idea that there's more going on than meets the eye. In college I majored in physics, because I loved the way science reveals things that are hidden from ordinary view. In grad school I studied computers to find out how machines could do such amazing things. Psychology was always an interest, because the mind, too, is a vast, unknown land. In all these disciplines, I discovered that close observation, pointed questions, and sustained reflection were the keys to unlock the gates.

When I stumbled onto Buddhism, I was delighted to find a whole new set of mysteries to explore. From the age of twenty-eight, I began to dedicate my life to learning what I could from teachers and meditation, including a year in Asia as a Buddhist monk. Many of the teachings I encountered made good common sense, and I was grateful for their emphasis on wise choices in speech and action. Meditation was a marvel that brought me a measure of calm, but my conceptual mind was most intrigued by things I couldn't quite understand, like not-self, enlightenment, nirvana, and emptiness. It seemed that comprehending these subjects must be necessary to realize the path of transformation and freedom, but however much I thought about them in the beginning, I couldn't penetrate them. Still, the glimmerings of these mysteries inspired me, and I was determined to explore them further. After some years, I began to teach what I had learned, primarily through leading silent retreats in the Insight meditation tradition.

The word *mysteries* has long had religious connotations. In both ancient and modern cultures, there have always been priests and priestesses, nuns, monks, and shamans seeking to learn from the mysteries and thereby shift their relationship to themselves and others, to life and to death. This book is intended for those today who are drawn to these subtle realms. Emptiness is the theme, as it is a core teaching closely connected to the other mysteries. For the truth of emptiness to reveal itself fully in our hearts and minds will require inquiry and reflection, as well as a deep intuition born from meditation, which is is simply another name we give to close observation. In truth the keys that unlock the mysteries of science also unlock the mysteries of spirit.

For two and a half millennia, Buddhist practitioners have explored emptiness and found the highest levels of happiness and freedom. This book is offered in the hope that it might encourage a few more people to take a few more steps along this sacred path.

INTRODUCTION

> When emptiness is possible, everything is possible.
> Were emptiness impossible, nothing would be possible.
> —Nāgārjuna[1]

EMPTINESS IS AN ODD TERM for the central philosophy of a world religion. It certainly lacks the emotional appeal of Hinduism's bliss and devotion, for instance, or Christianity's love and charity. It is not a word designed to attract newcomers. More than just austere, it sounds a little off-putting. Who would gravitate to a way of life based on what sounds like nothingness?

In fact, the insights pointed to by emptiness are deeply liberating and bring great happiness. They transform how we understand ourselves and life in profound ways. Many of those who have practiced the Buddha's teaching on emptiness regard it as the greatest gift he offered the world. Nonetheless, it is not an easy subject to approach.

When I first became interested in the concept of emptiness in Buddhism, I read a hefty volume with a respectable pedigree that defined emptiness as "the lack of inherent self-existence." I didn't doubt the author, but that definition didn't mean much to me at the time. Other works couch emptiness in terms of dependent origination, which is also intellectually challenging. The fact that so many books have been written about emptiness points to both the richness and the complexity of the subject.

Mingyur Rinpoche is a bright young Tibetan lama who, not too long ago, returned from a four-year personal retreat wandering the Himalayas. On his first visit to California in 1998, I had a chance to visit with him and show him around Marin County. As we drove I tried to strike up a conversation. "How do you find the West?" I asked. "Square and clean," was his reply. "Do you think Tibetans are happier than Westerners?" "Yes." End of conversation.

We reached our destination at the top of Mount Tamalpais and were walking along the trail around the summit, an asphalt track about six feet wide, when I thought I'd try again. "What is the difference between the Dzogchen view and the Madhyamaka view?" I asked, referring to two schools in Tibet that are considered to have different understandings of the nature of reality.

"Ah!" he said, now interested. "To understand that, you have to understand that there are eighteen different kinds of emptiness!" He sat down on the path right where we were and talked animatedly about the two views, concluding by saying something to the effect that the Madhyamikas think that the Dzogchenpas believe that something exists that doesn't actually exist, but that actually the Dzogchenpas don't believe that. Or something like that. The eighteen different kinds of emptiness went by quickly, but in any case it was a delight to listen to the young rinpoche.

I wondered at first if our word *emptiness* was a weak translation of some lofty ideal that had many rich overtones in the original ancient dialect, but that turned out not to be the case. In Pali, the Indian language in which the earliest teachings of the Buddha are preserved, the root word is *suñña*. (Please see the glossary for the pronunciation of non-English terms.) The Sanskrit is *shūnya*. Both words literally mean "empty." A line of advice frequently given by the Buddha to his disciples was, "There are these roots of trees, there are these empty huts. Meditate now, lest you regret it later." The word for "empty" here is *suñña*. As in English, it becomes a noun by adding a suffix: *suññatā* (Skt: *shūnyatā*), giving us "emptiness," the quality of being empty.

Over many years the word *emptiness* has taken on a number of meanings in Buddhism. The quality of something being empty is perhaps the simplest meaning. It is helpful to remember that when a noun is derived from an adjective, as *emptiness* is derived from *empty*, it doesn't mean that the noun refers to something that exists independently as an object on its own. It only means the noun is denoting the quality pointed to by that adjective. Just as it is not possible to find wetness apart from something that is wet, we don't expect to find emptiness as a thing that exists on its own. We could also talk about the roundness of a snow globe or of a pregnant woman's belly, but we are only saying that the objects are round. Emptiness here just means the quality of something being empty, like a jar, a desert, or the sky. With this meaning, *emptiness* functions, in a certain way, more like an adjective.

What might be understood as empty and what is it empty of? Let us begin by asking what it means to be a human being. Most people imagine that individual human experience revolves around a self, a notion that appears in our language through the terms *I, me, my,* and *mine.* Prior to careful investigation, we assume that the term *I* refers to an entity that can be found. The Buddha, however, discerned that our human experience is empty of a self. This is the liberating teaching of *not-self.* In this example, emptiness is more or less synonymous with the absence of a "self." This was one of the early meanings of emptiness in Buddhism.

Later Buddhist schools used the term *emptiness* to emphasize the lack of substance in the world. Just as twentieth-century quantum physicists exposed the lack of solidity in matter, the Buddha and his followers perceived this directly through meditation nearly 2,500 years earlier. This lack of substance is pointed to in the earliest Buddhist teachings and was explored more fully in succeeding centuries.

Another early usage of the word *emptiness* refers to a refined meditative state in which perception is greatly simplified. In a usual moment of experience, the many objects we perceive—sights, sounds, smells, tastes, sensations, and images—lead to thoughts and feelings about them. We hear a person's voice and imagine she is talking about us. We see a treasured possession and dwell on how it came to us. When perception is simplified so that we simply notice, for example, sound or sight, we are able to be present in a balanced and peaceful way. The full development of this approach was described by the Buddha as "abiding in emptiness."

A more colloquial use of the word *emptiness* evolved that points to the quality of mind when we are in touch with the present moment and not preoccupied with wants, needs, or issues of past or future. This mind is said to be empty in that it is not filled with extraneous thinking. Such a mind is attuned to the present with openness and receptivity. An empty mind moves easily to joy and contentment and moves slowly to reactive emotions like fear and anger. We might understand this as a less refined, everyday example of "abiding in emptiness."

There is a common misunderstanding about emptiness that I would like to dispel as we begin. Emptiness does *not* mean vacancy, nothingness, or the absence of conscious experience. As we've seen, emptiness is a property or characteristic of things that appear in the world. It is found within our human, conscious experience. There is a subtle meditative state called "the base of nothingness," which denotes an absence of sense contact. It is a significant achievement in concentration, but it does not bear in a central way on the meaning of *emptiness* as presented here. For the purposes of this book, emptiness is primarily understood as a property of things that appear in our world. Understanding emptiness brings freedom to our experience as we live consciously in the world.

Notwithstanding these definitions of emptiness or the eighteen kinds that Mingyur Rinpoche pointed to, we might say, simply, that emptiness means that the things of this world, including me, are not truly solid or substantial. In the beginning we are mostly unaware of the solidity we attribute to our self and the rest of the world, so even this description requires investigation. In fact all the definitions of emptiness have broad implications, because they go against fundamental assumptions we have of ourselves and the world, assumptions so pervasive and unexamined that we hardly know they are assumptions at all. Here is a brief summation of some of these implications.

We hold on tightly to things in an attempt to find security, but because the world is always in flux, this effort is ultimately unsuccessful. The thing we've clung to changes, and the clinging to what no longer is becomes a source of frustration and insecurity. Clearly seeing the fact of impermanence undermines our tendency to hold on, because we recognize that things will inevitably change. As we get older, for example, if we continue to wish that our bodies would stay as they were when we were twenty, we will suffer with every new wrinkle and pound. When we understand that change is inherent in the nature of the physical body, we can be much more graceful in accepting the aging process.

Seeing emptiness acknowledges this and takes it a step further. We also see that there was nothing solid to hold on to in the first place. It is not actually possible to cling to reality, because change is so rapid and universal that a grasp-able *thing* cannot be found anywhere. All that we can cling to is the memory of something fleeting. We understand, for example, that aging is going on in our bodies even at the cellular level. If cells are constantly dying and being recreated, how can our skin be expected to be constant for even one year? Moreover, within most cells, rapid chemical interactions are constant, as mitochondria burn the nutrients delivered to them. These bodily processes cannot be stopped or frozen even for a second.

When we see that this is true in every facet of life, it changes us deeply. We become less bound to the past and able to live more in the present. The heart can let go of what it has tried to store up. This shift comes as a great relief. We feel lighter, freer, and happier.

We explore emptiness not to construct another ideology but to bring greater freedom and contentment into our lives. The aim of all the Buddha's teachings is to convey a path out of suffering in all its many forms and into the greatest possible freedom, which he called nibbāna. The Buddhist path is different for each person, but there is a common trajectory for most of us, a series of steps in the seeing of emptiness and an accompanying series of releases. It is these insights and the resultant freedom that I do my best to describe in this book.

ABOUT THIS BOOK

One could talk about emptiness in a way that is highly philosophical and analytical. Instead, this book aims to be introductory and practical in nature, inviting you to discover the truth of emptiness in your direct experience. I offer pragmatic approaches that I have found helpful for myself and for students I've worked with in thirty years of teaching Buddhist meditation.

The book is divided into four major parts: Self, Phenomena, Awareness, and Compassion. Each part explores a key area of the implications of emptiness. Those familiar with the history of Buddhism may recognize that the first three sections parallel the evolution of Buddhist thought in India.

Buddhism began with Gotama Buddha's awakening and first teachings (ca. 445 B.C.E.) and the formation of the original Sangha (community of practitioners). After the Buddha's death (ca. 400 B.C.E.) some philosophical disagreements emerged, and over the next few hundred years, the Sangha splintered into about eighteen schools, including the modern tradition we know as Theravada, "the way of the elders." I will refer to these eighteen as the schools of Early Buddhism. Despite their differences, the eighteen schools all agreed on the central teachings of the historical Buddha, which emphasized the emptiness of our conditioned notion of self.

The Mahayana ("great vehicle") schools emerged around 100 B.C.E.–250 C.E. based primarily on the Perfection of Wisdom texts (Skt: *Prajñāpāramitā Sutras*) and the works of a teacher named Nāgārjuna. The teachings of these schools emphasized the emptiness of all phenomena, that is, the emptiness of objects as well as of self.

The Yogācāra ("practice of yoga") school, a branch of the Mahayana founded about 350 C.E., looked closely into the nature of awareness itself and found that it too was characterized by emptiness. This understanding became the basis for many later schools of meditation.

The first three sections of the book correspond to the emphases of those three schools. The fourth section of the book, Compassion, is relevant for all Buddhist schools—and indeed to anyone looking to live a life guided by kindness and wisdom.

SUPPORTIVE TOOLS AND PRACTICES

The Buddha's teachings are called the Dharma, a term that means "truth" or "law" or "the way things are." Traditionally there are three avenues to learning the Dharma based on what activity the understanding springs from.[2] These three avenues generally have differing degrees of power in their ability to transform us.

1. *Understanding from hearing.* This learning comes from hearing someone talk about the way things are or, in the modern day, reading about it. This gives us new information and leads to a certain kind of conceptual knowledge, but its effect is usually limited.
2. *Understanding from reflection.* We deliberately consider and think about the new information to see how it might apply to our own life and expe-

rience. We are still in the thinking realm, but we're reflecting under our own guidance in a way that feels new and direct. We might say that the first two avenues fall under the approach of rational inquiry.

3. *Understanding from meditative insight.* This way of learning occurs through the arising of an intuition that reveals a new way of seeing the world. While meditative insight will eventually express itself in words, it first emerges as a flash of pure seeing. Insight is essentially nonconceptual and has the greatest power to transform us. The primary style of meditation taught in classical Buddhism is called insight meditation (Pali: *vipassanā*) because of its emphasis on this third kind of understanding. Meditative insight can't be willed, ordered, forced, or commanded. It blazes forth when the conditions are right. An essential part of conditions being right is that we have previously seeded the ground with the two avenues of rational inquiry: hearing (or reading) and reflection. Meditation then adds the qualities of stillness and presence, which lead to fresh and creative ways of understanding. When the time is right, insight arises as this third kind of learning.

In a public talk a few years ago the Dalai Lama explained succinctly how these three avenues work together. He quoted an old Tibetan master talking about his own practice: "When I meditate, I bring to bear my study and critical reflection. When I study, I bring to bear my meditation and critical reflection. When I reflect, I bring to bear my study and meditation."[3]

We need all three avenues of learning to fully understand the truth of emptiness. This book can itself be a source for study, and I will also recommend other readings. In these pages you will find some reflections to carry out on your own. You will probably form your own ideas and questions to consider further. Reflection will greatly strengthen your confidence in your understanding and lead onward to insight.

Some of the explorations in the book will be most accessible to those who already have a Buddhist meditation practice. We encourage you to take up a meditation practice, if you haven't already, that will foster the kind of intuitive realizations that can most deeply free the heart and mind. Simple meditation exercises suitable for new meditators are included in this book, but because this is not primarily a meditation guide, we recommend that you find either a teacher who can provide detailed guidance or a book specifically about meditation practice.[4]

The inquiry into emptiness is not a one-day or one-week adventure. Most of us find that new understandings keep coming over a lifetime of study, reflection, and meditation. With them comes an ever-growing sense of freedom and ease in life, as well as more heartfelt connections with other people, creatures, and physical nature. The entire process, which we might describe as the awakening of wisdom, is possible only because of the vast, inherent richness of your heart and mind. If you sincerely want to understand, and you pose the right questions in a sustained way, the mind with its profound intuitive powers will respond with wisdom and insight. The keys that unlock the mysteries are observation, inquiry, and reflection.

A NOTE ON SOURCES

Among the eighteen schools of Early Buddhism, each had its own canon of texts that included monastic rules, discourses of the Buddha, and a psychological schema. From all these schools only one entire canon has survived to the present day, that of the Theravada School. It has come down to us in Pali, a language of ancient India similar to Sanskrit. Much of the Pali Canon is purported to be the authentic words of Gotama Buddha from almost 2,500 years ago. While this is impossible to verify, recent work comparing these texts with fragments of other canons found in China and Tibet support the view that the Pali Canon does include the essential components of the Buddha's teachings from his lifetime.

In this book I will use the texts of the Pali Canon for quotations attributed to the Buddha. When a phrase appears here such as, "the Buddha said," it means that such a statement can be found in the Pali Canon as representing the words of Gotama Buddha. While errors have certainly crept into these texts over the years, I take the discourses (Pali: *suttas*) of the Pali Canon to be as complete and reliable a guide to the teachings of the historical Buddha as can be found today.

In Mahayana texts like the *Prajñāpāramitā Sutras*, statements are often presented as having been spoken by the Buddha himself during his lifetime. Many of these statements represent deep spiritual wisdom. As to their authorship, however, I follow Edward Conze, a scholar who translated many of these texts into English, in his assertion that the Mahayana texts were created by other authors hundreds of years after the Buddha's death.[5] The consensus among Western scholars agrees with this assessment. Conze suggests that the words were put into the mouth of the Buddha to give the later texts the same authenticity as the original discourses.

Similarly, it is clear that Nāgārjuna's works and the key texts of the Yogacarins were created long after the Buddha's time. This does not make them any less powerful or diminish their value for the sincere practitioner, but it can be helpful to recall that they are not the actual words of Gotama Buddha.

A NOTE ON TERMS

The ancient languages of Pali and Sanskrit were very precise in their descriptions of the human mind and meditative experience, much more so than English is today. Western culture unfortunately has little understanding of many of the states that the Buddha was pointing to. We can expect that over decades some of the ancient words will migrate into English, as they have into modern Thai and Burmese—though we are not there yet (notwithstanding a perfume named Samsara, and the like).

Good translations are helping us read more accurately in English what the Buddha meant. I will generally try to use a single English word throughout this work to translate a single Pali word so that we can develop a more precise English vocabulary for these teachings. Unfortunately, sometimes the full meaning of a Pali word cannot be adequately conveyed by one English word. For example, the Pali term *dukkha* is usually translated as "suffering," but it actually indicates the entire range of the uncomfortable experiences in life, from intense suffering to pervasive insecurity to mild discontent. Other English words bring in connotations that are not present in the original Pali term and so can be misleading for English speakers. For example, "concentration" is the generally accepted translation of the Pali *samādhi*. However, concentration connotes an exclusive focus of attention, a sense that is not present in *samādhi*. An English speaker who wishes to understand the Dharma will still benefit from learning some of the classical terms.

When a Pali word is used in this book, it will generally be in italics and will also appear in the glossary, where its pronunciation will be indicated. As for diacritical marks, which are key to the correct spelling for scholars, we will follow a middle path. For Pali or Sanskrit words that have passed into or are passing into English (e.g., Theravada, Mahayana, nirvana, samsara, and the word Pali itself), we will not use diacritical marks at all or treat them in italics. For words that are not widely used in English, we will preserve the diacritical marks (such as those that indicate a long vowel) that an English speaker will need to pronounce the word in a more or less acceptable manner, but otherwise phoneticize those words. For example, while the word for "emptiness" in Sanskrit with full diacritical marks is *śūnyatā*, for ease of pronunciation by a general reader, we will be rendering this as *shūnyatā*.

PART I:

SELF

1. THE WORLD IS EMPTY OF SELF

All yogas have only one aim: to save you from the calamity of separate existence.

—Sri Nisargadatta Maharaj[1]

WE LIVE IN AN AGE when concern for the self has risen to unprecedented levels. Families and communities are disintegrating, and with them go our nearest opportunities for generosity and service. The social contract to care for one another is under attack. The planet's environmental health is in crisis, while many remain oblivious or indifferent. Materialism is widely honored and rampant. Compromise is becoming a distant memory. In our culture now it sometimes seems that all that matters is *me: my* wants, pleasures, needs, opinions, and rights.

Excessive self-concern is, of course, not a new phenomenon. It has always been a destructive aspect of human nature. But social structures that once limited its expression are now breaking down, and we are left more and more to face the naked manifestation of this force. There was once a time when no one would have dared to say, "Greed is good," but now this expression is seen as little more than the frank admission of a common ethic.

Buddhism views excessive self-centeredness as the primary source of suffering, causing us to act in ways that harm ourselves and others, from infidelity and dishonesty to murder, terrorism, and war. The habit of self-concern creates pain in our closest relationships, gives rise to greed and hatred, and torments our hearts on a daily basis. There is no way to a true and lasting happiness without seeing into and eventually overcoming this force.

Fortunately Buddhism doesn't stop with the diagnosis. It offers a radical therapy for overcoming self-centeredness by questioning the very idea of a self. Throughout his teaching career, the Buddha returned to this point again and again. He said that in our obsession with self, we are like a barking dog tied to a post, running endlessly and fruitlessly around a single point,[2] yet we fundamentally misunderstand what it is. "In whatever way they conceive of self," he said, "the fact is ever other than that."[3]

THE LANGUAGE OF SELF AND NOT-SELF

As we've seen, the self is designated by words like *I*, *me*, and *mine*. This sense of self, or "I," seems unmistakably real, yet when we look for it directly, it is elusive. William James said, "When I search for my self, all I can find is a funny feeling at the back of my throat." The Dalai Lama said that when something seems clear to us but we can't find it, that is a sure sign of delusion. The self is not real in the ways we take it to be.

The Buddha was asked by his cousin and longtime attendant, Ānanda, "Venerable sir, it is said, 'Empty is the world, empty is the world.' In what way is it said, 'Empty is the world'?" The Buddha replied, "It is, Ānanda, because it is empty of self and of what belongs to self that it is said, 'Empty is the world.'"[4]

The world is empty of self. Sometimes this is explained as the Buddhist teaching of no-self. Yet it seems inarguable that someone has written these words and someone else is reading them! What is the meaning of the puzzling assertion of no-self? This is the question I'll try to answer in part 1 of this book. To the extent that we can intuit the absence of a self, as opposed to merely believing in it as a doctrine, we will understand a key aspect of emptiness. The two understandings—(1) the absence of self and (2) emptiness—are mostly used synonymously in this part of the book.

THE CONVENTIONS OF "I" AND "MINE"

As we explore the assertion that the world is empty of self, we need to distinguish between our everyday use of the words *I* and *mine* and the reality these words point to. The Buddha did not tell us never to say these words in any type of conversation. He said that a wise person can use these terms without being confused by them.[5] Our speech would sound absurd if we did not use the words *I* or *mine* out of a fear of being "dharmically incorrect." We'd have to resort to cumbersome expressions like "the speaker" or "the one standing here."

It's fine to say "I" and "mine," "you" and "yours," as long you understand that these terms are merely *conventions* of our social contract that identify where an activity is taking place or where ownership is assigned. With these useful conventions, you end up in your home and I end up in mine, after driving our respective cars. Life would be too chaotic without these conventions and the language we use to communicate about them.

Similarly, there is a conventional manner in which we can talk about an individual having a unique way of being that we might call an identity. We all have characteristics of height, weight, age, ethnicity, gender identity, sexual orientation, and personality that allow us to describe ourselves in meaningful and authentic ways. The teaching on the absence of self does not take away or disregard these useful forms of description. But it does point to the need not to stop at the conventional description and take it as an ultimate truth—because doing *that* will lead to suffering.

The problem arises when we take conventional language to mean more than it can. By repeating "I" and "mine," and describing ourselves as being a certain way, we've come to believe that something real is being pointed to that isn't actually there. Buddhist practice helps us free ourselves from this delusion and see things as they actually are. In the process we find a more expansive and generous way to relate with the world.

NO-SELF VERSUS NOT-SELF

There is a debate in the Western Buddhist world on how to translate this key teaching on the absence of self. Some teachers call it "no-self" and others call it "not-self." The Pali term is *anattā* and could be translated either way: *attā* means "self" and the prefix *an-* is a negation. Those who translate it as "no-self" say this is a pithy expression that directly points to the insight that the world is empty of self, that no self can found anywhere. Those who call it "not-self" are fond of saying (and as far as I know, this is true) that there is no passage in the Pali Canon in which the Buddha categorically states, "There is no self." They quote a particular discourse in which the Buddha is asked by a wanderer from another sect whether there is a self or not, and he refuses to answer. The reason he later gives for his silence is tied to a subtle philosophical principle in vogue in his day.[6]

I think these points are interesting but not terribly significant. Philosophically, saying "the world is empty of self" is a clear statement of absence, and so I believe the translation "no-self" is a valid interpretation. However, the most compelling argument for using "not-self," I find, is that it shifts the discussion from a philosophical position ("There is no self") to a point-by-point investigation of one's direct experience ("The body is not the self"). A philosophical position can be taken as something we *ought* to believe, and if we don't we're not good Buddhists.

Buddhism is not particularly concerned with beliefs, because beliefs don't liberate us. The Buddha was interested in having us develop *understanding* to lead us out of suffering. When we consider statements such as "The body is not self" or "Anger is not self," we have specific objects to contrast with what we take a true self to be. That is why I find the "not-self" language more inviting and provocative, and I will use this translation most of the time in this book.

Our misunderstandings around the nature of the self are reflected in and also conditioned by the way we use language. In this section we'll look at some of the ways we use the words *I* and *my* in English that don't make logical sense. We'll also explore what is considered real in Buddhism so that we have a reliable foundation for investigation, and we'll see how the sense of self gets constructed again and again out of these foundational building blocks. We will see why the Buddha said that we don't need to see these basic realities as self and what our experience might be if we stop doing that. When we know for ourselves the emptiness of self that the Buddha pointed to, we will be in accord with the old Sri Lankan monk who said, with great amusement, "No self, no problem!"

MEDITATION

Mindfulness of Breathing

Here I'll begin to introduce some simple meditation exercises that can help clarify key points in the text. Most of these meditations involve mindfulness, an important factor of mind that we might define simply as "knowing what your experience is in the present moment." This first exercise focuses on the experience of breathing.

- Sit quietly on a cushion on the floor or in a chair. Keep your back fairly straight but not rigid, so you feel alert but also relaxed. Let your hands rest in your lap or on your thighs. Gently close your eyes.
- Feel your body in this sitting posture. You know that this is your experience of sitting in the present moment, so we can call this "mindfulness of body posture."
- As you feel your body, pay attention to what happens when you breathe in. Just feel the body as an in-breath enters. Now pay attention to what happens when you breathe out. Feel the body as the out-breath exits.
- Continue to feel the body as you notice each in-breath and out-breath. If your attention wanders off into a train of thoughts, don't worry. When you notice that has happened, gently return the attention to connect with the next in-breath or out-breath. Continue paying full attention to breathing as you feel it in the body. This is called "mindfulness of breathing."

2. THE FAULTY LOGIC OF "I"

*Of course the bird we see and hear exists. It exists, but what I mean
by that may not be exactly what you mean.*
—Shunryu Suzuki Roshi[1]

WESTERN CULTURE DOES NOT GENERALLY QUESTION the substantial
nature of the self. The self seems self-evident (as it were) and inarguable. We may
find it absurd when someone suggests that perhaps the self doesn't exist: there are
trees, there are birds, there are people, and there is me.

Buddhism is not disputing the basic reality of the existence of different
objects or beings—but there is more subtlety to this question than we may at
first realize. In fact significant problems arise if we take at face value the existence
of "I" as suggested by our culture. Let us explore what we mean when we use this
word "I."

SELF-IDENTIFICATION

Suppose I were to ask, "How old are you?" You might answer promptly, "I'm
thirty-seven," or whatever. Then let me ask, "What color are your eyes?" And
again the answer comes easily, "My eyes are blue," or brown or green. The answers

arise naturally and immediately. But if we look at each of these responses in detail, we discover something odd. If you say, "I'm thirty-seven," you really mean this body is thirty-seven years old—don't you? You don't necessarily mean that *all* of you is thirty-seven. Are your thoughts that old? What is the age of the mood you're feeling right now? Perhaps it came on today, an hour ago. So when we say, "I'm thirty-seven," "I" is taken to be the body. This tendency to equate oneself with an aspect of our experience is called *identification*—in this case, identification with the body.

When you say, "My eyes are blue," however, the "I" is not the body ("eyes") but the owner of the body: *"my* eyes." "I" as owner is a different form of identification. Feel into the sense of "I" as the owner of the body—"it's *my* body"—and inquire, "Where is that owner located?" Are you able to pin down an owner? Is the owner inside the body or outside? Is the owner all the space inside? These are some of the questions the Buddha pointed to 2,500 years ago. Which are you really—the body or something separate that somehow *owns* the body? These are two different things. Is it possible to be both?

We can find the same confusion around the mind. If you say, "I am happy," you are equating "I" with happiness, an emotion or a state or mind. A minute later you might talk about "my joys and my sorrows." Now you are the *owner* of the emotions. These are two more ways to self-identify. Are you the emotion or are you its owner? Can you be both?

"I" AS THE OBSERVER

There is one more place the "I" lays claim. "I" is sometimes felt as the observer of the whole show. It can feel as though there's a small entity located inside the head, a couple inches behind the eyes. This being is the center of everything; it watches sights, hears sounds, smells odors, thinks thoughts, and feels emotions. This "I" seems to stay the same over time through many changing experiences. It appears to accomplish this by remaining separate from what is observed. It feels as though this observing "I" was with us in grade school, is here today, and will be a couple of inches behind our eyes until we die.

The identification here as the observer is, in reality, taking as "I" the activity of consciousness, the faculty of mind that receives or knows the sense impressions that arise moment after moment. Consciousness may feel like a permanent, stable aspect of our experience, but the Buddha said that consciousness arises and passes with each new sense impression and that we can verify this through meditative insight. We will return to this type of identification later—because it is perhaps the most difficult to see through. For now we'll simply note it as another way the "I" is equated with an aspect of experience.

We've now found five meanings for "I"—as the body, the owner of the body, the emotions, the owner of the emotions, and the observer. Which are you, really? You might reply, "I'm all of them. I'm my body, and it belongs to me. I'm my thoughts and feelings, and they belong to me. And I'm something apart from them, watching it all. I'm everything you've said all wrapped up in one."

QUESTIONING THE LOGIC OF "I"

We've now arrived at the conventional understanding of the self. In this culture, when we talk about what "I" am, it's this whole package. This is what we mean by "a person," and it's what we mean by "I." We've now arrived at a place where, upon looking closely, the absurdity of conventional understanding becomes apparent.

How many selves are you? Are you a self as the organ of your liver and also as the emotion of compassion? Are these the same "I" or different? Are you a self as your political view and also as the consciousness that hears a birdcall? Are these the same "I" or different? Are you a self who is changing every moment, as the body does with its pulses, respiration, and digestion; or are you an ongoing self who is the stable observer of the changes? Are these the same "I" or different?

When we look into these questions what we find are little more than collisions of unexamined language habits around "I" and "my." One is reminded of the famous comment by Ludwig Wittgenstein that the self is only a shadow cast by grammar. We have found these terms useful to distinguish one person from another in social dialogue and to establish social guidelines around possessions. But by not examining the terms closely, we have stretched the idea of self so far that it does not actually make sense.

Just consider the sense we have that the body is me. I cross paths now and then with a friend at the gym who is also a meditator. One day he told me that he'd recently had an outpatient procedure at a clinic. He was fascinated by being able to watch his heart on an ultrasound monitor during the procedure and surprised to see his own heart beating in a perfect, steady rhythm.

At that moment he had one of those realizations that sometimes come in times of great openness. He said he looked at that beating heart and knew for a fact, "That's not me!" He'd had nothing to do with creating it or making it act like that. It was a part of the body simply doing its own work according to its own ways. The feeling he described on seeing this was a combination of excitement and relief.

It is not a problem to adopt a social convention that says that we will use the terms *I* and *my* when we speak to one another in order to distinguish where an experience is taking place. But it becomes problematic when we are lulled into the belief that these terms actually refer to some real thing that exists.

THE FLAWED ASSUMPTIONS OF "I"

The belief in a self carries with it four flawed assumptions that we have adopted unconsciously: continuity, independence, control, and singleness.

CONTINUITY

Continuity means that we take the self to be an entity that continues over time in some unchanging way through a multitude of changing experiences. We imagine the "I" wakes up each morning, eats breakfast, goes to work, comes home, eats dinner, and then goes to sleep. This "I" was born from our mother's womb and at some point will die from illness or injury.

Because we cherish the self, we find it frightening to consider that it will end at death. The anxiety we feel around our mortality is sometimes mild (if we are young and healthy) and sometimes acute (if we are old or ill—or Woody Allen). The assumption of continuity necessarily leads to the fear of death and thus involves some degree of suffering.

Of course there is some kind of continuity when a being exists over a span of years, but when we look closely, can we find a single thing that endures? In our belief, the self should be that thing, but locating such an entity is not easy.

INDEPENDENCE

When I referred earlier to the sense of "I" as observer, I noted that the observer seems to be lodged behind the eyes and feels separate from experiences that are being observed: "I" am seeing, "I" am hearing, and so on. This may begin when we are young as simply the way English grammar works, but when we tell stories like this for twenty or thirty years, it comes to represent reality for us and not just a convention of language.

My first year meditating, I practiced a kind of insight meditation based on a body scan. In this approach one systematically moves the attention through every area of the body, focusing for a while on each part and simply feeling without judgment the sensations (or absence of sensations) that are present. I sometimes engaged in this practice for ten hours a day several weeks at a time. I had ample time to investigate the details of every nook and cranny of the body, and I never found an observer anywhere. Later meditations showed that there is no such center to our experience. This "observer" is only a concept, an assumption not borne out in reality. There is no "I" standing apart from our experiences.

J. Krishnamurti, the Indian philosopher and sage of the last century, was fond of saying, "The observer *is* the observed."[2] This can be interpreted in a few ways, not all of which are accurate, so for our purposes I might paraphrase it as, "The observer does not exist apart from the observed," or "While observing, the observer is made up in part by that which is observed." When we are observing anger, we are, at least in part, that anger. When we are observing love, we are that love. What is in our experience is in us. We do not stand apart from the experience.

When we think that what we really are is separate from what we experience, we create an auxiliary entity that doesn't exist. We have to keep creating this "I" over and over to sustain the fiction of its reality. This requires constant effort that prevents the heart and mind from ever fully relaxing. Moreover, the identification with this entity that stands apart leads to a detached relationship with our experience that prevents us from feeling fully alive.

CONTROL

We believe that the self can exert a considerable degree of control over at least this body and mind, and we sometimes wish that the control could extend to others and the world. Many of the tantrums of a two-year-old are due to the frustration of this attempt to control the world. Our tantrums as adults are not so different.

Sometimes illness is felt as a great insult, because we see that we are not able to control even our own body. The Buddha was once challenged in debate by Saccaka, a follower of Jainism who vowed to refute the teaching of not-self. In reply the Buddha asked Saccaka if his body (here called material form) was under his control: "When you say thus: 'Material form is my self,' do you exercise any such power over that material form as to say, 'Let my form be thus; let my form not be thus?'"[3] When Saccaka would not answer, so the story goes, a spirit appeared above him holding a thunderbolt, ready to split the Jain's head in two. Saccaka finally agreed that he could not control his body and so could not actually regard it as his self. His head was spared.

We can discover this same lack of control any time we feel embarrassed about our body. How often have we felt ashamed that we aren't better looking or taller or finer boned or more athletic? Yet all these characteristics are beyond our choice or control. If we take responsibility for them, we have fallen under the false belief of controllability. This element of control also explains why for many people, the hardest place to accept the truth of not-self is in the area of volition or decision making. Surely if a decision is being made, we reason, there must be a decider, a controlling agent or entity.

SINGLENESS

The fourth assumption behind the notion of a self is that it is a single, unitary thing—not plural or manifold. Generally speaking, each of us feels that we are one person, not two or three or more. Those who believe otherwise are quickly medicated. Moreover, we believe this one person is unique in the world, perhaps in the whole universe.

When we take ourselves to be the body, the owner of the body, the mind, the owner of the mind, and the observer, we are trying to be many different things: eye, consciousness, liver, compassion, toenail, thoughts, anger. This might be all right if we feel that we are constantly coming and going, as all these things do by their nature of impermanence. But we combine the belief in singleness with the assumption of continuity. Is there an object that meets both these criteria?

APPLYING THE ASSUMPTIONS
TO OUR EXPERIENCE

Earlier I described six ways we can identify with parts of our experience: as the body, owner of the body, emotions, owner of the emotions, observer, or all of these. We must now ask if these six ways align with the four assumptions about the self: continuity, independence, control, and singleness. If a way of identification with our experience is not in alignment with an assumption about the self, then we cannot accept it as a valid definition of the self.

The body might appear to continue, but close inspection reveals constant change, aging, and eventual death and decay. It lacks independence, as it is built from air, food, and water. It is clearly out of our control, as even Saccaka attested. And it is not a single thing but a collection of manifold, quite dissimilar parts.

Emotions have even less continuity than the body, often changing by the hour. They generally arise in response to the immediate situation or a memory, so they are not wholly independent phenomena. Most of us are vulnerable to fear, anger, and jealousy, and so cannot control our emotions. Many different emotions come and go, so there is no singleness here.

The owner of the body, the owner of the emotions, and the observer cannot be clearly found, thus violating the assumption of stable continuity. Nor is the supposed owner or observer able to exert the desired control of experience. The owner or observer may feel to be independent and single, but if they cannot be located, we have to conclude that there is no owner or observer there.

The self as the assemblage of all the aspects of body, mind, owner, and observer is the notion most of us carry, but it fails all the assumptions: the assemblage changes moment by moment, is dependent because it is affected by outside conditions, is not in our control, and is not unitary but many different things.

Through this analysis we see that all our usual ways of identifying—of defining the "I"—don't quite make sense. How is it then that we keep having such a firm sense that this "I" is real? To see how this happens, we can start by looking close to home, in our direct moment-to-moment experience of body and mind. This examination takes us into the territory of meditation, so we will continue with simple instructions on mindfulness of body sensations and emotions.

MEDITATION

Mindfulness of Sensations

Begin by following the instructions in chapter 1 for mindfulness of breathing. Once you have connected to the experience of breathing in and out, then move your attention to notice other sensations in the body. For example, you might notice the touch of your palms against each other or your clothes, or the pressure where your buttocks rest on the chair or cushion, or some tension around the eyes or shoulders, or the beating of your heart in the chest.

Let the attention go wherever it is drawn in the body. When you notice a new sensation, just feel its physical nature in the body. It might be pulsing, tingling, vibrating, warm, cool, pressure, or lightness. It might be pleasant or uncomfortable. All of these are fine. Mindfulness knows the experience by feeling the sensation in the body, just as it is. You don't need to judge or change anything. Just know what it is you're experiencing.

Mindfulness of Emotions

As you're paying attention to the breath or to sensations, you might sometimes notice that you're feeling some mood or emotion. It could be sadness or anxiety, happiness or irritation, affection or dislike. When you notice a mood or an emotion, let the attention stay with that experience for a while. Allow yourself simply to feel that mood or emotion.

It is helpful to name the emotion you feel: anger, joy, contentment, and so on. You don't need to judge the mood or emotion or to change it. When you feel the emotion directly and know what you're feeling, this is mindfulness of emotions.

3. WHAT IS REAL?

The world is in you, not you in the world.

—Sri Nisargadatta Maharaj[1]

THE SENSE OF "I" is the foundation of nearly all of our thoughts and actions. We base our whole lives around the sense of "I," but as we're beginning to see, this sense may not be as reliable as we've taken it to be. If it is, in some ways, an illusion, where should we look for what is real?

The Buddha taught in order to ease the suffering of sentient beings, so how did he see a "sentient being"? We get the sense from many of his discourses that he did not see a "person" but a collection of elements.

The *Visuddhimagga*, or Path of Purification, is a fifth-century Sri Lankan text in Pali by Buddhaghosa Bhikkhu that collected many meditation techniques known at the time. In it the author says that an experienced butcher carving up the carcass of a cow would not call the parts "cow, cow, cow." The butcher would say, in today's words, "sirloin, tenderloin, rump." In the same way, Buddhaghosa says, for one who has thoroughly examined one's mind-body process, it would not occur to him or her to say "person, person, person." Rather the well-taught disciple would see the detailed components that make up a person. The Buddha generally described these parts as either the six sense bases or the five aggregates.

In this chapter we will explore both these schemata. As we learn to see the way the Buddha did, it can be transformative, because this seeing takes place without the veil of self.

THE SIX INTERNAL AND EXTERNAL SENSE BASES

In a teaching called the *Discourse on Totality*, the Buddha gave a pithy statement of what he considered to be real.

> Listen, monks, attend carefully, and I will teach you the totality [of things]. What is the totality? It is simply the eye and sights, the ear and sounds, the nose and smells, the tongue and tastes, the body and sensations, the mind and mind objects. If anyone were to proclaim a totality beyond this, that person would be speaking of something outside their knowledge.[2]

"I will teach you the totality of things." This is a bold statement. Yet the Buddha was confident in saying this 2,500 years ago. What are real are the six sense organs and their associated objects. In the Buddha's view, mind is the sixth sense; objects of this sense are primarily thoughts and emotions. The beauty of this statement is that it is very simple and at the same time clearly true. This simplicity strikes the opening bell for Buddhist philosophy, psychology, and meditation.

The discourse reveals a fundamental perspective that underlies the Buddha's teachings. The domain of these teachings is the immediate experience of a human being. Why? Because it is in the field of one's direct experience that suffering is born, and it is in the field of one's direct experience that suffering is ended. This was the Buddha's sole interest: "Both formerly and now, I teach only suffering and the cessation of suffering."[3]

When we look with a fresh eye, we see that our immediate experience is of the six sense organs and objects. The six senses describe a comprehensive field that includes all of our ordinary experience. This is the field that the Buddha is concerned with. In truth there is one other element not apparent in our ordinary experience that transcends the six senses: nibbāna. We will examine that element later.

THE SENSE ORGANS AND OBJECTS

Focusing on the way we apperceive the world through the sense bases (Pali: *āyatana*) offers a clear basis for discerning what is directly knowable, and thus "real," namely the sense organs and their objects. The organs are often called the "internal sense bases" or "sense doors," and the objects are known as the "external sense bases" or "sense objects." The language of internal and external is used in Buddhist texts even though some of the "external" objects, like sensations and thoughts, seem to be "inside." Even in the light of emptiness, we don't have to question the basic fact of the functioning of these sense bases.

In our experience, we mostly pay attention to the sense *objects*. This is especially true for meditators, who may have given many hours of attention to sounds, sensations, thoughts, emotions, and so on. It is the objects that seem to give us pleasure or pain and through which we seem to suffer loss. We seldom pay attention to the sense *organs* until they become uncomfortable (red eye, blocked ear, dry tongue).

Why are the sense organs in this passage from the Buddha's *Discourse on Totality* given the same importance as the objects? Why didn't he just describe our experience in terms of the sense objects? The answer is that sense objects don't appear without sense organs. The objects in our experience arise in dependence upon the organs, which are part of the body. The Buddha is emphasizing that without the body, there would be no human experience. This is a key point in his teaching of dependent origination, which we will discuss later.

USING THE SENSE BASES IN MEDITATION

The second power of the schema of the sense bases is that it offers a reliable guide for our meditation practice. Meditation is about coming to understand things the way they are, not the way we imagine them to be or would like them to be. What things appear that are to be understood? The sense doors and objects. So where should we focus our attention in meditation? On the sense doors and objects. In meditation we are not going to concoct elaborate theories about the beginning of the universe or the inherent flaws of social classes or the supposed divide between id and ego. We will simply pay attention to sights, sounds, smells, tastes, sensations, thoughts, and emotions as the way to stay most closely in touch with reality.

A key point in meditation then is to move our attention out of the conceptual acrobatics and fantastic proliferations of thoughts, and into what is real. This reminds us of the advice from the Gestalt psychologist Fritz Perls to "lose your mind and come to your senses." The Buddha does not ask us to lose our thinking mind altogether, because thoughts are essential for living in the world and for Dharma reflection, but we are encouraged to drop the unnecessary proliferations. When we do turn our meditative attention to the realm of thinking, it will be primarily to see each thought as an object arising in the present moment, persisting for a brief time, and then passing away. We are more interested in the *process* of a thought's arising and passing than in its *content*, which is often born of multiple associations far removed from the reality of the senses. In meditation, thought becomes just another sense object to be noticed, not engaged with.

SEEING THE NATURE OF WHAT IS

The third powerful effect of this schema is that we start to see the actual nature of things. This perception has long been obscured by our misguided ideas about reality. Now we see how changeable reality is. Every time we feel a breath, we notice that it has a beginning and an end. Every sound we hear starts and stops. Every sensation we feel changes under our gaze. Every thought that arises also passes away. In fact as we observe sense objects again and again, we find that not a single one lasts. Sometimes an emotion may last for hours or in rare cases for days, but eventually it changes or fades away. Even a persistent emotion like grief or depression goes through many variations in intensity in a day's time. The body may look similar from one day to the next, but it may have gained weight, sprouted facial hair, or reacted to an insect bite. Everything is changing. This truth of impermanence is a cornerstone of the Buddha's teaching. We suffer because we try to hold on to things that don't last.

Seeing change directly is an important perception, because concepts lead us into assumptions of continuity and permanence. We say "my body" and imagine it as an unchanging possession, or "my husband" and believe that he is the same person today as he was twenty years ago. We think "my house," but it's not constant: toilets start to leak and termites chew into the beams. The concept seems to promise an ongoing stable entity, but when we look closely, that entity is changing all the time. When we move from dwelling in static concepts to seeing the actual nature of what is, the truth of impermanence starts to sink in.

Understanding impermanence is a good example of the three avenues of learning we discussed in the introduction. You have probably heard about impermanence (learning by hearing) and may have thought about it (learning by reflection). But it is only when you witness change in your sense experiences over and over with a quiet, attentive mind (learning by meditative insight) that the truth of impermanence will penetrate and transform your habits of mind. We need this third kind of understanding to help us let go of our many attachments.

FINDING THE SOURCE OF SUFFERING

Fourth, the sense bases offer excellent direction on where to look for the genesis of suffering. As the building blocks of human experience, the sense bases are the places where craving fastens on, leading us into clinging and then suffering. Training ourselves to pay close attention to the sense bases, over and over, increases the likelihood we'll see how suffering is created and how it can be released.

THE FIVE AGGREGATES

The five aggregates (Pali: *khandha*) are another teaching model the Buddha employed to describe the reality of our human experience and the location of suffering. The sense bases and the aggregates cover the same territory of reality, but they divide it up in different ways.

The English term *aggregate* sounds rather technical—it makes me think of road-paving material—whereas *khandha*, a common word in ancient India, means "heap" or "bundle." Perhaps the closest rendering would be "the five kinds of stuff" that comprise us. However, *aggregate* is the term used most often to translate *khandha*, so I will use it here. This way of dissecting reality, unfamiliar to modern ways of thinking, requires some explanation. Let us look in turn at each aggregate and its meaning.

MATERIAL FORM

The first aggregate is material form (Pali: *rūpa*). Sometimes abbreviated as "form," *rūpa* refers to *all* matter, both internal and external. When we meditate, the term *form* is sometimes taken as synonymous with the body, because the body is such an important object in meditation practice. When used in this way, form includes the five physical sense organs. But the meaning of *rūpa* is much wider than this.

Rūpa also includes the entire universe of matter beyond the body, as well as sense impressions that arise within the world of matter, that is, sights, sounds, smells, tastes, and sensations. Hence, the aggregate of material form designates the body, the five physical sense organs and their objects, and the rest of the physical world.

The first five internal and external sense bases are all included within the aggregate of material form. But because sight is such a dominant physical sense, "form" is often associated specifically with seeing, and it is sometimes used in this context to mean "visible objects." In its widest meaning, the first aggregate, form, includes all matter and all physical sense impressions. So you might deduce that the other four aggregates have to do with mind, and that is correct.

FEELING

The second aggregate is feeling (Pali: *vedanā*). This specialized Buddhist term does not mean a feeling in the sense of an emotion. A better translation might be "feeling tone." It means the *quality* in each moment of sense contact as it is experienced in one of three ways: as pleasant, unpleasant, or neither pleasant nor unpleasant. (This last feeling tone may be called "neutral.")

Based on the pleasant and unpleasant aspects of sense experience, we form likes and dislikes. These then become the ground for painful reactive emotions like greed, hatred, and fear. Based on the neither-pleasant-nor-unpleasant aspect of experience, we form our "overlooks," the tendency to not even see people or things or events that don't excite our passions. Tuning out these things means that we are not paying attention to neutral parts of our experience, even though they are just as real as the pleasant and unpleasant. This is delusion at work.

I have seen the aggregate of *vedanā* explained by some Buddhist teachers as meaning physical sensations, but it's clear from the texts that *vedanā* applies to all six senses, not just the sense of touch. It's also sometimes described as meaning emotions, but the texts are clear that *vedanā* comes in only three flavors (pleasant, unpleasant, neither), not the myriad flavors of the emotions.

It's interesting that feeling tone is introduced as a mental component. We might assume that the feeling tone of a sense contact is inherent in the object. When we hear a pretty tune, it's natural to think that the pleasantness is an integral part of the tune, and that everyone would experience it in that same pleasant way. But when we observe the wide range of human tastes, we see that it's not always like this.

A convenience store in Southern California was having a problem with drug dealers in its parking lot. The presence of the dealers and their customers was keeping away paying customers. The store manager would call the police who would ask the group to leave, but soon they would come back. Then the store manager had an idea: why not play some music over the store's outdoor loudspeakers? He started playing tracks by Mantovani, a conductor who used the sound of swelling strings to dramatize movie scores in the 1950s and 1960s. My mother was fond of Mantovani, so I heard a lot of it growing up. To her the sound was very pleasant. However, the drug dealers did not find it at all pleasant and they cleared out.

Feeling tone is an individual response to each sense contact based at least partly on our own background, tastes, and conditioning. The contact can be either physical or mental. That is, we feel pleasure, pain, and neutrality in both the physical realm of the five senses and the mental realm of thoughts and emotions. We develop likes and dislikes, hopes and fears, through all six senses. One teacher described feeling tone almost as a verb, saying that we "feel into" a contact to define it as either pleasant, unpleasant, or neither.

I will mostly use "feeling tone" as the translation of *vedanā*, although I'll use "feeling" when the context makes clear that we are talking about the aggregate and not a synonym for emotion.

PERCEPTION

The third aggregate is perception (Pali: *saññā*), which in Buddhism means the activity of mind that recognizes an object. In the ever-changing stream of sense impressions that make up our experience, we are constantly singling some things out and naming them: "chair, tree, sweater, house, Mary." Naming is an act of recognition that places the object into a category we are already familiar with. Even if we don't say the word, the recognition process is still going on. Perception helps us to make sense of the myriad sense experiences by associating them with what is already known, by *re-cognizing* them.

The mind names objects so quickly and automatically that we may think that naming is built in to the sense contact. But that is not the case. Oliver Sacks, the neurologist and author, tells the story of a man named Virgil who had become blind when quite young and then as an adult had surgery to restore his sight. When the bandages were removed from his eyes, everyone expected him to exclaim with delight on being able to see again—but:

> He seemed to be staring blankly, bewildered, without focusing, at the surgeon, who stood before him. Only when the surgeon spoke— saying "Well?"—did a look of recognition cross Virgil's face. Virgil told me later that in this first moment he had no idea what he was seeing. There was light, there was movement, there was color, all mixed up, meaningless, a blur. Then out of the blue came a voice that said, "Well?" Then, and only then, he said, did he finally realize that this chaos of light and shadow was a face—and, indeed, the face of his surgeon.[4]

If we look freshly at our own visual field, perhaps with one eye closed, we might see that it is at root the same undifferentiated mass of form and color and movement that Virgil saw. But we have learned to interpret all those blotches with no apparent effort. Virgil, blind almost since infancy, had not. His eye organ had been repaired but his faculty of perception had not yet developed.

Perception is not always accurate. One fall day I was doing walking meditation outside at a retreat center when I heard the distinct sounds of drums and bugles coming closer. "A marching band," I thought, "coming up the street toward us." I stopped to listen more closely because it's not every day a marching band comes up the street. Slowly the drums and horns turned into the rattles and squeaks of a garden cart on two bicycle tires making its bumpy way along a gravel path a hundred feet away. The sounds had been heard clearly, but the perception—a categorizing that is inherently an interpretation—was faulty. This incident was just funny, but some misperceptions lead to real suffering, as when we perceive something dear to us to be lasting when it is not.

This definition of perception is different from its common usage in English. Merriam-Webster defines *perceive* as "to become aware of through the senses," and offers *consciousness* as a synonym for *perception*. The common understanding in English is that perception means the bare sense impressions that make up our experience, such as the visual object described as "form" above. However, in Buddhism, the bare sense datum is called a sight, sound, smell, taste, touch, or mind object. Perception refers to the act of conceptualization—naming and categorizing an object.

VOLITIONAL FORMATIONS

The fourth aggregate is called volitional formations (Pali: *sankhāra*). Sometimes we might just say "formations" if it is clear that we are talking about the fourth aggregate. There are three categories of volitional formations: mental, verbal (actions of speech), and bodily (physical actions). In a period of sitting meditation the most persistent of these categories is usually the mental. Here, mental volitional formations include all our thoughts; the wide range of our moods and emotions like happiness, fear, joy, desire, and so on; and subtle meditative states such as mindfulness, concentration, tranquility, compassion, and equanimity. What we commonly refer to as someone's "personality" is just the day-to-day manifestation in their life of the variety and balance among their volitional formations.

These formations are called "volitional" because they express our will or motivation in some way. A thought of desire expresses the will to have what is wanted, while a thought of generosity expresses the wish to help another. The refined meditative states do not come about by accident but only by deliberate, willed cultivation. Once activated, these volitions are more likely to arise again in future.

Just as the form aggregate covers a vast range of physical phenomena, so this aggregate covers a vast range of mental experience: love, cruelty, confusion, joy, tranquility, and so on. All the kinds of happiness we can imagine in the term "heavenly" are included in volitional formations, as are the intense miseries we ascribe to "hellish." The creative thoughts of Einstein and the murderous thoughts of Stalin are here. So also are Jesus's love and the wisdom of the Buddha.

CONSCIOUSNESS

The fifth aggregate is consciousness (Pali: *viññāṇa*). Consciousness may mean many different things in Western philosophy and psychology, but in Buddhism it is quite straightforward. It means the knowing quality of mind, that which receives or holds the impressions at the six sense doors. Consciousness is the most basic *knowing* of an object, before any words and before perception. Perception can act only after consciousness has revealed an appearance which can then be named. Every moment of sense experience has the element of consciousness within it. This is what it means to be a sentient being!

It can take some time in our practice to recognize the activity of consciousness. In paying attention to the breath, for example, we have mostly been advised to focus on the physical sensations arising with an in-breath or an out-breath. We have seldom been instructed to notice the process of consciousness that is also taking place. At first when we feel the breath we may feel that there is *only* a physical process taking place. But if we reflect, we realize that there is a mental component of the experience as well.

After the breath has disappeared, we can remember what it felt like. If there had not been a mental knowing of the experience of breath, we could not have formed a memory of it to store in the mind. We might also reflect that when we are asleep, the body still breathes but there is no conscious knowing of the experience. When we are awake, we consciously know of the breath if we attend to it. This knowing is mental. In time we can start to feel the mental activity of consciousness—knowing—as it is happening.

FIVE AGGREGATES—OR THREE?

These are the five aggregates the Buddha taught: material form, feeling tone, perception, volitional formations, and consciousness. Truth to tell, it is something of a strange list. It has none of the familiarity we experience in hearing about the six senses. Certainly matter, emotions, and consciousness are fundamental kinds of stuff, but what about feeling tone and perception? They are significant factors of mind, but why have they been singled out for such important treatment? Why were they not just included in the volitional formations aggregate? They are simply two more mental factors. Then we would have just three aggregates: material form, mental formations, and consciousness. This is a list we might relate to more easily: our experience is made up of the body with its sense impressions, mental states, and the knowing faculty.

In fact listing only three aggregates is the way reality is organized in the Abhidhamma, a section of the Pali Canon that is considered a technical manual of Buddhist psychology. Because of its respected standing in the Buddhist tradition, I will sometimes speak of the three components, or aggregates, as a simpler model that covers the same ground.

The six senses and the five aggregates encompass the entire range of our sense experience. The six senses are well suited for understanding the truth of impermanence and therefore learning not to cling. The five aggregates also play an important role in insight; their strength is in learning not to identify with things as being "I" or "mine."

Mindfulness of Sounds

We will continue to investigate the sense bases and aggregates through meditation. Sounds are a frequent part of our experience, appearing as objects of our ear organ in the six sense bases and as an aspect of form in the first aggregate. Mindfulness of sounds can be a useful way to bring a spacious quality into our meditation.

- Begin with mindfulness of breathing. Once you have connected well with the breath, shift your attention to hear all the sounds that are coming and going in your environment. There may be the sounds of nature, such as wind or birdcalls, or sounds in your home, like a fridge or dryer, or the sounds of cars and traffic outside.
- Let your attention widen to hear all the sounds around you in a 360-degree, panoramic fashion. Notice that you don't have to strain to hear sounds. If you just relax as you sit, all the sounds are heard spontaneously. Just stay receptive and you will know all the sounds.

Mindfulness of Feeling Tone

Feeling tone is the second aggregate and is included under mind objects in the sense bases. It's an interesting phenomenon because it forms the basis for our likes and dislikes.

- Begin with mindfulness of breathing. Then whenever a sensation in the body or a sound draws your attention, let that new object become the focus for your meditation. When you feel a breath or a sensation, or hear a sound, notice whether that contact feels pleasant, unpleasant, or neutral. This is its feeling tone.
- Once you have noticed the feeling tone, you can let the atten-

tion go back to noticing breath, sensations, or sounds. Every time your attention lands on one of these objects, first notice the object and then notice its feeling tone: pleasant, unpleasant, or neutral. Continue to notice these pairs: a sense object and its corresponding feeling tone. The latter is mindfulness of feeling tone.

4. THE FIVE AGGREGATES ARE NOT SELF

When you do not think yourself to be this or that, all conflict ceases.
—Sri Nisargadatta Maharaj[1]

FROM OUR OWN innate tendencies and the repeated use of language, we have adopted—without reservation—the belief that the body, thoughts, and feelings are "me," and that everything outside the body is "not me." This fundamental sense of duality creates a split in our experience that leads us to feel disconnected from the rest of creation, with the consequent feelings of loneliness, isolation, anxiety, and longing. We are examining the belief in a self in order to see through this duality, because beyond it is the promise of much greater wholeness and connection. To see fully the emptiness of self, we need to look into all the corners of our being—because the sense of self is very good at appearing to be reformed while merely finding subtler places to take a new birth. The Buddha often used the five aggregates as the model to offer a thorough analysis of the myriad ways we identify as self as well as the way out of identification.

In the last chapter we saw that the five aggregates correspond to the totality of a person's sense experience. Please note that there is a common word that is not among the five aggregates: "me." There is no entity at the center that owns them or stands apart from them or *to* whom the aggregates are happening. If the aggregates cover everything that is real, then what appears is only form, feeling, perception, formations, and consciousness. We don't see "I" anywhere, and we don't need to add it.

In conventional language we apply the term "I" to a partial collection of the aggregates: the body and the four mental aggregates. The rest of the material world is regarded as "other." But even within this conventional designation of a self, there is not any single thing that we can put our finger on and say, "Here is the 'I.'" What we call a being or a self is just a collection of parts—aggregates—put together in a certain way for a moment. There is no ongoing entity that is the center, or essence, of the collection.

The classical analogy used for this situation is that of a chariot, which is made up of a cart, wheels, axle, yoke, and reins. The chariot functions as a unit, but when considered closely, it is only a collection of parts assembled in a particular way. If you took the chariot apart and laid the parts on the ground, would you still call it a chariot? I don't think so. There is no one thing called "chariot" beyond this assembled collection of parts. But *chariot* is a useful word, a useful concept, and sometimes a useful contraption.

So it is with the word *I*. It is a useful term, but it doesn't point to any actual entity. The conventional "I" is just a collection of parts: body, mental factors, and consciousness. We lay claim to the individual aggregates or to the whole collection as "I" or "mine," but there is no evidence for this claim.

THE AGGREGATES AS NATURE

The way we identify with the aggregates is experienced differently for each aggregate. In this section, we will explore some of the common ways that identification happens and in each case why that identification doesn't exactly make sense. We will see that, far from being personal, each aggregate is merely an aspect of nature. In this section, I'll use the simpler schema of three aggregates: body, emotions, and consciousness.

THE BODY

Each aggregate is a conditioned thing that follows its own laws. Take the body for example. We call it "me," but it is just a phenomenon of physical nature. It has had its own life quite apart from our conscious volition. It formed years ago as a single cell from the union of our father's sperm and our mother's egg. That cell divided, then those cells multiplied and specialized for nine months in the womb. Since emerging into the wider physical world, the body has been nourished by milk and food, water and air, and it has grown bigger, stronger, and older. And here we find it today, shaped and colored the way it has been by our genes and other natural forces—and we lay claim to it as self.

We may feel a lot of pride in our body if others consider it attractive, or we may feel shame if they don't. We may wish that the body were taller or shorter, darker or fairer, lighter-boned or broader in the shoulders. But none of that was ever up to us. "I" didn't even get a vote. The body was birthed and lives its own physical life according to its own physical laws. The basic body we have was never under our control. Of course its appearance has been influenced by our choices in diet, exercise, and health care, but these variations are minor compared to what we were given.

I had the good fortune to practice as a monk for some time in the monastery of Ajahn Buddhadasa, one of the great forest masters of the last century in Thailand. Living close to nature was integral to the way he learned and taught. He put it this way: "This body came out of nature, is part of nature, never departed from nature, and belongs to nature. So give it back to nature. That will be a big relief for you."

It is truly a great relief to let go of the belief that "I" am responsible for how this body looks. We see that the body has been created out of countless causes and conditions that were never within our control. Feelings of pride or shame about the body are based in the unconscious assumption that we should be able to control the body's appearance.

EMOTIONS

Emotions, a subset of volitional formations, can be equally sticky as a source of "I." When we start to become mindful of emotions, we can see how we react to the different emotions that visit us. We want to feel happy, strong, confident, and joyful, so when these emotions come, we usually feel good about ourselves, as though "I" made this emotion happen. We don't want to feel fearful, confused, anxious, or depressed, so when these emotions come, we usually feel bad about ourselves, as though "I" made this happen. But is our emotional life really under our control? Do "I" make these emotions come and go?

Not really. Emotions, like the body, are the outcome of countless causes and conditions, including our culture, upbringing, traumas, successes, failures, health, past mind states, and recent events. Each of these experiences has conditioned our emotions in specific ways. When a mind state arises in the present, there is no agent called "I" who out of free choice has willed it to come, nor is there an "I" who can always choose to make it either last or go away. We find ourselves unable to control the presence or absence of most of our emotions.

Like the body, emotions follow their own laws and their own nature. Just as the body is an integral part of physical nature, we could say that emotions are simply a part of human nature or, more precisely, mental nature. Until enlightenment, all human beings have in their makeup the same wide range of emotions: happiness and unhappiness, joy and sorrow, hope and fear, and so on. All these are part of our mental nature, just as eyes and ears, or stomach and liver, are part of our physical nature. Trying not to feel some of these emotions when they are present makes as much sense as trying to take one's eyes out.

Emotions are not generally under our control, and so they cannot be considered as a self. Yet they often play the most central role in who we take our self to be. We think, I'm a happy person or an angry person or a kind person or a fearful person. We often have strong feelings about who we take ourselves to be emotionally, but this type of self-description can be very constricting. We become hurt when others see us more critically than we see ourselves, or glad when they see us in a more flattering light. Of course no one feels the same way all the time. If I hold to a fixed view that "I am a kind person," then when anger arises, I might not be able to accept it as an authentic feeling.

As we observe emotions over many hours of mindful attention, we see that all our moods just come and go. They don't usually last very long. One arises, influences us, and passes away. Then the next arises and passes, and the next, and so on. We can't hold on to the pleasant ones, because they are impermanent. We don't need to coax the painful ones to go away, because they too are impermanent. Emotions are like the weather; sometimes it's sunny and sometimes cloudy, wildly variable and out of our control. We could get caught up and spun around with each one, but it isn't necessary that we do so. If we stop resisting or trying to control them and simply be with each one with balance as it expresses itself, we are far less likely to be disturbed by their presence or absence.

When we understand emotions as part of nature and see their impermanence clearly, we can no longer claim them as who we *really* are. All humans have them, and none of them lasts for long. To say "I am a happy person" is like saying "California is sunny." This is true—except when it's not. Nature is always changing. The mind and emotions are constantly in flux. The mind, in fact, changes even more quickly than the body does.[2]

CONSCIOUSNESS

We often identify our sense of "I" with consciousness. When we see, we think, "*I* am seeing." When we hear, we think, "*I* am hearing." The sense of "I" as the observer—"I" *am* seeing—can be the most compelling entity of all to identify with. In fact there is no separate "self" having the experience of seeing or hearing. The aggregate of consciousness is simply receiving a sense impression. *Consciousness* sees. *Consciousness* hears. When we add "I," we introduce an unnecessary element that doesn't refer to anything that actually exists. Of course it's fine to say "I am hearing" as a convention, to contrast with another person who is speaking, but we don't need to add the word "I" when talking to ourselves about the experience of hearing or seeing.

Consciousness is also nature. The body is a part of physical nature and moods are part of mental nature. We identify with both body and moods, and we're concerned with how others see us in these areas. We take these two aggregates personally. They represent the core of our personality, and we build our self-image around them. We think they are what makes us unique. Consciousness as *viññāṇa*, the bare knowing of a sense object prior to naming or labeling, is another aspect of mental nature, but unlike the body and moods, we don't take consciousness personally. When we understand this function of mind, there is no reason to suppose that our consciousness is any different from anyone else's. It's not as though I have a really great *viññāṇa* and yours is quite puny. Consciousness as *viññāṇa* seems to be the same in all of us. When we examined the assumptions implicit in the idea of self, we saw that my self should be unique, different from anyone else's. The contents of consciousness may be different from one person to the next, but consciousness itself is not. Consciousness fails this test, and so it is not suitable to be considered my self.

SEEING WITH WISDOM

In many discourses the Buddha suggests to his disciples not to claim the five aggregates as self or as belonging to self. Here is a representative teaching, one that occurs in a few discourses. The Buddha is addressing a group of practitioners. (Scholars say that *bhikkhu*, which usually means "monk," in this context refers to any serious practitioner, lay or monastic.)[3]

> "Bhikkhus, what do you think? Is material form permanent or impermanent?"
> "Impermanent, venerable sir."
> "Is what is impermanent suffering or happiness?"
> "Suffering, venerable sir."
> "Is what is impermanent, suffering, and subject to change fit to be regarded thus: 'This is mine, this I am, this is my self'?"
> "No, venerable sir."[4]

This sequence is then repeated for the other four aggregates of feeling, perception, volitional formations, and consciousness, so that the disciples are led to see the totality of their sense experience as not-self.

We need to explain the use of the words *suffering* and *happiness* in this discourse. *Suffering* is the translation of the Pali word *dukkha*, a significant term in the Buddha's teachings that actually has a broader range of meaning than simply "suffering." It covers the whole spectrum of what we might call the unfortunate aspects of living, which can range from a mild sense of incompleteness or a state of irritation to the most intense experiences of bodily pain and mental anguish. Because some pain is inherent in living, the Buddha characterizes the life of the senses as not entirely satisfactory, as *dukkha*. It is the lack of satisfaction that leads most of us to a spiritual path. In Buddhism the entire goal of the spiritual life is to end this sense of unsatisfactoriness by finding an unshakable peace, called nibbāna (Pali) or nirvana (Skt.). In this passage we should take the word *dukkha* to indicate this inherently unsatisfactory nature of life as experienced through the six senses.

The word translated as "happiness" is the Pali term *sukha*, which also has connotations of pleasure and contentment. In this passage, its contrast to *dukkha* means that we should consider "happiness" to point to a lasting happiness that would remove any underlying unsatisfactoriness. Therefore, to bring out the full meaning of the Pali, we might translate the Buddha's second question as, "Is what is impermanent ultimately unsatisfying, or can it lead to lasting happiness?" The practitioners' response then becomes, "Ultimately unsatisfying, venerable sir."

The Buddha is not saying that all sense experience is miserable or that there is no happiness or pleasure in life. Far from it. In many discourses he talks directly about the pleasures that can be found through the senses. However, he also states clearly that sense pleasures can only give limited fulfillment; they cannot overcome the basic unsatisfactoriness of conditioned life caused by its changing nature.

THIS IS MINE, THIS I AM, THIS IS MY SELF

Having guided the bhikkhus to see their sense experiences as ultimately unsatisfying, the Buddha then asks them whether the sense experiences are valid grounds for identification, or ownership. Each of the phrases he uses in the third question is significant. "This is mine" expresses ownership. We own things first of all, because we desire them or some aspect of them. Because of the underlying motivation of desire, we become *attached* to these things. We've invested emotional energy into them remaining the way they are now. When they change or are broken or decay or die, as inevitably they will, we'll suffer because the attachment will be broken too. This is the basic cycle to which the Buddha is pointing.

Ajahn Chah, a great forest master of Thailand in the twentieth century, described this well, referring to a glass of water that he was drinking from.

> You say, "Don't break my glass!" Can you prevent something that's breakable from breaking? If it doesn't break now it will break later on. If you don't break it, someone else will. If someone else doesn't

break it, one of the chickens will! Whenever you use this glass you should reflect that it's already broken. . . . Develop this kind of understanding. Use the glass, look after it, until, one day, it slips out of your hand . . . "Smash!" . . . no problem. Why is there no problem? Because you saw its brokenness before it broke![5]

The activity of attachment, also called clinging or grasping, is born from desire and is at the root of an unsatisfactory relation to life. Ownership is rooted in craving (Pali: *taṇhā*).

The second phrase, "This I am," points to the activity of identification. We feel "I am this body," or "I am angry," or "I am the observer." When the body is threatened, "I" am threatened. If our emotions are criticized, "I" am at risk. As Maharaj points out in the epigraph at the start of this chapter, conflict comes when we assert, "I am this," because "this" is always changing and hence unreliable. Identification is imagining that I am a particular fragment of what exists, which is small, limited, and bound to decay. This is simply a way of conceiving of self (Pali: *maññanā*)—and we could say it is actually a form of conceit (Pali: *māna*), a technical term indicating the deep tendency to take oneself to *be something*.

The third phrase, "This is my self," is similar to the second phrase but leads in a slightly different direction. "This is my self" means we have a particular *view* about the self, about where "I" resides. At the time of the Buddha, Indian society was crowded with philosophical and religious teachers and sects, all promoting their opinions and arguing against others. Many of these views had to do with what defined the self. Unlike, say, political views, a view about the self is at the center of our very existence and can shape our life in strong ways. If the view is incorrect, we may live our entire life in an illusion. In addition to a consciously adopted philosophical stance, such a view may also include beliefs about the self that we've taken on without noticing.

PERSONALITY VIEW

As the discourse continues, the Buddha enumerates twenty ways we can form a view about the self, based on the aggregates. This is called a self view or personality view (Pali: *sakkāyadiṭṭhi*). Here is how we form a self view around the aggregate of form, which in this context means the body:

> An untaught ordinary person . . . regards material form as self, or self
> as possessed of material form, or material form as in self, or self as in
> material form. . . . That is how personality view comes to be.[6]

These comments may sound cryptic, but if you read them slowly, substituting "body" for "material form," you'll see that we have already met a few of them.

"Regards material form as self" is the view *"I am* the body." This view is limited, because the body is limited. The physical body is born in separation, lives in separation, and dies in separation. By equating the body with "I," this view leads to fear and isolation.

"Regards self as possessed of material form" is the view "*I am* the owner of the body," though somehow separate from it. As in all ownership, desire is behind this view—and a very strong one at that, since we tend to cherish and protect the body. We regard the body as the most important possession of all, and we suffer when it changes through aging, illness, or death.

"Regards material form as in self" could be the view *"I am* the entire range of conscious awareness," within which the body is one object. Awareness is seen as vast and all-encompassing. Awareness includes the body, but identifying as the particular (the body) is rejected in favor of identifying as the knowing of all. "I am nothing small and limited, I am the vast expanse of awareness like the sky." It is true that awareness includes everything, but again, assigning "I" to it is unnecessary. Such a view inclines us to a disconnection from the pesky realities of corporeal life, work, and relationship.

"Regards self as in material form" could be the view "*I am* the observer," located perhaps inside the head. We might identify with the observer as a way of trying to stand apart from experiences in order to control them and gain a sense of continuity. This view can lead to timidity and to shrinking from life.

Defining the self in any one of these four ways in relation to the body is limiting. The Buddha goes on to apply the same four patterns to the other four aggregates of feeling, perception, volitional formations, and consciousness. We won't go through these in detail, but you might like to reflect on some of them around emotions and consciousness. Five aggregates by four patterns gives twenty ways to form personality views. And every one of them is incorrect. So what is correct?

A well-taught noble disciple . . . does not regard material form as self, or self as possessed of material form, or material form as in self, or self as in material form. He does not regard feeling as self . . . perception as self . . . formations as self . . . consciousness as self . . . That is how personality view does not come to be.[7]

SEEING AS IT ACTUALLY IS

When personality view is not formed, there is the freedom of being unconstrained, unlimited by identification with a fragment. In fact, according to Buddhist teachings, personality view is one of the fetters that is eliminated in the first stage of enlightenment, called stream-entry (Pali: *sotāpatti*). The Buddha concludes:

> Therefore, bhikkhus, any kind of material form whatever . . . should be seen as it actually is with proper wisdom thus: "This is not mine, this I am not, this is not my self." Any kind of feeling whatever . . . Any kind of perception whatever . . . Any kind of formations whatever . . . Any kind of consciousness whatever . . . should be seen as it actually is with proper wisdom thus: "This is not mine, this I am not, this is not my self."[8]

For much of the discourse, the Buddha was questioning the bhikkhus, encouraging them to investigate their experience rather than declaring what was so. But now at the end he stresses seeing "as it actually is" in relation to the aggregates. He states unequivocally that no self is to be found within the five aggregates. Moreover he tells them that in order to see in this way, they must see "with proper wisdom." The depth of insight into not-self can't be willed. It will come only when wisdom has been developed sufficiently. Recall that we need to use three avenues to develop proper wisdom—hearing (or reading), reflection, and meditation.

That discourse is one of the most complete teachings on not-self to be found in the Pali Canon. With every component that can be found in a being, the Buddha trains us not to see that as self. We can imagine that as he enumerated all the incorrect views and then this correct view, his listeners must have been keenly engaged in reflecting on their own experience in the light of this advice. At the end of this discourse, "through not clinging, the minds of sixty bhikkhus were liberated from the taints." That is, sixty disciples reached full enlightenment.

Is it possible for a human being to be so wise that he or she no longer holds the body or mind as self? Consider the advice the Buddha gave a group of disciples who were practicing in a park in the city of Sāvatthi that had been gifted to the community.

> "Suppose, bhikkhus, people were to carry off the grass, sticks, branches, and foliage in this Jeta's Grove, or to burn them, or to do with them as they wish. Would you think, 'People are carrying us off, or burning us, or doing with us as they wish'?"
>
> "No, venerable sir. For what reason? Because, venerable sir, that is neither our self nor what belongs to our self."
>
> "So too, bhikkhus, form is not yours, feeling is not yours, perception is not yours, volitional formations are not yours, consciousness is not yours: abandon them. When you have abandoned them, that will lead to your welfare and happiness."[9]

In this passage, to "abandon" the aggregates means simply to stop clinging to them. Of course one must still look after one's body, mind, and actions with care—but with training, one can look on this body and mind as dispassionately as one would look upon the grasses and sticks of a grove of trees.

Another story from the early days of the Sangha shows us that this is more than a theoretical possibility. An arahant monk named Adhimutta was captured by bandits, who told him they would kill him. The monk showed no sign of fear or terror. The bandit chieftain, much surprised, asked the monk why he did not tremble. Adhimutta replied in verse:

> There is no mental pain
> To one with no expectations.
> All fears have been transcended
> By one whose fetters are extinct.

It does not occur to me "I was,"
Nor does it occur to me "I will be."
Mere formations get destroyed,
What is there to lament?
When one sees with wisdom
This world as like grass and twigs,
Not finding anything worthwhile to hold to as mine,
One does not grieve.[10]

Upon hearing these words, the bandits laid down their swords and let Adhimutta go. Such is the power of the mind liberated from the concept of self.

MEDITATION

Choiceless Attention, or Mindfulness of Changing Objects

In our earlier meditations, we deliberately chose to focus on one aspect of experience at a time: body posture, breath, sensations, emotions, sounds, or feeling tone. As we explore identification with the aggregates, we want to meditate in such a way that we can be aware of anything that arises. In this exercise we will not exert choice around where our attention goes.

- Begin with mindfulness of breathing. When you have established mindfulness of the breath, let go of the breath as a chosen object. Where does your attention go now? It might notice an in-breath, or a sound, or a body sensation, or an emotion, or a feeling tone. In the next moment it might land somewhere else. Wherever the attention lands—that is, whatever you notice—allow that new object to be the focus for mindfulness, for as long as the attention naturally remains there. When the attention moves again, mindfully pay attention to the new object it has found.
- In this way we allow the attention to roam freely through the sense doors, but we stay in touch with it by noticing where it is landing, moment after moment. This requires a fresh and alert interest in our experience. Everywhere attention lands, we can become mindful of that new sense contact.
- If you start to feel confused and lose the ability to be present, return the attention to the breath for a while. When you feel that you are centered, once again allow the attention to move as it will, being mindful of each new experience.

5. CREATING A SELF

If you want to understand your mind, sit down and observe it.
—Anagarika Munindra[1]

WE'VE NOW SEEN that the logic of self is not trustworthy, that the sense bases and aggregates are the real elements of human experience, and that the self is not to be found within them. In this chapter we explore how the sense of *being* a self or *having* a self is so pervasive. How have we come to believe so strongly in something that is, in fact, illusory? Even after we start to question the solidity of the sense of self, why do we keep falling into it? To answer these questions we'll look at two different mechanisms. One has to do with our thoughts, the other with the activity of attachment.

CREATING SELF BY THINKING

As I've noted, full understanding of not-self or emptiness needs to be developed through hearing (or reading), reflection, and meditative insight. This chapter will be more meaningful if you approach it in a meditative frame of mind. Without some degree of steadiness, you won't be able to see thoughts clearly and can be swept away by their flood.

Beginning instructions in insight meditation tell us to direct our attention in a continuous, sustained way to a simple sense experience in the present moment, like a breath, sensation, or sound. Although the instruction is simple, it is not always easy to carry out. We might feel one breath or sensation and then not notice another for several minutes, because our attention has been captured by a succession of passing thoughts. In such cases, we'll eventually come back to the present moment and reconnect to the breath or sound—but the time spent drifting can be rather long.

While the wandering of attention can be frustrating, we learn important lessons from it. The first is that it is not possible, at least in the beginning, to control one's mind. This can be humbling, but it is an important lesson because it reveals the limits of our will.

PAYING ATTENTION TO THOUGHTS

When our attention is not in the present moment, where does it go? We observe that it gets diverted into all kinds of thoughts that apparently are more interesting than a breath or a sensation—thoughts of past or future, work or family, self-image or fantasy. These thoughts do not occur in a clear, linear, or logical pattern; they are chaotic and jumbled, leaping wildly from one topic to the next, sometimes accompanied by great swings of emotion. We might enjoy an image of lazing on a tropical beach in one moment and in the next be gripped by anxiety about a presentation at work. There are strong forces at work in the mind that are not controlled by our conscious intention.

We may wonder if we are failing at the meditation when we spend so much time thinking—and I'd like to say clearly that this is not the case. As long as we are willing to reconnect with the present moment each time we wake up from one of the thought excursions, the meditation will continue to develop. The instructions suggest that the attention should be continuous, but this is seldom possible—and that's fine too. If we are willing to come back to the simple experience of breath or body, to start again, then we will progress.

Once we've found a little stability in being in the present, we begin to notice subtler aspects of our experience, like our state of mind. What is the mood in this moment? Is it sad or excited? Nervous or peaceful? Resentful or grateful? It's important to understand the effect that moods have on us, because they so strongly influence our happiness and unhappiness as well as our interactions with others. Instructions for this kind of meditation, called mindfulness of emotions, were offered at the end of chapter 2.

As we start to pay attention to our moods and their shifting range of power, beauty, and pain, we notice that they are often linked to our thoughts. A long train of thoughts about our partner can perhaps leave us feeling a mix of affection, regret, desire, and annoyance. Thinking about work can lead to pride and satisfaction or embarrassment and anxiety. A fantasy can be quite enjoyable but then leave us deflated and enervated when we emerge.

To understand our emotions, we have to keep looking closely at our thoughts, because the two work together to bring us into states of happiness or misery. Understanding this is helpful and can motivate us to bring more care to the process of thinking.

THOUGHTS ARE NOT THE ENEMY

When we first begin the practice of meditation, we may imagine that thoughts are the enemy. They seem to take us out of the present moment, stealing our attention away from the chosen subject and derailing our practice. When we have a moment of calm, it may be so satisfying that we think this peaceful state is the whole point of practice. We might imagine that the way to meditate successfully is to stop thinking. A teacher's praise of tranquility may even contribute to this belief. So it is quite natural to think that thoughts are merely an obstruction to be overcome and discarded—but this attitude itself becomes a problem. It isn't possible to stop thinking through willpower, and the effort to do so only ties us up in knots.

The deeper purpose of meditation is not simply to enjoy moments of calm, as rewarding and meaningful as they are, but to understand deeply how our minds lead us into unhappiness so that we can stop the activities that lead to those states. To reach this understanding, we have to learn to observe thoughts with as much presence and discernment as we bring to the seeing of breath and emotions. Instructions on practicing mindfulness of thoughts are at the end of this chapter. This is a fascinating exploration, because all our big choices in life, as well as many small ones, begin with a thought. When I was a senior in college, I had a strong thought of wanting to see Asia. This thought became a seed that continued to grow. The next year I found myself in Malaysia on a two-year teaching assignment with the Peace Corps.

THE PROLIFERATION OF THOUGHTS

When we look closely, a thought is not very much: just a fleeting string of words or images generated in the mind. It's far from solid. Yet thoughts exert such power in our life! They lead to important choices, influence our relationships with others, and lift us to heaven or toss us down to hell emotionally. How have such insubstantial phenomena managed to gain so much power over us? The Buddha gave a penetrating analysis of the mechanism of thinking in a pithy discourse called *The Honeyball.*[2]

A man approached the Buddha and asked in an aggressive tone what he taught. The Buddha said that he taught that one does not argue with anyone in the world and that "perceptions no longer underlie" such a wise being. The visitor harrumphed and departed, seemingly frustrated that he couldn't get an argument going. But the reference to perceptions in the Buddha's reply was intriguing even to his disciples, who later asked him what he meant. He said that it could be explained by the following sequence.

> Dependent on the eye and forms, eye-consciousness arises. The meeting of the three is contact. With contact as condition, there is feeling. What one feels, that one perceives. What one perceives, that one thinks about. What one thinks about, that one mentally proliferates. With what one has mentally proliferated as the source, perceptions and notions tinged by mental proliferations beset one with respect to past, future, and present forms cognizable through the eye.[3]

This passage packs in a lot of Buddhist psychology. Let's look at it line by line.

> *Dependent on the eye and forms, eye-consciousness arises. The meeting of the three is contact.*

Form (*rūpa*) is the first aggregate, meaning physical matter. Here it means a visible object. Consciousness (*viññāṇa*) is the fifth aggregate and means the faculty of mind that knows or registers the bare data revealed by the senses. There are six types of consciousness for the six types of sense experience: the five physical senses plus the mind, with its objects primarily of thoughts and emotions. When three things come together—eye, object, and eye-consciousness—that is called a moment of contact (Pali: *phassa*). Contact can occur at any of the six sense doors.

With contact as condition, there is feeling.

When there is sense contact, we feel something impacting us. The impact may be light and subtle, like a distant birdcall or the touch of a feather, or it can be intense and overwhelming, like scalding bathwater or a nearby gunshot. With each impact there is a quality of feeling, or feeling tone (*vedanā*), the second aggregate. Hearing a birdcall might be felt as pleasant while a gunshot is usually sensed as unpleasant. The touch of a feather may be so subtle that it is felt as neutral. The point is that with every contact there is an associated feeling tone, which can be pleasant, unpleasant, or neither. This feeling tone conditions our likes and dislikes, hopes and fears.

What one feels, that one perceives.

When we feel the impact of a sense contact, our attention is drawn to that experience. That object is singled out from the field of experience and becomes the focus of attention, at least for a moment. When we focus on an object, the mind will try to recognize it. We place the sense experience into a category we've created and used before: birdcall, feather, water, gunshot. This act of recognition or naming is perception (*saññā*), the third aggregate. This usually happens automatically, without any effort on our part. Occasionally we have a sense contact and don't recognize the object. When that occurs, we are usually drawn to investigate the object further so that we can place it in a familiar category.

What one perceives, that one thinks about.

Once we have noticed the object and put it into a familiar category, we roll out the rest of our conceptual apparatus and incorporate this object. We think about times we've heard the bird before or remember a hawk's feather we once found on a trail or imagine a favorite hot tub or speculate about who fired the gun, or a million other permutations and scenarios. We don't do this with every object we perceive, but in most waking moments, we are thinking about some object we have perceived. What the Buddha is pointing to here is our habitual tendency to move from direct sense experience into thinking about that experience.

> *What one thinks about, that one mentally proliferates.*

As thought kicks in around a fresh perception, it generally diverges further and further from the original object and the reality of the moment. Once in meditation I came out of a vacation fantasy and wondered how I had gotten there. I retraced a train of thoughts that had gone from a door slamming down the hall (accurate perception), to imagining who had done it (initial thought), to judgments about that person, to a teacher they reminded me of, to a friend in that teacher's class, to a trip we'd taken together, to a breakfast buffet at a hotel in the tropics. From a nearby door to halfway round the world in six steps! Our thoughts engage in this type of free association all the time. This kind of endlessly diverging stream of thoughts is called in Pali *papañca* and can be translated as "conceptual (or mental) proliferation."

> *With what one has mentally proliferated as the source, perceptions and notions tinged by mental proliferations beset one with respect to past, future, and present forms cognizable through the eye.*

Here is the kicker. We may have thought that our habit of turning perceptions into thoughts was a kind of innocent pastime—but now the bill comes due. Other perceptions and thoughts now *beset* us, quite apart from our wishes or intentions. Who has not experienced this? We start out thinking about a small incident with our partner, and before long a blizzard of thoughts has come storming in about past and future: arguments, regrets, plans, hurts, disappointments, therapy sessions, divorce, child custody, and so on. We find to our horror that we can't stop the thoughts, and the accompanying flood of emotions does not dry up quickly. We are spinning in a stew of our own making. To a greater or lesser extent, this is our condition much of the time when our attention is not clearly focused.

If we retrace the chain of events as the Buddha describes them in this discourse, we see three distinct stages. The first is rather automatic: a sense contact arises, we feel the impact, and the mind recognizes the object. This all occurs naturally and inevitably: just steps in the ongoing links of cause and effect that is life. The second stage is volitional: we think about the object we've recognized. This comes out of our own will and to some extent our own choice. We like to think. We not only acquiesce to thoughts but encourage them. At this stage we are still the active agent. But in the third stage we become more of a passive victim as the *papañca* we've activated takes on a life of its own, swirling out of control like the broom in the Disney cartoon of the Sorcerer's Apprentice in the movie *Fantasia*. Thoughts and perceptions beset us and bring with them a raft of disturbing emotions.

HOW PROLIFERATIONS CREATE SELF

As we see all this thought activity and its disturbing nature more and more clearly, we begin to wonder, How did this come to be? What's behind this pattern? Is there a thread that strings all the beads together? Is there a theme common to them all?

As we look, we find that all the beguiling narratives are basically about "me": what I like, what I don't like, what I want, what I fear, what I hate, what I believe, what I'm like. These I-thoughts are frequent and compelling—just try giving them up for two minutes. We sense that they are being thrown up by some strong motive force like a turbocharged engine. What is behind all this power? It is the belief in a self, in the story of "I, me, mine" that we tell ourselves over and over. We do this to convince ourselves that we are real in the way we imagine ourselves to be. But this self is a fiction. There isn't actually an entity that corresponds to this fabrication.

To convince ourselves that the imagined self is real, we tell the I-story continuously, using past and future, likes and dislikes, hates and loves, views and beliefs, engaging our deepest emotions to keep us turning on this hamster wheel. It's not a pleasurable or satisfying habit. In a recent study, participants were asked to stop all activities and simply be with their thoughts for six to fifteen minutes. Most subjects either rated this as difficult or didn't find the experience enjoyable. A number of the subjects, including two-thirds of the men, were offered an opportunity for distraction by giving themselves an electric shock, and chose to do so.[4]

This habit of thinking doesn't make any sense, one might say. Why would we engage in thought activity that is so often restless, upsetting, disturbing, and painful? Because the alternative is feared to be even worse. And what is the alternative? It is seeing an aspect of the truth of emptiness. If we didn't keep up the drama of the I-story, there would be a space in the mind. Eventually this is greatly liberating, but in the beginning it can seem, well, too empty. Thoughts are the first of the two main ways we create a self and fill the space.

CREATING SELF BY HOLDING ON

The other major strategy we employ to construct a sense of self is holding on to things. In Buddhism, an attachment is a relationship we form by taking hold of something we've experienced and not being willing to let it go. We form attachments to people, places, things, and experiences. The length of time we're attached to a thing can range from seconds for a handsome face we pass on the street to a lifetime in the case of our body. The reason this is so important in Buddhism is that when we are attached to something, we become dependent and lean on it, and when it changes, part of our foundation is shaken. When change comes to a major attachment, we can suffer a lot. The Buddha considered attachment to be the source of suffering.

Mara is a malevolent figure in Buddhist lore who tries to lead practitioners away from the noble path into negligence and unhappiness. Shortly before the Buddha's awakening, Mara attacked him with several armies to persuade him to abandon his quest. In modern terms, Mara is sometimes understood as a force within one's own psyche that leads to suffering. About attachment, the Buddha said, "By whatsoever a person clings to in this world, by that Mara will track them down."[5] That is, when we cling to anything, at some point in time, the clinging will become either a test of our commitment to awaken or else a source of suffering.

The list of attachments for most of us is long. To get a sense of its scale, ask yourself, What in my life would I be upset about if it changed? We might include our health, the health of those we love, our marriage or friendships, home, job, savings, car, possessions, status, reputation, weight, appearance, eyesight, mental acuity, and more. Take a few minutes to reflect on this and see what comes to mind.

At age twenty-nine, before he left home on a quest for liberation, the Buddha saw a few of his own deeply rooted attachments and let them go.

> I too am subject to aging, not safe from aging . . . When I considered thus, the vanity of youth entirely left me. . . . I too am subject to sickness, not safe from sickness . . . When I considered thus, the vanity of health entirely left me. . . . I too am subject to death, not safe from death . . . When I considered thus, the vanity of life entirely left me.[6]

In a powerful statement of nonattachment, Sāriputta, one of the Buddha's two chief disciples, once emerged from meditation and shared with the other monks an understanding he had reached:

> Friends, when I was alone in seclusion, a reflection arose in my mind thus: "Is there anything in the world through the change and alteration of which sorrow, lamentation, pain, displeasure, and grief might arise in me?" Then it occurred to me: "There is nothing in the world through the change and alteration of which sorrow, lamentation, pain, displeasure, and grief might arise in me."[7]

This is a powerful testament to the unshakability of Sāriputta's liberation.

In Western psychology, attachment refers to the wholesome bond a child forms to its parent or caregiver, which is necessary for the development of trust in a healthy human being. This is different from the way the word is used in Buddhism. Of course even a healthy child does become attached in the Buddhist sense to her or his parents, but a healthy adult grows out of that childhood dependency, at least to some extent, and the liberated person grows out of it completely.

DEPENDENT ORIGINATION:
SEEING ATTACHMENTS BEING FORMED

Our strongest attachments are usually in areas of life we've been involved with for some time. The moment the attachment formed may be too long ago to recall clearly, and it's likely we've rebuilt the attachment many times since. Meditation offers the clarity of mind that can help us see an attachment forming or re-forming in the present moment. The practice of choiceless attention, also called mindfulness of changing objects, described at the end of chapter 4, helps us see this. Practicing choiceless attention, we are mindful of whatever sense contact draws our attention. We can investigate that sense contact in the present moment to try to understand where attachment might form.

Dependent origination (Pali: *paṭicca samuppāda*) has been called the most profound of all the Buddha's teachings. He laid out a chain of twelve links of cause and effect that describe the origin of suffering in vivid detail. Tibetan artists depict this sequence in a widely known painting called the Wheel of Existence.

To explain dependent origination fully would require more detail than this book allows. Of the twelve links, the first five and the last three take us into territory that is more philosophical than our concern here. So I will focus on the four central links, which are experiential in nature. They are contact, feeling, craving, and clinging.

Contact

The first of the four central links of the wheel, or chain, of dependent origination is contact (Pali: *phassa*). You will recall that contact means the coming together of three things that make a sense experience appear to us: sense organ, sense object, and sense consciousness. Contact may occur in any of the six senses and is purely a momentary happening. If contact seems to be ongoing, that is only because we are not seeing the rapid arising, passing, and rearising of the sense impression. Contact is the first moment of the encounter with a new sense impression, and so it is the beginning of our relationship to the experience. In a meditative state, one can attend mindfully to this first moment of contact.

Feeling

Contact is followed by the next link in the chain, feeling (*vedanā*), which is also the second aggregate, as we saw in the *Honeyball* discourse. These two factors—contact and feeling—are linked in a relationship that might be described as "contact *conditions* feeling" or "dependent upon contact, feeling arises." We don't describe it as "contact *causes* feeling," because other factors are at work too, like our personal background and tastes, and also because the causal relationship of later links is even less direct.

Feeling has the quality of being pleasant, unpleasant, or neither. Every sense contact brings with it one of these three feeling tones. If, in meditation, we notice the moment of contact, then we are prepared to also notice the associated feeling tone. You could softly name it as pleasant, unpleasant, or neutral, as explained in the instructions for the meditation on feeling, at the end of chapter 3. We tend to like what is pleasant and dislike what is unpleasant. If our relationship with the sense experience were to stop here, we wouldn't have a problem. But if we're not paying close attention, feeling tone easily leads to the next link in the chain.

Craving

The third link is craving (Pali: *taṇhā*). You may know this word from the Buddha's teaching on the four noble truths, where it is named as the cause of suffering—not a good reputation to have! In dependent origination too it is a pivotal link in the generation of suffering. Craving is the yearning for something. It can be more of something or less of something, but we want *something*. We can feel this urge over and over when we meditate. The moment is not quite satisfying in itself and we want it to be different. It is not actually that the moment is inherently flawed—rather it is that we have a deep-seated tendency to *think* it is flawed.

Mingyur Rinpoche says of our tendency to find fault:

> We continue to stick with misguided views. These views all share one misunderstanding: the belief that there is something wrong with the present moment. Whatever comes up, we identify a problem with the present moment.[8]

We might say that there is an underlying mood of insufficiency or discontent that leads us to want a different moment than the one we are with.

Feeling conditions craving, or we might say craving arises based on feeling. When the ingrained tendency to want meets the feeling tone of a new sense contact, we tend to react in a predictable way. A pleasant feeling ignites greed: I want more of that. An unpleasant feeling ignites aversion: I want that to go away. A neutral feeling activates delusion: I can overlook that. These reactions of greed, aversion, and delusion are the different forms taken by *taṇhā*, the force of craving.

In Pali *taṇhā* was originally a common word that simply means "thirst." This is a powerful word for the Buddha to use for the cause of suffering, because thirst can never be fully and finally quenched. If we satisfy it now, it will come back again. It is this relentless, restless quality of wanting the Buddha was pointing to. We translate *taṇhā* as craving, which emphasizes the activity of desire or greed, generally considered to be for pleasant experience. However, craving encompasses all three forces of greed, aversion (or hatred), and delusion. With greed I want more of what is pleasant. With aversion I want the unpleasant to go away. In both cases I want the moment to be different from the way it is. Craving also includes delusion, because when we are fixated on pleasure and pain, the neutral experience is regarded as worthless and uninteresting, and so we ignore it. Neutral contacts, however, are just as real as pleasant and unpleasant ones, and it is the job of clear mindfulness to see what *is*, regardless of its valence.

Once craving is activated, we are on the road to suffering. One more step is needed to firm up the situation.

Clinging

The fourth link is clinging (Pali: *upādāna*) or, as it is sometimes translated, grasping. This refers to the activity in the mind that fixates on an experience and takes hold of it. Grasping might refer to the immediate act of taking hold, while clinging might mean the tendency to keep holding on to something that has previously been grasped. Grasping is the origin of attachment, and clinging is the ongoing activity of attachment. Both meanings are included in the Pali term *upādāna*. Craving (the third link) almost always leads to grasping. We can feel the fixation taking hold as it happens in our direct experience. Sometimes meditators ask, "Who is it that is grasping?" But this is not a suitable question. In the light of not-self, there is no one doing the grasping. Grasping is only an activity in the mind.

As a simple example of grasping, if we have a delicious meal at a restaurant, we will often make an effort to store the name of the restaurant in our memory (or on our phone) so we can repeat the experience. Eating the dish we ordered (contact) led to a pleasant taste (feeling), which led to wanting more (craving), which led us to hold on to the name of the restaurant (clinging). This is not to judge or condemn any step in the process. It is not a problem for most people to have a good meal or to go back to a good restaurant. But we are interested in learning about how the mind works, and this is a rather harmless example of our tendency to try to repeat or sustain pleasant experience. Other pleasant experiences can lead to more unsettling forms of attachment, such as addictions to alcohol, drugs, sex, television, money, or power. The mechanism is the same for all of these; only the intensity changes.

You might think that we cling only to pleasant experiences since they stand a chance of gratifying us, but we also grasp unpleasant experiences—though that grasping takes a different form. For example, after a long run we discover a new pain in our knee (contact). All our attention may be drawn to that painful sensation (feeling). We start to feel some fear about its condition (craving) and keep the situation in our mind through many thoughts (clinging): Will I have to stop running? Do I need to see a doctor? Should I get an MRI? Will I ever walk again? We can dwell on these kinds of thoughts for quite a long time as the knee now occupies center stage in our mind—proof that we have taken firm hold of it through grasping and clinging. Again, I am not judging the process. If our knee has been injured, we need to take care of it. But we do not need to obsess about it.

Let's summarize how these four links of the chain of dependent arising work together. If we're awake, contact is happening at one or more of the six sense doors. That contact brings a feeling of pleasure, pain, or neutrality. Based on the feeling tone and an underlying sense of insufficiency, craving inclines the attention to this experience out of some kind of wanting. We lean into the experience out of craving. Grasping fixates and takes hold to try to make the relationship ongoing. If we were to reflect, we would know that the sense impression is impermanent, but we have forgotten this. Grasping is like trying to freeze the experience. Now we have solidified around what might have been a fleeting sense impression. What exactly has become solid? The sense of self. Let's see how this happens.

CLINGING CREATES SELF

Once we have grasped something, we think about it—a fact we can verify in our meditation. Because the grasping came from underlying urges that were not well understood—craving and a sense of insufficiency—it is inevitably colored by the unconscious forces of greed, aversion, and delusion, which give it an emotional investment on our part. In other words, grasping is not a neutral, unfeeling activity but is deeply rooted in unresolved forces in our heart and mind. As we continue to hold on to the thing, we turn it over in our thoughts, and our thoughts are also colored by the same craving and sense of insufficiency. Proliferating thoughts beset us—thoughts about I, me, and mine. So when we grasp, we create anew the sense of self. In fact grasping is identical to creating the sense of self. The sense of self arises through grasping.

As we've seen, the Buddha described seeing the five aggregates with proper wisdom: "This is not mine, this I am not, this is not my self." He goes on to say:

> It is when one knows and sees thus that in regard to this body with
> its consciousness and all external signs there is no I-making, mine-
> making, or underlying tendency to conceit.[9]

Note that the Buddha expresses this in terms of verbs: "There is no I-making or my-making." This makes it clear that the sense of self is not intrinsic to human experience but is being generated by us moment after moment through our own mental activity when we're not seeing with proper wisdom. We engage in I-making (Pali: *ahaṁkāra*) when we take the "I" to be something, and we engage in my-making (Pali: *mamaṁkāra*) when we take something to be "mine." Together we could call I-making and my-making the activity of *selfing*. We understand *conceit* in this passage to mean a general sense of self. When we see with wisdom, we do not generate the sense of a self.

It is so easy to engage in selfing. When there is a mood of sadness, we immediately think, "I'm feeling sad." The "I" is born in that moment as the one who is sad. If we don't think that way, then the "I" doesn't come into being. When there is a pain in the knee, we immediately think, "My knee hurts." The "I" is born in that moment as the owner of the painful knee. Without selfing, that "I" doesn't come into being.

We see in these two simple examples how the "I" is inserted as an addition to a simple contact such as a volitional formation of sadness or a physical sensation of knee pain. If we examine our thoughts and speech, we can see this taking place again and again. The "I" is constantly defining itself in relation to something that exists: I think, I feel, I hurt, my home, my partner, and so on. An interesting question for reflection is: Does the sense of "I" ever arise on its own, without reference to an object of one of the six senses? Can you find such an "I"? What is its nature?

This question has been intriguing meditators since the time of the Buddha. There is an account in the Pali Discourses of a monk named Khemaka, who is a "nonreturner," which means he has reached the third stage of enlightenment, a very high attainment. The monk tells a group of other bhikkhus that the sense of self is still with him even though he does not identify with any of the five aggregates: "Friends, although [the notion] 'I am' has not yet vanished in me in relation to these five aggregates . . . , still I do not regard [anything among them] as 'This I am.'"[10] He calls this sense of "I am" a form of conceit and compares it at his stage to the scent of a lotus that cannot be traced to the petals or the stalk or the pistils but is nonetheless present in the flower. As he was describing his understanding, Khemaka attained full liberation—as did sixty other bhikkhus who were listening.

Khemaka as a nonreturner had reached a level of subtlety with respect to the "I" that most of us have not yet found. He no longer identified with any of the aggregates yet still had an I-sense. When we are nonreturners, we too can focus on this more subtle sense of self. For our purposes now, it is enough if we can see the self being born again and again by claiming the aggregates as "I" or "mine."

Some births are pleasant, as when we get a new job or a new friend, and some births are painful, as when a partner leaves us or our new car gets in an accident.

SELFING LEADS TO SUFFERING

Once a new self has taken birth, it will inevitably die. That is the truth of impermanence, of trying to hold on to changing conditions. Some births are painful to begin with: getting bad news or not getting what we want. Other births are pleasant to start with but become painful when they die: a friend disappoints us or the job goes away. Ajahn Chah said that grasping either pleasure or pain is like picking up a poisonous snake. If you grab the head, it will immediately bite you. This is grasping pain. If you grab the tail, eventually the head will swing around and bite you. This is grasping pleasure.[11]

Either way, the sense of self is problematic; birth is suffering either now or later. Sometimes the suffering is subtle and we hardly feel it, as when the cookie tin goes empty. At other times the suffering is intense, as in death, divorce, or bankruptcy. In every case, the suffering is built on the precondition of our having grasped at a passing experience at one of the six sense doors. A chain of feeling-contact-craving-clinging, of which we weren't fully mindful, led to the birth of a sense of self and then, inevitably, to suffering.

This picture of the human condition may seem bleak, but not every link in the chain is inevitable. Sense contact and feeling take place all the time, but we don't have to generate craving around them. Nor do we need to continue to grasp the aggregates as *who we are*. Understanding this opens the doorway to freedom.

Mindfulness of Thoughts

If we're not mindful, when thoughts arise we tend to get swept up in their content and spin out in proliferation. In the meditative approach, we see a thought simply as a present-moment phenomenon that arises, persists, and passes away. Doing this, we can maintain mindfulness even when thought is present.

- Begin with mindfulness of breathing. When you have established some mindfulness, let go of the breath as a focus. Simply wait attentively and notice the first thought that comes. Pay attention from the first moment of its arising until it has ended. See if it is possible to stay mindful all the way through one thought. When it has ended, return your attention to the breath.
- Now let go of the breath and see if you can notice two thoughts in a row while remaining mindful. Return to the breath.
- Now let go of the breath and see if you can notice every thought that comes in the next, say, fifteen seconds. If you get lost in the content of the thoughts, return to the breath and try again to notice two thoughts. Then try once again to notice every thought for a short time. By building up gradually, you will find a greater ability to be mindful of thoughts without becoming lost in their content.

6. WHEN THE AGGREGATES FALL APART

And what is death? The passing away of beings, their perishing,
breakup, disappearance, mortality, completion of time,
the breakup of the aggregates.
—The Buddha[1]

IT IS PROBABLY CLEAR by now that the emptiness of self in this world is revealed through a deconstruction of what we normally call "a human being" into the various impermanent components of experience, especially the five aggregates. When the aggregates combine into a living, breathing, speaking, and acting person, it can seem that a solid being exists there. When the various parts are analyzed in detail, however, no abiding entity can be found.

One of the most dramatic examples of deconstruction comes from witnessing death. At the time of someone's death, the coherence of the aggregates is broken up. The body, or form, persists, but the mental formations and consciousness seem either absent or disconnected from the form. The assumption we held of an integral entity within the living being is shattered. The unity is no longer. When the aggregates come apart, we have to confront the constructed nature of what we have taken to be someone's self. This was brought home to me powerfully through two encounters with death. One was the death of an older sister; the other was witnessing autopsies in Thailand. Each encounter was profound and brought a different insight about the aggregates.

MY SISTER'S DEATH

I had two older sisters. Linda was seven when I was born, and Judy was five. At age fifty-one, Judy died suddenly and unexpectedly. Her death was hard for me. We were close, and I had no warning, no time to prepare. I was plunged into two months of grief during which the world seemed a dark and gloomy place. I felt a lot of sadness for her husband and children, because she was the spark and heart of the family. But I also felt the loss myself. Judy was a big personality who expressed great warmth, humor, and joy. I missed her.

At the same time, a dharma thread piqued my interest. What happened to Judy? Where had she gone? Where was she now? She'd been a solid presence a few days earlier, and now there was just this lifeless body. What was going on? For the first time, I let in the age-old mystery of death. It had sunk in its teeth, and I needed to understand.

By then, I was familiar with the Buddhist teachings on not-self, but in my limited understanding I had ascribed (quite naturally) to my sister a strong sense of solidity. Clearly there was more for me to see. I took up the five aggregates for reflection, using the simpler version of just three aggregates—form, mental formations, and consciousness.

I began by focusing on the sense I had of my sister's self, since its absence was now so puzzling to me. When I called her to mind, I would envision her body, which was usually in motion, and her face, which was often animated with smiles and laughter. Everything she did was emphatic. As I reflected on these memories and images, I started to tease apart my perception of her body—form, or *rūpa*—from my perception of her thoughts and emotions—mental formations, or *sankhāra*—and I realized that what I'd thought of as Judy's personality was really the volitional formations I saw in her: her thoughts, moods, emotions, speech, and actions. In general we describe someone as warm or cold, generous or stingy, smart or deluded, based on the volitional formations we observe in them.

I began to see that what I had taken as Judy's solid self was actually a joining together of two components: her body as it was animated by her personality. It slowly dawned on me that this pairing was not intrinsic. She might have looked the same but have had a different personality, or she could have had the same personality in a different body. Nor was this pairing irrevocable; clearly after death the two were no longer joined. Her body was still there, but the personality was gone. I'd fused them in my mind; now I saw that the connection between body and personality that I had lumped together to make Judy was not solid at all, but almost accidental.

An insight formed itself into words: What dies is only what is born. The body dies because it has been born. A particular thought or emotion can die, but that is happening all the time anyway. Personality is not an enduring object but is made up of one moment after another of laughter, petulance, wit, sulking, teasing, caring, and so on. A personality, we might say, is always being born and dying. There is some overall consistency to someone's personality, but that just means that similar patterns of changing formations occur and reoccur. No formation is fixed. (We'll look at this in more detail when we talk about karma.)

My sister, I now saw, was an ongoing body, which had to die at some point, coupled with a different stream altogether that was the constantly shifting parade of her thoughts and moods, expressions and emotions. Of course, when the body dies there is still a great mystery about what happens to this stream of volitional formations: Do they stop altogether or continue in some way? I couldn't say for sure, but that question was not so urgent just then. The question that was burning for me at the time was how Judy had been so solid and was now so gone. I had understood something in a new way that helped to settle this question for me.

This insight also changed how I see myself. I too am not a single fusion of body and formations. The body is going to die; the formations will do whatever they do. There is not a single "I" to be found there. Understanding these two streams as separate strands of a "being," each following its own laws, was freeing for me. It helped me to let go of some of the attachment to this body, and it left me lighter and more trusting about the formations of the mind. The freedom I felt was pointed to directly in a poem written by Ajahn Mun, a greatly respected Thai forest meditation master, sometime after his enlightenment. The poem is called "Verses on Liberation from the Khandhas (or Aggregates)."

> Once you know the nature of the five khandhas,
> The heart will be pure and clean, free from stain with no more issues.
> If you know in this way it is supreme because you see the truth,
> And gain release.[2]

OBSERVING AUTOPSIES

My other encounter with death had taken place years earlier. I was in my early thirties and living as a monk at my preceptor's monastery just outside of Bangkok. One of the privileges of being in robes in Thailand is that we were allowed to be close to dead bodies on numerous occasions. In some rural monasteries, cremations were held in an open area, with the corpse placed on a large pyre of wood that was then set on fire. We could view the body both before and during the burning. We were instructed by our teachers to reflect on impermanence and the eventual passing away of our own body. Contemplation in charnel grounds and cemeteries has been encouraged since the time of the Buddha. It appears as a central practice of mindfulness in the *Discourse on the Foundations of Mindfulness (Satipatthāna Sutta)* in the Pali Canon.[3]

Close contact with corpses is not so easy in population centers, so there is now an urban alternative: the morgue. In Bangkok, one of the large downtown hospitals allowed monastics to observe autopsies performed by the coroner. I went to the hospital on a weekday morning and was admitted to the morgue. There on a stainless steel table lay the nude body of a young woman who had drowned in one of the city's canals. The hair on her head had been cut off; the scalp was shaved clean. I was allowed to stand at the table directly beside the corpse, though I was not permitted to touch it. This alone was a breathtaking education. I had never been next to a dead body before. In the West it seemed that as soon as someone died, the forces of medicine and law combined to whisk the body quickly out of sight, as though death was a calamity best ignored in polite society. I felt a mixture of awe and fascination standing next to the body. This was someone who had been as alive as I a few days ago, and now the body was missing the element of vitality. Of course I was reflecting that one day my body would be like this too.

After a few minutes, the coroner wheeled the table into the operating theater. A few of us monastics took our seats in the tiered rows of the theater along with a number of medical students. The coroner gave a brief account of the woman's death and then began the autopsy. I was not at all prepared for what happened next (in fact if you are squeamish about body parts, you may want to skip the next two paragraphs—but, in the time-honored Buddhist tradition, I encourage you not to).

The first organ the coroner wanted to examine was the brain. He made a deep incision into the scalp above one ear, then ran his scalpel over the top of the head to the other ear, neatly dividing the scalp into two halves. Then with his two gloved hands he took a firm hold of each half and pulled in opposite directions. As the front section peeled away, what I had taken to be the young woman's face became separated from the skull and was pulled down, exposing the bone of the skull. The back section separated in the same way. Now the whole crown of the skull was cleanly exposed. The coroner took a handsaw and sawed completely around the crown. Then he removed the top portion so that we could all see the brain, which he took out, examined, and weighed.

The coroner's next area of interest was the abdomen. He made another deep cut in the skin, starting just below the throat and extending down to the belly. Separating the two flaps of skin at the chest revealed the rib cage, which he sawed open to reach the main organs: the woman's heart, lungs, stomach, liver, intestines, and so on. He cut out each large organ, examined it, and weighed it. When he finished, he packed all the organs, including the brain, back in their previous locations and sewed up the cuts in the skin. Everything was again packaged something like the way it had been before.

I had been in retreat at the monastery for several weeks leading up to this day. I was very attentive. My mind was open and my heart was engaged. I found that I was a little shocked by the incisions in and sawing of this recently living woman. Maybe I was expecting some atmosphere of reverence—instead these actions reminded me of meat being cut in a butcher's shop. At the same time I knew that the coroner was just doing his job and that the body wasn't experiencing any physical discomfort. In a short while I began to believe that the shock was an integral part of my learning. I needed to have the body deromanticized, needed to see its meaty nature, to help cut through some of my cherishing of it.

After completing the first autopsy, the coroner returned that body to the morgue and brought out a second body, then a third. He went through three complete autopsies that morning, following the same pattern of incisions to remove and weigh the organs. After the third procedure I left the hospital to catch a bus back to the monastery.

I was standing at a bus stop on the edge of Sanam Luang, a large grassy parade ground in the heart of Bangkok, in something of an altered state. I would say now that the experience had blown my mind. I wasn't exactly shaken—it had been too interesting for that—but I was deeply moved by the contrast with life. I watched all the people going by: an old woman carrying a bag of groceries, children kicking a ball around, students loaded down with books, a couple walking hand in hand, and I couldn't help but imagine them dead, just like the bodies I'd been with. There seemed such a slight difference between life and death; the transition could happen in any second. The phrase that came to mind was, *walking corpses*—"We're all just walking corpses!" I floated in the silent mystery of that way of seeing all the way back to the monastery, struck over and over by our shared predicament.

The living and the dead were so alike. The difference I perceived was that with the living, there was some kind of light that shined out through the eyes. In the dead, that light had gone out. What was the light? It seemed to me that it had something to do with consciousness, *viññāṇa*, the fifth aggregate. There was a brightness of knowing—the spark of conscious experience, joined with the body—that was present in the living and not present in the dead.

THERE IS ONLY THE PRESENT

I saw that conscious knowing was purely a thing of the present moment. For the living, the senses were functioning and contacts were being known. That knowing had nothing to do with past or future. There was the body, which was purely present, and there was consciousness, which was also purely present. Thoughts and feelings also came and went, but they seemed like minor players, small ruffles on this fundamental ground of body and consciousness. Body and consciousness, only in the present.

But we have this peculiar faculty called memory. Memory retains and stores up fragments of what consciousness experiences; then we build all kinds of concepts around these fragments. We call that the "past" and believe that it's real. Extrapolating from some selective elements of memory, we imagine that certain things will happen at some other time. We call that the "future," and we believe that it's real. But past and future are only concepts. They don't truly exist. The past is gone and the future hasn't arrived. What is real is the present moment. Body and consciousness are real, and so are thoughts and feelings. The three aggregates are real and present. But there is nowhere behind us called the "past" and nowhere in front called the "future." When we remember something from the past or imagine something in the future, in either case it is a thought in the present moment.

This understanding was very freeing. Normally we feel burdened by past and future. After a certain age, the past can weigh on us like a ball and chain: mistakes we made, disappointments we had, people we lost, opportunities we missed, successes we couldn't repeat. Among the most oppressive things about the past are the character traits we haven't been able to change. It sometimes seems as if the past is controlling our present. While the past tugs at our feet, the future weighs on us from above: *Will I ever find a partner? What if I lose my job? Where will the money come from? How can I help my son with his addiction? Is this lump something serious? Who will look after me when I'm old? What will dying be like?* And on and on.

When we see that these are just thoughts, and that our feelings are being generated by these thoughts, we also see that it's possible not to take them all so seriously. We can come back to the present and see what is real and what is speculation. Of course there are many times when we need to remember the past or imagine the future. It's helpful to recall where we live and that we agreed to pay the electric company on the first of the month. In order to take a trip, we may need to look at a plane schedule or reserve a car months in advance. These are all useful and necessary activities. But once we understand how past and future are generated from thinking, we can engage in planning and remembering with clarity and balance. Memory and imagination can serve us without ruling us.

The perception of walking corpses came out of a close contact with death, but the insight it revealed about life doesn't depend on the nearness of death. That insight was seeing that each human existence is basically a body plus consciousness, and both are completely in the present moment. This was freeing because the present moment is much lighter and more bearable than the weight of past and future we call to mind. We can develop this way of seeing by consciously reminding ourselves of it. I offer some reflections here, based on the two kinds of truth: conventional designation and a more fundamental reality.

REFLECTION 1: A FRIEND'S STORY

Bring to mind a friend you know well, someone you have very positive feelings for. Feel that affection. As much as possible, let conflicts stay in the background. As you recollect your friend, bring to mind what you know of that person's life situation and background:

- current joys as well as struggles
- family situation, including intimate relationship, parents, and children
- health, including any physical limitations
- livelihood and financial outlook
- past successes and failures
- personality with its strengths and weaknesses

Reflect until you've brought together a comprehensive portrait of this person. Hold your friend and all this information charitably, without much judgment. Notice that a large part of what you've brought to mind is around the person's past and future. This is the "conventional" view of your friend.

When you feel ready, move on to the next reflection.

REFLECTION 2: THE FRIEND IN THE MOMENT

Pause for a minute or two. Let your mind clear by paying attention to your breathing: in, out, in, out. Allow the thoughts to settle. Now bring your friend to mind again. This time imagine that you are meeting her for the first time. Perceive her in the present moment as only her body plus consciousness: her form plus that bright light that is shining forth through her eyes. Hold this perception for as long as you can. If thoughts about her past or future come in, let them pass and return to seeing her as just body plus consciousness. We will call this the "fundamental" view. It doesn't depend on fabrications of memory or imagination, which are subject to many whims and vagaries. Does it feel different to see her in this way?

Next, ask yourself, Which reflection gave a lighter, freer, less constricted feeling about your friend? In which view was your friend freer to feel, move, breathe, change? Was it the usual way, the conventional way, with the additions of past

and future, with prior associations and conclusions? Or was it the more fundamental, with your friend seen in her basic nature of body and consciousness? The
conventional view sees in terms of a being with an assumed personality based on
a continuing existence over time with past and future. The more fundamental
view, which we could also call a dharma view, is seeing in terms of the aggregates as they are in the present moment. We are not trying to ignore your friend's
thoughts and feelings, but by framing it in this way, you can see these as impermanent and lighter. If we choose to, we can learn to see this dharma view more
and more.

REFLECTION 3: YOUR STORY

Repeat reflection 1, but with yourself as the subject. Bring to mind your sense of
yourself, perhaps with an image of yourself in a relaxed or happy setting, or just
feeling yourself as you sit here now. Hold yourself with a sympathetic, nonjudg-
ing attitude. Recall the main outlines of your situation and background: joys and
struggles, family situation, health, livelihood and finances, successes and failures,
personality. All this makes up the conventional view you have of yourself. Stay
in touch with this sense of yourself in all its rich variety. Many different feelings
may come about all these areas of your life. Try to be with the feelings without
running off into thoughts of praise or blame. Hold yourself with care and charity. When you feel ready, and certainly within a few minutes, move on to the
next reflection.

REFLECTION 4: YOURSELF IN THE MOMENT

Bring yourself to mind again, perhaps with an image or by just feeling yourself
sitting. Be sympathetic. Try seeing yourself as simply the body—this form that
is sitting—plus consciousness—this alert knowing that is always there when
we're awake. Notice how each of these components occurs only in the present
moment without referring to the past or anticipating the future. Thoughts and
feelings will continue to come and go; let them come and go without following
or needing to hold on. Return to this present-moment sense of the body and of
knowing. Rest in that perception for as long as you are able. How does it feel to
see yourself in this way?

Having engaged in both reflections on yourself, which one feels freer? The conventional view, which holds all the past and future? Or the more fundamental view, which is simply about what is here now? Most people find it at least a little freeing to be able to see themselves in the moment without the weight of past and future. This way of seeing is what the Buddha was pointing to in teaching about the five aggregates, and it can be developed as an ongoing practice using these reflections or others you may create.

THE CONVENTIONAL AND THE ULTIMATE

The conventional view of a human being as a single entity continuing unchanged over time does not hold up in the light of impermanence and death. The Buddha taught the five aggregates so we can free ourselves from the bondage of taking self to be something it isn't. To see a being in terms of the five aggregates leads to a lighter, less burdensome relationship to life. It is also closer to the way things fundamentally are.

We don't want to hold the fundamental, or ultimate, view as superior or the conventional view as inferior. We need them both. The conventional view is useful in the realm of society, work, and relationships. The problem comes when we think that it tells the whole truth. It doesn't. The ultimate view tells the rest of the truth, and it is the discovery of this "other half," we might say, that frees us. Nāgārjuna, one of the most important philosophers in the history of Buddhism, sums this up well:

> The Buddha's teaching of the Dharma
> Is based on two truths:
> A truth of worldly convention
> And an ultimate truth.[4]
> Without relying upon convention,
> The ultimate cannot be taught.
> Without understanding the ultimate,
> Freedom is not attained.[5]

As we mature in Dharma understanding, we want to be able to see from the conventional perspective when that is helpful, especially in relation to others, and to see from the ultimate perspective when we need to rediscover freedom.

7. BEYOND SELF

What is inside is me,
What is outside is mine—
When these thoughts end . . .
Freedom dawns.

—Nāgārjuna[1]

WE HAVE SEEN that the self is not an intrinsic entity but is born again and again from specific acts of grasping and conceptualization called "I-making" and "mine-making." In this chapter we want to explore how this activity of *selfing* might stop and what the experience is like when it does. The Buddha pointed to the key elements in this development: "Whatever streams there are in the world, mindfulness blocks them. They are stopped by wisdom."[2] Mindful attention can slow down the flow of selfing, and understanding can stop it altogether. As mindfulness and wisdom become strong, the outcome is the dawning of a great sense of freedom.

For most practitioners, understanding the truth of not-self is not an instantaneous, one-time occurrence. When we start to meditate, we might think that a big "explosion" should happen when we sit. When it doesn't, we think we must be doing something wrong. It's true that big insights do occasionally come along that can affect us deeply, transforming the way we see the world and bringing a wonderful sense of release. But the understanding of not-self most often matures through small insights over years of study, reflection, and meditation. These insights add to one another in a cumulative way to loosen the bonds of the sense of self.

A great variety of experiences come to meditators over the course of practice, especially during silent retreats. Many practitioners come to me during retreats and say with great enthusiasm, "I've just had an *anattā* experience!"—meaning an experience of not-self. Their enthusiasm always delights me, because their love for the practice will sustain them along this path. After expressing my delight, I generally listen with interest to the details of the experience, asking a few questions and perhaps offering ways to explore it further. But before they leave, I generally correct their language.

"You know, you didn't just have an experience of not-self. You were already having an experience of not-self and you're still having one right now." They may look a little puzzled. "All along, there hasn't been a self there—today you recognized that. So what you had was really an *insight* into the ongoing truth of not-self. You had a not-self insight." They always get it.

This is also true for you, the reader. It's not that one day you will have an experience and suddenly the self will go away. There is no self here right now. There hasn't been one your entire life. Yet everything works fine, just the way it has always worked. Any idea of getting rid of the self or destroying it is a misunderstanding. A short poem from the author Wei Wu Wei points to this.

> Destroy "the ego," hound it, beat it, snub it, tell it where it gets off?
> Great fun, no doubt, but where is it? Must you not find it first?
> Isn't there a word about catching your goose before you can cook it?
> The great difficulty here is that there isn't one.[3]

Questions tend to arise at this point along the lines of "If there is no self, who makes decisions?" or "If there is no self, who is reborn?" or "If there is no self, who inherits the karma of my actions?" These questions are all based on identifying self with one or more of the aggregates. In each case, the aggregate functions quite well on its own without the need of a superfluous self. We'll take up all these questions in detail later.

Not-self insights come in a variety of flavors. Gradually becoming familiar with not-self is like seeing a jewel with many facets. As meditation and life experiences tumble over and around, different facets of the jewel come into view. Among the multiple avenues through which insights into not-self are revealed are impermanence; calm; unification of mind and its three subcategories of investigation, concentration, and loving-kindness; spaciousness; and enlightenment. And this list is by no means exhaustive. Some of these insights and the conditions that shape them are described below.

IMPERMANENCE

The insights into impermanence and not-self are closely linked. Deeply seeing change in the present moment can lead directly to seeing not-self. One of the classic insights into impermanence is seeing arising and passing away. Here is what the Buddha said about this:

> And what is accomplishment in wisdom? Here a [person] is wise; he possesses the wisdom that discerns arising and passing away, which is noble and penetrative and leads to the complete destruction of suffering. This is called accomplishment in wisdom.[4]

Later commentaries, such as the *Paṭisambhidāmagga* and the *Visuddhimagga*, call this the knowledge (Pali: *ñāṇa*) of arising and passing away, a key step in their accounts of the path to enlightenment. This is not a theoretical or conceptual knowing. It comes from the direct observation of one's moment-to-moment sense experience. Everywhere the attention is directed, the meditator sees the arising and passing away of that very experience. Mahasi Sayadaw, perhaps the most influential meditation master of the twentieth century, put it this way:

> One's knowledge remains concerned exclusively with the arising and passing away of the processes noticed. For then, at each act of noticing, one sees: "The noticed object, having arisen, disappears instantly." . . . In this way one understands by direct experience how bodily and mental processes arise and break up from moment to moment.[5]

This kind of insight becomes an avenue to seeing not-self, because it is so clear that everything we experience has no continuity at all but is simply arising and passing moment after moment: sounds, sensations, thoughts, emotions—going, going, gone. Eventually even the noticing mind is seen as arising and passing. As we saw in chapter 2, continuity is a key criterion for the establishment of self. In the light of the momentariness of arising and passing, there is nowhere to locate an ongoing "I."

Some Buddhist teachers describe this insight into arising and passing as a "small enlightenment" and suggest that once a meditator has seen in this way, eventual enlightenment is assured.

CALM

When we first experience calm in meditation, it can feel like a revelation. Our busy lives in the modern world don't lend themselves to this state of mind. Fast-paced societies have bred in us fast-paced nervous systems that are not easily slowed down. Hours of sitting still in meditation, however, start to change that.

When we meditate, the rapid flow of thoughts starts to ease up. There is more space between thoughts, and the words themselves come more slowly, as though we're on vacation in a warm climate. The body relaxes. The heart rate slows and the breath becomes longer. It feels as though more space has opened in the mind. This discovery of calm is one of the great rewards of meditation. It nearly always feels satisfying. We may sense, accurately, that this is only the beginning of what is possible through meditation.

As calm develops further, we start to get the first direct taste of a certain kind of emptiness. Not as much activity is taking place now. Body and mind are tranquil, like a calm lake. In the absence of restless activity, some support for the "I" has gone away. In discussions of practice, meditators will often report that their sense of the self has become weaker. There can be a little unease because the seeming solidity of "I" is getting undermined. Sometimes they are not sure what to do next. In most cases the meditator just needs to be assured that the development of calm is a good thing, that they can trust it, and that it can take a little while to get used to. The instruction is generally to keep doing what they've been doing in meditation and simply allow any unsettledness to be there as well.

Usually the meditator at this point is familiar with the teaching of not-self and recognizes for herself that the calm is teaching her something about that. She is starting to see how much of the sense of self is dependent on the restless activity of thinking, which stirs up emotions and bodily energy as well. It becomes clear that the sense of self is not a steady ongoing presence but rather something that fluctuates, growing stronger or weaker at different times. This understanding opens the meditator further to the possibility that the sense of self could go away altogether. In the first experience of calm, however, there is usually still some sense of self as the observer of the more subtle activities of mind and body.

When the sense of self weakens or falls away in meditation, this is not to be confused with an unhealthy psychological condition or a depersonalization disorder—those states are characterized by confusion and disorientation. The meditative loss of self, usually preceded by calm, is born from clarity and understanding.

UNIFICATION OF MIND

Another avenue to seeing the absence of self is the development of an attention that has become unified, so that the totality of the mind is interested in and engaged with the present experience. Attention can be so complete that there is no room for stray thoughts, projections, or even unconscious views to influence our perceptions. When the mind is unified, there is less division between self and other, between subject and object, and between inside and outside. The gap of duality is bridged in the mind that has become whole.

The unification of mind can come about in three ways—through investigation, concentration, and loving-kindness. Each imparts a different flavor to the seeing of not-self.

INVESTIGATION

We may live much of our lives in a state of distractedness, not actually present for the moment as it occurs, but lost in past or future. T. S. Eliot in *The Four Quartets* used a marvelous phrase to describe this kind of mind: "distracted from distraction by distraction."[6] How adrift have we become? We are so distracted we don't even realize we are distracted; we've forgotten what wholeness of mind feels like.

What is it that occupies our distracted attention? Is it a great matter of life and death, or the future of the planet? Hardly. It is mostly trivia that occupy us. The always-on Internet circus, the latest sporting event, our social media accounts, hundreds of channels of satellite television, and so on.

When we become truly interested in an experience in the present moment, our attention collects naturally and easily around it. Not long ago I was riding a bike down a quiet country lane in Massachusetts when an adult black bear walked slowly out of the woods and sat down in the middle of the road. My attention became very focused! The bear made itself quite at home on the pavement. Alert, but not afraid, I stood by my bike and with no forced effort watched the bear for several minutes. We both might have stayed like that for a long time but for a car that drove up and eventually around the bear, prompting it to move on.

We can become similarly interested in any moment of experience and collect the mind in the present. We don't need a bear or even something dramatic to prompt us. It could be the smile on the face of a child, the new moon setting just after the sun, or the miracle of a single breath as we're meditating. As we draw our attention closer to that sense experience, we let go of distracting thoughts and come into greater wholeness in the moment. Many people listening to the Buddha's teachings during his lifetime reached significant stages of awakening, due I believe to the high degree of interest and attention evoked by his words and presence.

We can choose to develop this kind of attention by deliberately investigating our experience in a meditative way. That is, we look more closely at experience in order to better understand the nature of things: body, mind, sense experience, aggregates, craving, grasping, and so on. We are trying to learn not by thinking about things but by a direct observation of the immediate present. This kind of investigation naturally comes out of mindfulness practice.

Seeing without a Seer

Once when I was a monk in Thailand I was sitting at the top of a small mountain on the island of Koh Samui with two other monks. We got to talking about the relation between subject and object as we understood it from our meditations. We realized that somewhere along the way we had all picked up the view that subject and object always go together, that any time there was the sense of an object there had to be the sense of a subject felt as "I." We became interested in the question, Can we notice an object without giving rise to a subject that is felt as an "I"? Does the perception of an object necessarily lead to the creation of a sense of self? One of the other monks, speaking from his own experience, said that he had had a clear sense in recent sittings of hearing a sound without any sense of an "I" accompanying it.

This was intriguing to me. I didn't have a strong opinion on the matter so I was free to play with it. Sitting right there I started to investigate the sense door of seeing. I looked at a forested mountain across the valley and repeatedly paid close attention to the arising of contact and perception, taking the green shape of the hill as something familiar, though without always using a word for it. I had the sense a few times that I could confirm what my friend was saying, that there could be an object without a sense of "I." Maybe there could be seeing without a seer! This was exciting in a way that may only be appreciated by longtime meditators. I wasn't going to declare myself highly transformed, but I did appreciate how keen the observing mind could become when we sincerely want to understand our experience here and now.

This reminded me of a time in college when I was just becoming interested in Buddhism. I read what I could find at the time, which was mostly D. T. Suzuki and Alan Watts. I would walk around the campus alone at night and think about what I had read. The question that interested me most was that of self or no-self. One night I sat in the middle of the school's well-lighted main quad and puzzled over this question while I stared at the physics building, where I had spent many hours in classes. My interest was keen and wholehearted, drawing all my attention into the moment. All of a sudden my conceptual apparatus fell totally away and the sight of the building stood out vividly, all on its own. This altered perception lasted only a few seconds before my normal habits of thought returned.

When they came back, I was most struck by two things. First was that my sense of self had been absent, even if briefly. The sense of myself as someone sitting watching the physics building had completely fallen away for a few moments; only the building stood out, in all its brick-and-concrete glory. For that brief spell, I knew there was no "I" watching or sitting or doing anything at all. Second, that brief experience had been completely exhilarating and I wanted more.

At the time my only Dharma resources were a few books. I didn't have a teacher or spiritual friend I could talk to about this odd occurrence, nor did I have a meditation practice to lend it meaning or support. It stayed in my mind as an unusual event. Later I came to understand it as an early *anattā* insight. It was not earth-shaking, but it was one in a series of many moments of seeing beyond self that have added up to changing the way I relate to myself and to the world.

As I read more, I found that the self has been falling away from meditators for a long time. This was written by the eighth-century Taoist poet Li Po:

> The birds have vanished down the sky
> Now the last cloud drains away.
> We sit together, the mountain and me,
> Until only the mountain remains.[7]

CONCENTRATION

Concentration (Pali: *samādhi*) is a key word in meditation and one that is easily misunderstood. It refers to a mind that has become collected, composed, or brought together. Collectedness restores a power to the mind that we give away when we incessantly pursue the distractions of past and future. In the Pali Discourses, a synonym for concentration is the unification of mind. A unified mind is a powerful agent. As we just saw, investigation can also collect the mind's distracted energies and bring them together, but the collectedness of investigation will disappear when interest wanes or the specific inquiry ends. The composure of concentration, once established, is more stable and long-lasting.

As a translation, *concentration* is probably not the best term to convey the meaning of the Pali term *samādhi*. In English *concentration* refers primarily to the mental factor of attention, or focus, indicating the ability to stay on a single object or topic. A student might say, "Can you turn the music down? I'm trying to concentrate on my homework." In this usage, even a present-moment experience like music could be seen as a distraction to the single chosen focus.

But in meditation, concentration denotes the collected quality of the mind itself, regardless of its focus. It is quite possible for the mind to be highly concentrated with or without a single ongoing focus for the attention. For example, in mindfulness of breathing, a very narrow focus on the breath at the nostrils may be sustained for hours at a time. But in the practice of choiceless attention, we allow the focus to shift to a new object in every moment. It is important to understand that both methods can be used to develop high levels of *samādhi.*

This linguistic confusion is not helped by the fact that a synonym for concentration in the classical texts is one-pointedness (Pali: *ekaggatā*). Some commentators have taken this to mean that there must be only a single ongoing focus (for example, breath at the nostrils) in order to generate a one-pointed mind. However, Ajahn Sumedho, the senior Western monk in the Ajahn Chah lineage, defines *ekaggatā* as "the one point that includes everything." We might say that the one point that includes everything is the present moment. So one-pointedness is developed when our attention is fully in this moment.

Because of the different meanings between meditative language and ordinary English, "concentration" is not an ideal translation. "Collectedness" or "undistractedness" might render the meaning of *samādhi* more clearly. However, Buddhist writers have been using the word *concentration* for more than a hundred years, so I will too. We just need to remember that this refers to a unified mind and not to a single, exclusive focus of attention.

Concentration is a highly valued meditative state that appears in many of the Buddha's lists of wholesome qualities to be cultivated (for example, eightfold path, five spiritual faculties, seven factors of enlightenment). *Samādhi* is the last factor in the eightfold path, which means it is the culmination of the section on meditation. It is developed by frequent moments of mindfulness, which can eventually become continuous. Although mindfulness has received more press coverage, concentration is the brighter star of the meditation show. It is what leads onward to wisdom: "Knowing and seeing things as they really are is the purpose and benefit of concentration."[8]

The collected mind feels strong and steady, stable and not easily shaken. Calm is usually an aspect of such a mind, and now calm has developed into an even more refined quality called stillness. In stillness, we feel imperturbable. Thoughts, moods, and sensations may still arise, but we see them clearly and so they don't disturb this underlying stability. We feel a deep sense of peace. Interest comes naturally, because this state is so refined and beautiful. It's not that all the contacts are pleasant—there may be discomfort in the body in a long sitting, for example—but we feel a great sense of appreciation while dwelling in this quality of mind.

When thoughts and moods are quiet and interest is high, this is an ideal setting for intuition to arise and insights to flower. This is when we are able to see things as they really are. Many *anattā* insights are born from such states.

Nothing There

Several years ago I was teaching a month-long retreat at Spirit Rock in Woodacre, California. One of the meditators had a capacity for strong concentration, so I was guiding her to develop the four *jhānas*, states of deep concentration often recommended by the Buddha. She had made steady progress through the first three and was now exploring the territory of the fourth jhāna. She came in one day for our practice discussion, sat down, and exclaimed, "There's nothing there!" She laughed. "I was sitting in the fourth jhāna and everything was really quiet. There weren't any thoughts. I could hardly feel my body." (This is not uncommon in strong concentration.) "I looked around [inside] and I just wasn't there any more. And it hit me: There's nothing there!" She was close to tears in telling me this, partly from joy and partly from the shock of this discovery.

She didn't mean that literally nothing was present in her experience at that time. She could still feel her body and hear sounds and know that her thoughts had calmed. She meant there was nothing else there. She had seen that her experience was completely empty of the self she had always assumed was present. That absence was what made it feel like there was nothing, compared to the normal weight of self, which definitely feels like a something. Even a normal experience of sense contact is relatively light; the sense of self is the burdensome weight. It is as though when we meditate we usually bring with us the whole baggage of our history and plans and place the pieces all around us: parents, old relationships, job prospects, housing problems, money worries, and so on. "There's nothing there!" points to the lightness we feel when all that load is seen not to be actually present. All we have are the light contacts of the present moment.

She said she then imagined her partner of many years to see if she could find some substance: "But there's nothing there either!" She checked other areas of seeming security in her life: also nothing there. These were life-changing insights. It is not possible to see the world in the same way again after this kind of understanding. Her attitude was very accepting of these insights, welcoming in fact, even though they were taking away refuges and beliefs she had leaned on for her entire life. The freedom this discovery brought her was already greater than any imagined loss.

The Buddha's Instruction to Bāhiya

There is a famous account in the Pali Discourses that brings this out clearly. During the time of the Buddha, an ascetic named Bāhiya was living on the west coast of India. He was an advanced practitioner in a non-Buddhist system and had many followers, but he was not altogether free. When he learned that there was a liberated teacher in the north, he left his small hut right away and traveled hundreds of miles on foot to meet him. He came upon the Buddha while the teacher was wandering for almsfood in the city of Sāvatthi. Bāhiya approached the Buddha and asked for teachings. The Buddha said the time was not convenient as he was engaged in his alms round. Bāhiya asked a second time and was again refused. He asked a third time, pleading, "It is hard to know for certain, venerable sir, how long you will live or how long I will live. Please teach me the Dhamma." As was often the case, when asked a third time the Buddha consented.

> This is how you should train, Bāhiya. In what is seen, let there be just the seen. In what is heard, let there be just the heard. In what is sensed, let there be just the sensed. In what is cognized, let there be just the cognized. Then, Bāhiya, you will not be in that. When you are not in that, there is no you there. When there is no you there, then you are neither here nor there nor in between. This, just this, is the end of suffering.[9]

Bāhiya understood the Buddha's teaching and was immediately liberated. The two men went their separate ways. Shortly after, a cow protecting a young calf gored Bāhiya and killed him. His plea to the Buddha proved to be timely!

In all the Pali Discourses, the instruction to Bāhiya is one of the most concise and powerful pointings to the liberating potential of the truth of not-self. First the Buddha tells Bāhiya to train to see each sense experience as only the bare experience, whether it be the seen, the heard, the sensed (that is, the other three physical senses), or the cognized (that is, objects of mind). Doing so, Bāhiya's sense of self will not arise in that moment.

Then the Buddha explains the significance of this instruction: "Then you are neither here nor there nor in between." No sense of self is established anywhere. There are only the sense bases. There are only the aggregates. One is seeing things just as they are. There is no "I" standing to one side or the other to claim or identify with them. When we see in this way, if our minds are as ripe as Bāhiya's, this alone can liberate us.

Bāhiya penetrated to the truth of things because his mind was so well prepared. In fact the Buddha called Bāhiya his foremost disciple in understanding quickly.[10] Most non-Buddhist meditations at the time were designed for concentration, so it is likely he had already attained proficiency in that state. The purity of his mind, as implied by the devotion of his supporters and his renunciate lifestyle, also supports the conclusion that he had skill in concentration. For this reason, I offer this story as an example of the power of the concentrated mind when paired with the faculty of investigation. It's also a potent reminder of the urgency that comes when we consider our own mortality.

LOVING-KINDNESS

Love unites families, friends, partners, and even adversaries. It unites the emotional heart with the rational mind, and the heart/mind with the body. In its deepest movements, love unites the individual with the world. It erases divisions and makes us whole.

In the Buddha's teachings, the quality of love is awakened and developed primarily through the practice of loving-kindness (Pali: *mettā*), one of four qualities called the divine abidings (Pali: *brahma vihāra*). The other three are compassion, appreciative joy, and equanimity. The divine abidings are so named because they are heavenly states that can be developed to such a degree that they begin to feel like home. Sharon Salzberg likes to say, "They are our best home." From ancient times, there are practices to evoke each of these four states. I'll introduce a traditional practice for the cultivation of loving-kindness at the end of this chapter. Instructions and descriptions for all four divine abidings can be found in Sharon's book on this theme.[11]

When I was practicing loving-kindness over a long period of time, I could feel the slow, steady growth of a kinder disposition toward myself and all the people in my life. As I brought myself and other individuals to mind, I found that my usual judgments began to fall away and I was able to look on us all with much more friendliness. I could still see our faults and weaknesses—I wasn't blind—but it became surprisingly easy to hold our flaws in a larger attitude of sympathy.

I also experienced some side effects of the meditation that at first seemed curious. As I was sitting, I continued to notice sounds: a bird calling, footsteps in the hallway, a car passing by on the street. But strangely the sounds didn't seem to be outside me. I knew that conventionally speaking they were definitely outside my body. But oddly, it felt like they *were* me, just as much as the sensations that were arising and passing in my body.

These weren't momentary, mystical experiences. They would last for quite a while and there wasn't anything otherworldly about them. The state of mind was pleasant but not especially exhilarating. There was no bright light. I wasn't merging with the energy of the cosmos. I felt completely grounded and sensible. Yet something had loosened around the boundary between myself and the world that I'd usually taken to be fixed.

I believe the boundary was eroded by love. As I grew more familiar with the experience, it seemed to grow out of the spirit of friendliness that the meditation was engendering. Myself, other people, birds, cars—all were drifting into and through this warm space of sympathy that knit us all together. Where I stopped and these other things started was not so easy to say.

Neuroscientists have discovered a type of brain activity they call the "default-mode network." The network "appears to be most active when we are least engaged in attending to the world or to a task. It lights up when we are daydreaming, removed from sensory processing, and engaging in higher-level 'meta-cognitive' processes such as self-reflection, mental time travel, [and] rumination."[12]

This sounds like *papañca*, conceptual "proliferation." The default-mode network "is charged with holding the entire system together" and "is thought to be the physical counterpart of the autobiographical self, or ego." Researchers hypothesize that this part of the brain keeps the boundary line between self and other active. Judson Brewer, a neuroscience researcher at Yale, found the default-mode network to be less active in long-term meditators.

These studies suggest that in meditation, as in some mystical experiences, the sense of a dividing line between self and other is not so strong. I would add that this feature may be enhanced if the meditation we are engaged in is that on loving-kindness. If we are paying attention, this softening of the boundary can support the insight that the self is not clearly defined as being anywhere at all: neither here nor there nor in between.

SPACIOUSNESS

Sometimes in life or in meditation, our awareness seems to expand and become vast. We could be walking by the sea, gazing out from a mountaintop, or meditating outdoors listening to the sounds of nature. In such instances, the space around us seems huge, even limitless, and our own awareness seems just as large. We'll explore this phenomenon further in the section on awareness, but for now, let us note how vast awareness can help us see the self in a new way.

First of all, spaciousness can put our preoccupations into perspective. Our personal problems and even our sense of self can seem small in the context of such vastness, a tiny piece of a much bigger picture. This perspective brings a great sense of ease.

Second, that space—especially if developed through a sustained meditation— can be a fertile field for insight. When the pressures of self-concern are lifted, we are better able to see things as they really are. With a sense of spaciousness, sense contacts are felt less intensely. A teaspoon of salt in a glass of water makes the water taste salty, but a teaspoon of salt in a lake is imperceptible. Sense experiences in a field of vast awareness have a weaker impact.

We could describe this as the thinning out of sense experience. As sense experience becomes thinner, there is less structure on which to hang an "I." With less intensity of contact, there is not as much hope or fear. The mind relaxes more easily; the sense of self weakens. At times, spaciousness can be so great and sense contact so light that one simply knows that no self is there. If it were, the self would feel far heavier in the lightness of that moment.

ENLIGHTENMENT

Traditionally, enlightenment is understood as a direct realization of the unconditioned or, one might say, an immediate personal experience of nibbāna. In the Theravadan tradition, one's first realization of nibbāna is called stream-entry, and one who has attained this is called a stream-enterer (Pali: *sotāpanna*). One has entered the "stream of the Dharma," the flowing waters of profound wisdom. Stream-entry has a transformative effect on one's relation to self. The ability to believe in a self, also called the "personality view" (Pali: *sakkāyadiṭṭhi*), is uprooted from mind, never to return in quite the same way again. One sees through the self so thoroughly that one never again believes it truly exists.

The uprooting of personality view, however, does not prevent the *sense* of self from returning again and again. In fact the sense of self, also called "conceit" (Pali: *māna*), does not completely go away until full enlightenment. It's as though the stream-enterer knows better but keeps forgetting. One has seen the truth of things, but old habits of mind persist. This forgetting is an aspect of ignorance (Pali: *avijjā*), which is not uprooted until full enlightenment. So for a stream-enterer, the sense of self will reappear again and again. Sometimes this sense will be weak and can be easily seen through and released. At other times, strong clinging will lead to a strong sense of self which is understood as deluded but is still not released. We'll talk more about enlightenment in chapter 13.

Many avenues lead to the truth of not-self. We practice to keep learning in all these areas, allowing each insight to chip away the bonds of self. Some insights might be dramatic, but many will come in ordinary circumstances to our ordinary mind. We can trust that wisdom is continuing to grow and that the growth of wisdom leads to greater freedom and awakening. In time, the understanding of not-self becomes the way we see the world. It has to be like that. If that were not the case, we would have to rely on altered states of experience for our freedom, and that would not be freeing at all.

MEDITATION

Loving-Kindness

This meditation is the traditional way to develop feelings of loving-kindness, also called goodwill, for oneself, other individuals, and all beings. Like the mindfulness practices, it is best carried out while you are sitting quietly and feeling comfortable.

- Gently close your eyes and bring to mind your sense of who you are. You might feel your body and mood here and now or remember a place where you feel happy. When you feel connected to yourself, say quietly the following phrase: "May I be well, happy, and peaceful." Continue to stay in touch with the sense of yourself and repeat the phrase, feeling a sincere wish for your own welfare. Carry on for a few minutes.
- Now bring to mind someone you naturally care for or love. Bring to mind an image of them or remember times you've been together. When you feel connected to them, repeat the same phrase for them: "May you be well, happy, and peaceful." Do this for a few minutes.
- Now let your goodwill expand as far as you can imagine to include all beings everywhere. Reflect that all living beings only want to be happy and don't want to suffer. In this we are all alike. Send your wishes for their welfare in all directions, repeating the phrase "May all beings be well, happy, and peaceful." Do this for a few minutes.

8. BEARING EMPTINESS

In all our searching, the only thing we've found that makes all the
emptiness bearable is each other.

—Carl Sagan[1]

DR. SAGAN WAS talking about the emptiness of space but the same issue arises
in discovering the emptiness of self. We've already talked about the liberating
power of insights into not-self. It can feel as though we've put down a great burden, one that we'd carried for so long we didn't even realize we were carrying it.
There is potential for great freedom in these insights. But it's also true that these
insights can be unsettling, frightening, and discouraging. Sometimes they offer
more than we'd bargained for. The self is the main project we've been embarked
on for most of this life and, according to the Buddha, many prior lives as well. It
is the foundation of almost every choice we make and everything we do. It is the
fixed point around which everything else revolves. When its status is challenged
and its very existence threatened by Buddhist inquiry, it's no wonder that some
big pieces of the mind's furniture start to shift.

Often in a retreat, a meditator who comes to talk about not-self insights will
walk in trembling. The lightness that comes from letting go of the self is usually felt as a great freedom, and at the same time it can feel like a serious loss of
ground, as though the carpet has been pulled out from under oneself. Where is

the foundation I've built my whole life around? Where is the glue that holds all this together? What do I stand on now? These are not theoretical questions; they are felt viscerally. At this point, a meditator often feels insecure, exposed, and vulnerable. The title of Milan Kundera's novel captures this well: *The Unbearable Lightness of Being.*

FEAR AS PART OF THE PATH

Anxiety and fear are normal and even traditional aspects of the path to awakening. The *Visuddhimagga* talks about a stage of insight knowledge (Pali: *ñāṇa*) called dissolution, in which the meditator experiences the rapid passing away of phenomena everywhere the attention is directed. This is said to occur sometime after the earlier insight into arising and passing. The text says that at this stage the meditator understands a new aspect of emptiness from his or her personal, direct experience. At this point the meditator may pass through periods of anxiety, fear, and even terror at the groundless nature of things.

There is something primal about the fear that arises here. We all have a deep longing for safety and security, but we also know that the universe we live in is uncontrollable and unpredictable. We are vulnerable to pain, injury, illness, loss, and death. Human beings in all cultures have tried to solve this problem through systems such as armies, agriculture, religion, philosophy, science, and psychology. But in the millennia of recorded human history, no easy solution has been found. (Buddhism and some other spiritual systems do offer a real resolution to this insecurity, but the work getting there is not easy.) As individuals we still carry a deep wish for security and an underlying fear of what might happen. This primal fear is exposed at this juncture in the journey of seeing emptiness. The insight into the selfless, dissolving nature of things reveals that there is not a solid scrap of mind or matter to take hold of.

Freud once defined *neurosis* as the refusal to suffer.[2] Likewise we might say that constructing an ongoing self out of grasping and personality view is designed to keep us from feeling the primal fear of groundlessness. The self can be seen as a defensive maneuver against emptiness. However, at this point along the path, the defenses have come down. Krishnamurti said that we don't have to search for the truth—to see the false as the false is to discover the truth.[3] We have seen the falseness of the old notions of self and there is no way to undo that seeing. Chögyam Trungpa Rinpoche compared the practitioner at this point to a snake that has crawled into a long thin tube of bamboo. Even if it wanted to back out there's no room to turn around. For better or worse, we have invited emptiness in and now there's no turning back. The only way through is to keep going forward to the end.

Tibetan Buddhists speak of learning to bear the truth of emptiness. At this point in our journey, we need to bear the fear and anxiety that come when the ground is pulled out from under us. The practitioner has to be willing to go through these experiences, unpleasant as they are. It helps to know that this is not the end of the path. If we can open to these states with mindfulness and feel them fully, they too will pass away, exhibiting the same impermanence as all conditioned things.

LOSING OLD IDEAS OF SELF

We must also be ready to bear an experience of loss. We've invested a lot over many years in the project of the self—personal history, self-image, plans, ambitions, career, family, and more. Some decisions in these areas may have been made from clarity and wisdom, and we may still feel aligned with them, even as our understanding of selflessness deepens—but it is also possible that some choices might have been made from self-centered desires that no longer seem valid. We may have acted out in relationships to get attention, taken a high-paying job to create status, chosen an attractive partner to make us look good, craved approval because of a lack of self-love, acted cruelly to others out of blind anger, drunk too much to keep from feeling despair, or searched incessantly for sex to defend against loneliness. With a greater understanding of self and not-self, some of these actions and motives fall away.

Life begins to change. We see the false as false. We let go of old habits. Our values shift. We're no longer in tune with certain old friends, and we move on. We don't enjoy the same entertainments we once did. Loud gatherings start to feel oppressive. Some previously enjoyable pastimes now seem like distractions. We may feel we've become a different person. Things are falling away not because we think they should but because they don't fit anymore. Our life simplifies so we can focus on things that really matter to us.

This is a natural process, described in Buddhism as renunciation (Pali: *nekk-hamma*). It's not an act of will or discipline, to give things up out of a belief that they aren't good for us or are "not spiritual." Some things just fall away because they no longer bring as much satisfaction as our new way of seeing. The Buddha put it this way in the *Dhammapada*:

> If, by giving up a lesser happiness,
> One could experience greater happiness,
> A wise person would renounce the lesser
> To behold the greater.[4]

Even though we wisely choose these changes in our life and don't want to return to our old habits, there may still be some sadness around their passing. We do not want to call the old pleasures back, but we sometimes miss the kick they gave us. Trungpa Rinpoche called this "nostalgia for samsara." We notice some longing for the old, but we don't let it command us. We know that simplifying our life is the path of wisdom.

THE LOSS OF MEANING

Another deep shift starts to register around meaning. What will give meaning to our life when the "I" is not there? The project of the self had its own embedded meaning even if it came from delusion. We were on the path to getting rich or famous, perhaps, or married or popular or powerful. We were on the road to becoming someone. This is the territory of egoic gratification: sense pleasures and becoming someone. These goals provide a strong motivating force that gives our life direction and meaning. When that whole aim comes into question, it's not that we become boring and give up all enjoyment, but we no longer make pleasure and *becoming* the main projects of our life. We move away from building up ego and toward a search for greater meaning. True meaning looks after the long-term welfare of ourselves and those around us. As the Dalai Lama put it, "We are visitors on this planet. We are here for ninety or one hundred years at the very most. During that period, we must try to do something good, something useful, with our lives. If you contribute to other people's happiness, you will find the true goal, the true meaning of life."[5]

As we begin to orient our life around more genuine meaning, it may not be clear what activities will best express our new direction. We may feel caught between two lives. A lot of the false has fallen away but the truer expression has not yet manifested. The shift in values takes place deep in the roots of our personality, and we can feel somewhat adrift while it is unfolding. This is a time that calls for patience and trust, which we might also call faith.

SEEING DELUSION MORE CLEARLY

Selfing has not ended yet. As we continue to observe selfing—I-making and mine-making—we see increasingly clearly the pieces that make them up—identifying with body and moods, craving the pleasant and despising the unpleasant, claiming personal history as "who I am," owning things. These activities are not as satisfying as they once were, because we've seen the strings that make the puppet dance. We're not taken in as easily, but we are still sometimes taken in. This can be an awkward moment along our path of practice, because we are seeing our own confusions so clearly, yet they do not entirely cease. "These are my old habits of mind? Was I always this deluded? Oh no, nothing has changed!" It can be discouraging to see the old patterns come back, even when we now know their limitations. We'll talk more about this in the next chapter, but for now the important thing is that we are seeing the delusions clearly, and with continuing mindfulness, the patterns will grow weaker and weaker over time.

To summarize, the gathering insights into the emptiness of self bring their own difficulties. We may feel:

- ungrounded
- like we are dissolving
- frightened
- nostalgic for the old self
- like we are lacking in meaning
- discouraged by our delusions

While these experiences can be extremely uncomfortable, they are all natural and none of them is truly a problem.

THE WAY THROUGH

We won't always feel this way. This is an important stage in practice, but it is only an intermediate stage. We have come a long way from the blind identification and clinging we began with, but there is still more work to do. This transition can be hard to bear, and traversing this stage may take some time. Three qualities have the capacity to help us bear the burden of emptiness and make this transition workable: compassion, patience, and faith.

COMPASSION

Compassion (Pali: *karuṇā*) is the second of the divine abidings and is closely related to loving-kindness, the spirit of friendly acceptance we can bring to ourselves and all other beings. Compassion is what loving-kindness becomes when it sees suffering. Love takes on a different flavor around someone who's in pain. Its joy is tempered by the other person's sorrow, but that doesn't mean that we fall into suffering too. Compassion, like love, is a heavenly state. Our heart resonates with the suffering we see but is not overwhelmed by it.

In the work of bearing emptiness, compassion for yourself lets you hold your own difficulties in a large and caring container. You acknowledge that it is difficult, and you can accept that burden without judgment or depression. You can feel a tender caring for yourself just as you would for a child who is in pain. The ability to be compassionate toward our own suffering is a profound strength we can find in ourselves and develop even more fully. It's a tremendous support along the entirety of the path. There is a meditation practice for compassion, as there was for loving-kindness. We'll explore this more in the meditation at the end of this chapter.

PATIENCE

Patience (Pali: *khanti*) is that inner quality that lets us meet unfortunate circumstances with a tranquil heart. *Khanti* does not mean simply waiting, as the English term *patience* might sometimes imply, because that could involve a certain degree of resignation or even inward irritation: "Okay, I'll try to be patient while this customer service rep puts me on hold for another fifteen minutes!"

Sometimes translated as forbearance, the true meaning of *khanti* is that we maintain a sweetness of mind even in situations that are not to our liking.

On a visit to Thailand in my early twenties, I was struck by this quality in a Thai woman working in a travel agency. A Western customer was unhappy with the ticket she had bought and was complaining loudly and aggressively. Whether there were grounds for her unhappiness, I couldn't tell. The agent on the receiving end of the tirade did not react with anger, frustration, or condescension. Instead the Thai agent continued to address the customer with genuine respect, listening carefully, not interrupting or turning away, and even smiling at times. I learned many lessons from people in Thailand, and for me this was a revelation: that one could be inwardly composed and truly kind in the middle of an angry harangue. This was patience at work! Eventually the customer was satisfied.

In bearing emptiness, patience reminds us that all the work doesn't need to be accomplished this minute, that difficulties are also impermanent, and that the journey is best furthered by staying peaceful.

FAITH

Faith is one translation of the Pali word *saddhā*, which means, literally, "to place one's heart upon."[6] Faith in the Buddha's teachings is not about blindly believing in a doctrine or a dogma. In fact, the Buddha criticized those who cling blindly to views and opinions. Faith is about a growing trust in a reliable source that leads to greater happiness for ourselves and others. Classically, this source is found in the triple gem: the Buddha, his teachings, and the community of committed practitioners. We feel an initial trust on hearing Buddhist teachings and then develop a firmer faith as we put the teachings into practice and verify them for ourselves. We see the beneficial outcomes in others who are walking the same path. This deepening quality of trust allows us to relax into our experiences on the path whether they are pleasant or not.

In this stage, as we struggle with the difficulties of bearing emptiness, we need faith in order to keep going. That is why it is so important at times to talk with a teacher who has been over this terrain herself or himself. The teacher tells us that if we keep going on the path, these difficulties too will be understood and mastered. The teacher reassures us that we can do this. As Bhikkhu Bodhi writes, "Liberation is the inevitable fruit of the path and is bound to blossom forth when there is steady and persistent practice. The only requirements for reaching the final goal are two: to start and to continue. If these requirements are met there is no doubt the goal will be attained. This is the Dhamma, the undeviating law."[7]

If we will just continue, the liberating power of emptiness will continue to work on us. At this moment, only the obstacles are apparent. Eventually, everything will fall into place in its own time.

MEDITATION

Compassion

Like the meditation on loving-kindness, the compassion practice works by bringing to mind oneself, other individuals, and all beings, and wishing for an end to their suffering.

- Gently close your eyes and sit comfortably. Get in touch with a sense of yourself as an individual person. Let your reflections include a few of the difficulties you are currently facing in life, though not necessarily the most challenging ones. As you connect with yourself, allow yourself to feel a tender caring for the difficulties you are going through. Repeat the phrase "May I be free from my suffering." Do this for a few minutes.
- Now bring to mind someone you know well and care about. Remember their good qualities, and also recall some of the difficulties they're facing in life. As you connect with them, repeat the phrase "May you be free from your suffering" for a few minutes.
- Now let your imagination expand to take in all beings everywhere. Remember that all beings encounter a mix of pleasure and pain in life. Have some care for the painful aspects of life. As you connect with them, repeat the phrase "May all beings be free from their suffering" for a few minutes.

9. KARMA: PATTERNS OF BECOMING

It is more important to teach Westerners about karma than
about emptiness.

—His Holiness the Dalai Lama[1]

WE MAY HAVE seen through the belief in an ongoing self many times, but one
of the more convincing arguments for its reality is the relative stability of our
personality, our way of being in the world. We appear to be the same person
through different situations, with different people, over the course of years. We
have a wide range of moods and behavior, so the personality is not fixed, but it
is remarkably consistent. We don't wake up one morning and find that we've
become the Dalai Lama. We might experience a spacious meditation that transcends personal boundaries, but when we meet our partner, we seem to reassem-
ble into the same person with the same reactive tendencies. When we are trying
to change and develop more wholesome character traits, this can feel frustrating.
The personality can be stubborn in its resistance to reform.

Personality is a big part of who we take ourselves to be, that is, of our self-
image. We tell ourselves that as a person, we are generally a certain way, which
may include positive and negative descriptors. We think we are kind or mean,
generous or stingy, lovable or worthless, capable or incompetent, funny or

boring, smart or stupid, confident or anxious, and so on. Often our parents, teachers, or siblings gave us these labels when we were young, and we simply accepted them. The characteristics we include as part of our self-image may not be present in every situation, but we hold on to this image because some common traits do appear often. There is usually some truth and some fiction in the way we see ourselves.

Another part of self-image is our body. We may have concluded that we are attractive or unappealing, fat or skinny, too short or too tall, too dark or too light, or that our nose, mouth, hands, or feet are too big or too small. These assessments can greatly impact our sense of confidence and self-worth. Spiritual practice is unlikely to change the body all that much, so our work as Dharma practitioners is to recognize that what can change is this self-assessment. With greater acceptance, we don't need to judge our body as inadequate.

WHAT IS PERSONALITY?

In this chapter we want to investigate this phenomenon of the personality and its consistency. What is it we call personality? How did it get to be this way? Why does it seem to repeat itself over and over? Is long-lasting change possible? If so, how can we effect it? We touched on some of these questions in the previous chapter. Now let us look at them in more detail.

Personality, as the word is commonly used, means a person's collective habits of acting, speaking, thinking, and feeling. This definition includes both outer expressions of speech and action as well as inner movements of thoughts and feelings. The outer expressions are prompted by prior inner movements. When we speak or act, it is because there has first been some inner motivation like love, restlessness, anger, generosity, desire, or compassion. A person's wholesome and unwholesome qualities can be summed up in what we call *character*. This word brings something of an ethical dimension to a discussion of personality. I will use *character* and *personality* more or less interchangeably.

So *personality* as I am using it means one's actions, speech, thoughts, and feelings. This is akin to the description of the fourth aggregate, volitional formations (Pali: *sankhāra*)—an alternate translation for *sankhāra* is karmic formations.

These words are all closely related: personality, volitional formations, and karma. To understand personality more deeply, we need to understand what is meant by karma, one of the major teachings of the Buddha and one that is widely misunderstood in the West.

KARMA AND INTENTION

Karma is a Sanskrit term; the Pali equivalent is *kamma*. We will use both terms interchangeably, with a bias toward the Sanskrit because karma has become a common term in English. In Sanskrit, *karma* is a common word that simply means "action." At the time of the Buddha, action was a spirited topic for debate because different spiritual teachers taught very different things about actions. Some said that there was no result from actions, which meant that one could do anything—kill and steal and lie, or be very kind and generous—and there were no consequences for the actor either way. Others said that our futures were predetermined, so that from a spiritual perspective there was no point in any action or effort such as ethical conduct or meditation. Others said that by acting well we could be reborn in favorable circumstances and that by acting badly we could be reborn in unpleasant circumstances. All of these were speculative views; none of the teachers or traditions knew their view to be a fact.

The Buddha cast a unique and original light on the question of action when he declared, "It is volition that I call kamma. For having willed, one acts by body, speech, or mind."[2] All the other traditions had focused on the action itself. The Buddha's insight was that the key to understanding action lies in the volition (Pali: *cetanā*) that gives rise to the act. This force of volition can also be called intention, urge, impulse, motivation, or motive. He said that an unwholesome volition is one that is rooted in greed, hatred, and delusion, while a wholesome volition is rooted in their opposites: renunciation, loving-kindness, and wisdom.[3]

Here is the key teaching: actions done from a wholesome intention give rise to future results that are "wished for, desired, agreeable," while acts done from an unwholesome intention give rise to future results that are "not wished for, undesired, disagreeable."[4] This connection between intention and results is what is generally known as the law of karma. Put simply, good intentions give rise to good results; bad intentions give rise to bad results. For the Buddha this was not a speculative view but something he could see directly.

Action can take place in body, speech, or mind. The Buddha outlined what he considered ten unwholesome and ten wholesome acts in these areas. In bodily acts, three actions are considered to spring from unwholesome intentions and therefore are considered unwholesome conduct: killing a living being, taking what is not given, and sexual misconduct. Four kinds of speech are considered unwholesome: false speech, malicious speech, harsh speech, and gossip. Three kinds of mental actions are unwholesome: covetousness, ill will, and wrong view. The ten wholesome actions are to refrain from the ten unwholesome actions.[5]

KARMA AND HAPPINESS

It's not easy to live a life free from the ten unwholesome actions, but when we move in this direction we experience a much greater sense of harmony and an absence of conflict. The Buddha said that when one lives wisely in this way, one thinks: "I am endowed with blameless bodily, verbal, and mental action."[6] Such a person, said the Buddha, experiences happiness and joy. "This is called the bliss of blamelessness."[7]

The connection between actions and happiness is stated even more clearly in the opening verses of the *Dhammapada*, one of the most popular works in the Pali Canon:

> Mind is the forerunner of all things.
> Mind is chief.
> Speak and act with an impure mind,
> And sorrow will follow you
> As the wheel of the cart follows the ox.
> Mind is the forerunner of all things.
> Mind is chief.
> Speak and act with a pure mind,
> And happiness will follow you
> Like your shadow, unshakable.[8]

The basic notion of karma has gained widespread acceptance in the West, even if the understanding is a little superficial. Some years ago a friend and I were teaching a six-week meditation class in the maximum-security wing of a juvenile hall in Northern California. About a dozen young men attended. Some of them were gang members who had been charged with felonies such as murder and assault. When we reached the last class, we had to decide what message we wanted to try to convey about ethical conduct, well aware that the pronouncements of a couple of middle-aged white guys might seem completely irrelevant if not absurd to these children of the streets.

We decided to present ethical conduct as "the science of happiness": if you want to be happy, here's how you might think about it. After a short introduction, I asked if any of the men could relate to this somewhat foreign notion of karma. One of them immediately replied, "You mean, what goes around comes around?" "Yes, exactly," I replied. Everyone else nodded in agreement. A few weeks later another teacher who continued the class reported that some of the meditators had started to send thoughts of loving-kindness to members of a rival gang.

Our past actions influence our present to such an extent that the Buddha said that it's as though we are born from them:

> Beings are owners of their actions, heirs of their actions. Their actions are the womb from which they are born, their actions are their friend, their refuge. Whatever acts they perform, good or bad, of those they will be the heirs.[9]

One traditional formulation of the law of karma says that one's happiness or unhappiness depends on one's own past actions.[10] This phrase is often used as a reflection to develop equanimity as a divine abiding. Because it is often hard for Westerners to understand or accept this principle, we might sometimes substitute the reflection that one's happiness or unhappiness depends on one's habits of mind.

THE FACTOR OF VOLITION

The teaching on karma gives great weight to the notion of personal responsibility. But it would be a mistake to say only, "I am responsible for my happiness or suffering." This formulation leads to the question, "Which *I* is responsible: the past *I* or the present *I*? Is it the *I* who initiated the actions or the *I* who is receiving the results?" We need to understand the influence of all the laws at work, including not-self and dependent arising, which show that there is no individual agent behind action or upon whom the results of actions land. If there is no individual agent, then what is the *key* operative force here? As the Buddha said, the key is volition. Let's look more closely at this factor of mind.

The Abhidhamma considers volition to be a universal mental factor, which means it is present in every moment of conscious experience. What we intend is constantly changing but the factor of will is always present in some form. At one moment the volition may be to stand up, in the next to step to the desk, then to pick up the phone, then to say "Hello," and so on. Even if we are sitting still and not speaking, our thoughts and emotions are expressing motivations. A thought may express the desire to buy a new dress, to visit a friend, or to condemn a politician. The emotion of compassion expresses the will to care, while the emotion of anger expresses ill will. In meditation, the volition, we hope, is to keep our attention on our present experience, but that intention is repeatedly swept away by attractions to past and future, a different sort of motivation.

Volition is arising over and over, and in each moment it is influenced by other mental factors: desire, judgment, compassion, anger, wisdom, and so on. These factors are also arising and passing moment by moment. The karmic significance of an act has to do with the wholesome or unwholesome mental factors that form the volition behind that act. Action in the world is thus a complex undertaking in which mind truly is the forerunner. Different mental factors arise and pass and influence different moments of volition, which then give rise to actions of body, speech, and mind. This is all happening moment after moment, in every waking moment, without any self at the center of the sequence.

NO SELF IN VOLITION

Surely we would expect to find an "I" in an act of volition. Who decides to act? Who makes a choice? But if we look closely at a simple action, we see that a multitude of factors converge to bring it about. Let's say we are sitting in a room feeling a bit chilly and we decide to draw a shawl over our lap. In a normal account, that is all there is to say: "I felt cold, so I put on a shawl." But if we look more closely, with the eyes of meditative mindfulness, we see that there are more steps in the process.

First there is the recognition that one is sitting (mindfulness of body). Then at some point there is a sensation (contact) that we recognize as cold (perception). Cold is felt as unpleasant (feeling tone), and there is a reaction of aversion (volitional formation). Not seeing the reaction mindfully (delusion), we don't pause to investigate the feeling tone or formation, but rather distract ourselves (beginning of proliferation) with the mildly complaining inner voice, "I'm starting to feel cold," and perhaps we feel a little shiver (sensation). Perhaps some perception of "warm" then arises, either by feeling a part of the body that is well covered or by remembering how the room felt when we sat down. Based on the perception of warmth, a desire (formation) arises to experience being warm (sensation with pleasant feeling tone). Just as the earlier aversion was not seen mindfully as something to investigate, so also the desire for warmth is not seen mindfully or investigated. Based on desire for warmth and a touch of delusion (lack of mindful attention), a memory arises of the shawl lying on the sofa. Based on desire and memory, a volition arises and we turn our head to see the shawl on the end of the sofa (perception). Next the urge arises (volition) to reach for the shawl and cover our lap with it (action)—which we do.

In this entire chain of linked causes and effects, there is never a separate agent or self. Rather there is a back-and-forth dialogue between the body, perceptions, feeling tone, aversion, desire, volition, and action. Volition is just another factor of mind that arises based on prior causes and conditions. It then leads to action, in this case, of the body. It can be very tempting to identify with volition: "I decided to reach" or "I reached." But when we see the momentary nature of all the factors arising and passing, we see there is no continuity to volition either. It too arises, does its work, and passes away.

WHOLESOME KARMA AS THE PATH

The question is not, Do I want to create new karma or not? We are creating new karma in every moment because we are intending something in every moment. The question is, What kind of karma am I creating? And what kind of karma do I want to create? The recommended choice is clear. Since happiness will be born from wholesome intentions, then we want to have only wholesome states of mind as the source of our actions. But it is not easy to have only wholesome states of mind. Greed, hatred, and confusion continue to torment us.

Happiness will only be born from wholesome states of mind, but what are wholesome states of mind born from? This is the purpose of the path. The path is to clarify the heart and mind so that more and more we abide in wholesome states. This is called the purification of the mind (or of the heart/mind). Then our actions will be born from wholesome volition and will be the cause for our future happiness.

Seen in this light, karma becomes our best friend, because it shows us the way to happiness. Actions become our friend and our refuge, because they can lead us out of suffering. This is not a one-time effort or insight that affects a great shift from misery to lasting happiness. Rather this is the moment-by-moment path of practice that we will work with throughout our life until we are fully enlightened. In each new moment, we try to find the most wholesome state possible and let volition and action come from that.

This is what the Buddha described as right effort, the sixth step in the eightfold path.[11] Right effort is described as four specific practices:

- to *guard* against the arising of unwholesome states that have not yet arisen
- to *abandon* unwholesome states that have already arisen
- to *develop* the arising of wholesome states that have not yet arisen
- to *maintain* wholesome states that have already arisen

These four practices are sometimes summarized as: guard, abandon, develop, and maintain. We might sum them up as: always keep the mind in a wholesome place.

Karma and the eightfold path are deeply related. The proper understanding of karma leads us to undertake the effort of the path. Moreover, the path itself is a karmic unfolding. The power of the path, which is comprised entirely of wholesome factors, derives from the power of karma to create wholesome results from wholesome states.

Buddhism considers the law of karma to be simply another natural law of the universe, as universal as the laws of physics, chemistry, and biology. Whether you believe in karma or not, whether your culture or religion believes in it, the law of karma applies to you, as it does to everything. It is not, however, the only law of cause and effect.

OBJECTIONS TO THE LAW OF KARMA

People sometimes object to the teaching on karma because its assertion of personal responsibility seems heartless and uncaring—seeming to put too much responsibility on the individual's volitional actions and too little on circumstance or systemic factors.

The Buddha's teaching on karma does not discount other causes of suffering. In one discourse, the Buddha is specifically asked if all the pain that a person experiences is due to his or her past actions. The Buddha declares this to be a wrong view and mentions a number of other sources of pain, including illness, diet, climate, accidents, and assault.[12] Karma is one among several laws of the universe; it does not replace or diminish the others.

If we take the teaching of karma as an omnipotent force in our own life, we might feel guilty about the pain we find in life, believing that it must have come from our past actions. If we are suffering, we can be tempted to imagine what it was we did in the past to cause that pain. Even if we don't have the slightest inkling of what those actions might have been, we may feel guilty and judge ourselves harshly. This is an attempt to use karma as a rearview mirror: "Here's where I am today—let me speculate on how I got here." That might not be so helpful. Speculation and guilt are not compassion and understanding. They don't lead to wholesome states of mind and so fly counter to right effort, yielding no beneficial result. We simply don't know what connection there may be between our immediate present and specific past actions. This kind of imagining should be abandoned out of compassion for oneself.

Similarly there is no point in assigning blame to someone else who is having difficulties, thinking, "Well, they have brought this on themselves by their own actions, so it's their problem." Sometimes, if we know a person well, we may able to see with some accuracy the causes of their misery. We might watch a friend or family member make an unwise choice that we know will end in suffering. Often we are frustrated by our inability to change their decision and then watch help-lessly when the situation plays out as we expected. But even when we see that someone brought on their pain by an unwise choice, that doesn't mean that we should stop caring about them. This is the time they most need our compassion. Our judgments won't be helpful. In other areas of their life, we may not have any idea why things have ended as they have.

If we don't know a person well, we generally can't know the source of their unhappiness. To say that it is due to their past actions is just speculation. One example is the children who were killed in the Holocaust. Does the law of karma say that every one of those deaths was the karmic result of that child's own past actions? The Buddha never said anything like this, and we don't know it for our-selves. On a number of occasions the Buddha did say that he was able to see what past action had led to a specific individual's good or bad fortune, but most of us lack that ability. If we don't know, it is usually not helpful to speculate. The most helpful use of karma is not as a rearview mirror but as a tool to navigate going forward. When we understand that our present action will influence our future happiness, we then make the effort to choose wisely and act from wholesome intentions.

Another misunderstanding of karma is regarding it as a cosmic system of reward and punishment. "If someone's past actions caused their unhappiness, that person *deserves* to suffer." Karma is again seen as an uncaring doctrine that finds satisfaction in otherwise inexplicable punishment. There is, however, no such attitude of punishment within the teaching of karma or spoken by the Buddha himself. Karma is simply a natural law. To expect it not to operate would be like expecting gravity not to operate. To expect a happy outcome from an unkind act would be like expecting an apple to come off a branch and not fall to the ground.

The Buddha never showed a wish to punish or satisfaction in anyone's suffer-ing. His response to suffering was always compassion. I'm sure if he had known a way to remove the suffering of all beings, even the most hardened criminals, he would have done so immediately. We see this from his treatment of Angulimāla, a serial murderer who even tried to kill the Buddha. After stopping Angulimāla in his attempt to kill him, the Buddha gave him basic instructions in mindful-ness and admitted him into the community of monks. Angulimāla practiced diligently and not long afterward became fully liberated.[13]

SIX WAYS OF SEEING KARMA AT WORK

The basic teaching on karma is that wholesome volitions lead to happy results while unwholesome volitions lead to unhappy results. There are at least six ways we can see this law at work.

1. *Before we act.* As we are preparing to do something, we consider it by thinking about it. If we are considering doing something wholesome, such as giving a gift to someone in need, then the anticipation of that giving brings us happiness and joy. On the other hand, when we think of doing something unkind, even the anticipation brings some unease into the mind. If we can become mindful of that sense of unease, we can use it to examine our motives and make a wise choice.

Once I was on a conference call with other committee members of a retreat center. I expressed a difference of opinion with one of the members. A day later I received an email from that person that I considered disrespectful. My first impulse was to reply to the person and copy the other committee members. Generally this might be a good organizational principle and a way to keep everyone informed. But as I thought about sending the email, something made me uneasy. When I examined the unease, I saw that my motive for copying the other members was to expose the person's tone of disrespect so their credibility would be undermined. When I saw that this was not a respectful thing to do, I refrained from sending the email and called the person instead. We were able to talk through my feelings and the issue and restore our working relationship.

2. *While we act.* When we do something helpful, it feels good in the very moment of doing it. Some friends were moving into a new house and needed to stack three cords of wood to prepare for the winter. That's a lot of wood and a lot of work, so they emailed their friends and asked if any would be willing to help them. A number of people showed up on the day, which made the work not just easy but a delightful community experience. At the end of the day, naturally the hosts thanked the helpers, but perhaps surprisingly, a number of the helpers also thanked the hosts. They told the hosts that it had been a great pleasure to be able to offer

their service, an opportunity they wouldn't have had without the invitation. This was a good reminder of the joy we can have in giving.

Similarly, when we cause pain to someone else, there is pain for us in the act too. If the person causing the hurt is not sensitive enough to feel their own pain, the pain is there nonetheless, unfelt and unacknowledged. Sylvia Boorstein, an insight meditation teacher and colleague, put it very well, "Anyone causing great pain is himself in great pain."

3. *After we have acted.* If we have done something skillful through compassion or generosity, we will also feel happy when we remember that action. It can be a great pleasure to reflect on our acts of kindness. It needn't be egotistical. When we begin a period of loving-kindness meditation, we are often instructed to recollect our own good actions from the past. This brings joy and creates an atmosphere of appreciation of oneself that can be helpful for developing the friendly spirit of loving-kindness.

On the other hand, if we have harmed others in the past, we will feel bad when we remember those acts. Often in the prolonged quiet of a meditation retreat, some of these memories emerge, even if we haven't thought about them in a long time. On one of my early retreats, a lot of these came to mind—memories of saying something mean to a classmate in second grade, shooting a bird while hunting with my father, killing a chicken while overseas in the Peace Corps. When I reviewed these acts from a place of openness and compassion, I felt terrible. I lived with the pain of those regrets for some days in that retreat. Eventually the intensity of the pain diminished, but to this day I still feel remorse when I think of those actions.

4. *In our relationships.* Our actions come back to us as karmic results in the way people relate to us. The adage "As ye sow, so shall ye reap" is true in the field of interpersonal relationships. If we have been friendly, warm, caring, and generous to others, generally they will appreciate us, be happy to see us, and are more likely to respond with similar expressions of friendship and generosity. But if we've been quick to anger, judgmental, or blaming of others, they are not likely to welcome us or seek our company. They won't trust us or share their feelings or problems with us. The

world of human relationships, a mirror of our own inner lives, is also a field of karma.

Intimate partnerships offer a vital and dynamic opportunity to observe karma and its fruits. Relationships almost always develop sticking points, areas where the partners repeatedly come into conflict in ways that trigger the other's reactive formations, such as resentment, greed, jealousy, or insecurity. For example, your partner's spending habits might make you feel fearful about money, and when you express this, they become resentful of your control. Or your partner might make frequent sexual demands of you, and you feel resentful. When you tell them, they become insecure about their desirability. A partner likes to spend time with young, attractive members of your own sex and you feel jealous, but when you tell them, they feel angry that their freedom is being limited. Suffering mounts for both parties. The topic becomes a tightly wound knot; the slightest mention of it can throw both people back into painful reactivity. If you can be aware of the pattern and drop your reactivity, or even reach out with love, the knot can start to untangle. Because partners in intimate relationships spend a lot of time together, a change in one partner is quickly sensed, and often the other person will offer their own kind response. An act of love or care is often followed soon by its fruit.

5. *In habitual states of mind.* Volitional formations are creatures of habit. When we incline time and again to a particular way of relating to experience, to life, to the world, that response becomes more and more likely to be repeated in the future. Our habitual reactions wear grooves in the mind, which is why personality tends to repeat itself again and again. One person meets the world with unbridled optimism while another views it with cynical pessimism, because those are the grooves they have followed many times before. The Buddha expressed it like this:

> Monks, whatever a person frequently thinks and ponders upon, that will become the inclination of his mind. If he frequently thinks and ponders upon thoughts of sense desire . . . ill will . . . cruelty, then his mind inclines to thoughts of sense desire . . . ill will . . . cruelty. If he frequently thinks and ponders upon thoughts of

renunciation . . . kindness . . . compassion, then his mind inclines to thoughts of renunciation . . . kindness . . . compassion.[14]

The connection between the underlying intention and the pattern of reaction is expressed in the following quotation attributed to the Buddha. I doubt it was he who said it, but I think he would agree. "The thought becomes an intention, the intention manifests as an action, the action develops into habit, and habit hardens into character. Therefore watch closely the thought and let it spring from concern for all beings."[15]

Donald Hebb, an early researcher in neuroscience, discovered in 1949 something similar about repetitive patterns in the brain. His rule has been simplified as "Neurons that fire together wire together." This is what makes for the observable consistency in people's personalities. These repeating personality patterns can persuade us that there is indeed a stable, ongoing self in the center of someone. However, when observed closely, the habitual intentions are not steady or constant but like all formations are always changing, arising and passing, yielding to a new intention. The repetition is merely a phenomenon of karma as expressed in the habit of intentions. The mind's reactions may have been shaped in unskillful ways by this repetition, but we can now take advantage of the law of karma to shape our hearts and minds in a wholesome direction.

6. *In ways we don't understand.* The Buddha gave examples of karmic outcomes that may have taken years or even lifetimes to come to fruition. He mentions, for example, a gift to a great sage that led much later to someone's fortune, or an act of harm that led much later to that person's assault. Most of us, not being buddhas, can't see these connections. We will definitely not discover them by thinking about them. In fact the Buddha advised that there are four "imponderables," areas of knowledge that cannot be realized through mere thought. He said that one who thinks too much about these topics would "go mad and experience frustration." One of these imponderables is the workings of karmic outcomes, because they are so complex. They will always be beyond our rational capability. The other three imponderables are the range of mind of a buddha, the power of a concentrated mind, and the beginning of the universe.[16]

In summary, these are six ways then that karma can manifest: before we act, while we act, after we act, in relationships, in mental habits, and in mysterious ways. We can observe and verify for ourselves the workings of the first five; most of us cannot observe or verify the sixth. When someone says they don't believe in karma, it's usually this sixth kind of result they don't believe in. The other five make sense to almost everyone and can be verified.

We may never see exactly how specific wholesome acts lead to happy outcomes or how particular harmful acts lead to unhappy ends, yet this is the basic message of the Buddha's teaching on karma. Although critics may suggest that karma is a heartless doctrine, once we understand it we tend to feel that the opposite is true. A mechanistic world that lacked intrinsic morality would be heartless. But the Buddha's teaching on karma shows that morality is embedded in the very fabric of the universe. At the heart of this karmic law is a profound linkage between virtue and happiness. This remains a great cosmic mystery, but it is a tremendous source of faith for those on the path.

10. WHO IS REBORN?

I always knew I wanted to be someone but I see now I should
have been more specific.
—Lily Tomlin[1]

THE LAW OF KARMA is often linked to the teaching of rebirth, and for good reason. Sometimes the karmic result of an action will be experienced in the same lifetime. But in other cases, the karmic result will not play out entirely in one lifetime; the full consequences may not appear until a later birth.

I initially met the idea of rebirth with skepticism—I was a trained physicist after all. But having seen the validity of so much of the Dharma, I began to work with my skepticism as a kind of open question. I realized that I didn't need to believe or disbelieve but could continue to explore the question with an open mind. I found this to be a rich and rewarding inquiry. So I would encourage you also to keep an open mind on the question of rebirth as you carry out your own reflections and exploration of this topic.

As you inquire into this question, you'll naturally want to consider both points of view. Those who are skeptical of rebirth say there's no scientific proof and they can't verify it from their own experience. Western culture and some major religions do not endorse the concept. Even some Buddhists don't see its relevance for their own life or practice.[2] On the other hand, those who believe in rebirth note that it's mentioned repeatedly in the discourses of the Buddha as a truth he saw directly for himself. Respected teachers of our time, like the Dalai Lama and Dipa Ma, have spoken of clear memories of their previous lives. Meditation instructions in the *Visuddhimagga* tell how to develop the ability to see this for oneself, and many meditators today still carry out these instructions.[3] Some Western researchers have investigated many accounts of past lives and found no other way to explain their accuracy.[4]

The basic teaching of rebirth, according to the Buddha, is that after we die, unless we are fully enlightened, there will be a new birth connected in some way to this current one. That life also will be subject to death, and another rebirth, and so on. The cycle of birth and death will continue forever until we are fully enlightened. This is samsara, the never-ending round of being born, aging, and dying. According to the Buddha, karma plays a critical role in this round: our actions in this life greatly influence the conditions of our next birth. Generally speaking, wholesome actions now will lead to a happy rebirth. For example, the Buddha said that generosity in this life can lead to abundance in our next birth, not injuring living beings can lead to good health, and asking questions of wise people can lead to wisdom. Likewise, unwholesome actions generally lead to an unhappy rebirth. In light of this connection, he said, we should take special care with our actions while we are alive.

> Grain, possessions, money, all the things you love, servants, employees, and associates—none of these can you take with you. You must cast them all aside. But whatever karma is made by you, whether by body, speech, or mind, that is your real possession, and you must fare according to that karma. That karma will follow you, just as the shadow follows its owner. Therefore, do good actions, gather benefit for the future. Goodness is the mainstay of beings in the hereafter.[5]

In one discourse, the Buddha talks to a group of nonbelievers about the implications of this question. He points out to them that if his teaching on karma and rebirth is true, they would be wise to act in light of it. Good deeds will yield fortunate results for them in this life and the future, including a good rebirth. If they pursue good deeds and his teaching turns out not to be true, then they would still have lived an ethical and praiseworthy life and would be respected by their peers. In either case they would benefit. Therefore, it would be wise of them to act as though karma and rebirth are true. This discourse he called "an incontrovertible teaching."[6]

REBIRTH AND NOT-SELF

As we saw in the last chapter, the repetitive patterns of karmic acts lead to a consistency in personality that can lull us into believing in a stable, ongoing self. However, when investigated more closely, there is no actual stability to personality but only the appearance and reappearance of patterns whose actual makeup is impermanent volitional formations. In a similar way, the reappearance of a being, or rebirth, can make us think that there is something stable and ongoing—a self who journeys from one life to the next. This view can be summed up in the question, If there is no self, who is reborn? Or in another form, Where is the self that continues?

Buddhism considers these questions to be wrongly put. They are like the question, Who is it that grasps? There is no "one" who is reborn or, for that matter, who is born at any time, since all birth is rebirth. Birth is just another event in the unending chain of causes and conditions that lead to effects. In this chain, karma plays a critical role. There may always be a great mystery around birth, as there is around death, but some things in the teachings seem clear. Let us look into the mechanics of cause, effect, and rebirth as described in the Pali Discourses.

When we examine cause and effect in just this lifetime, we see that there is continuity in the patterns of our experience, even though no one thing continues. Moment after moment, sense experiences arise and pass. Each experience in each new moment arises conditioned by what was in the previous moment. This moment fades and conditions the following moment. In this way, the past makes its imprint on the present, and the present upon the future. No one thing lasts across the three times, from past to present to future. Nothing endures, but patterns are perpetuated as each moment "rubs up against" and conditions the next.

According to the texts, this is what happens in rebirth also. When a being dies, there is some continuation of moment-to-moment experience during the time following death. That continuity of experience becomes linked to a new body, which becomes the previous being's next birth. Nothing among the aggregates has endured, but some stream continues in a new channel, influenced by the old. This is the same way experience is happening for each of us right now. As expressed by Ajahn Amaro, the abbot of Amaravati Monastery in England, "The process of going from one life to the next is not very different from the process of going from one moment to the next in this life."[7]

The aggregate of consciousness plays a key role here. Consciousness is not lasting either, but rather arises and passes with each new moment of sense contact. So it is this impermanent consciousness that forms the link to the new life. In one discourse, the Buddha says that "the nutriment consciousness is a condition for the production of future renewed existence," in other words, rebirth.[8]

A few discourses discuss the process in more detail. In one, the Buddha says that "the conception of an embryo in a womb takes place through the union of three things: the union of the father and the mother, the mother's season, and the being to be reborn."[9] In another discourse, the Buddha explains the role of consciousness more clearly: "If consciousness were not to come into the mother's womb, would name-and-form develop there?" A bhikkhu replies, "No, Lord." "Therefore consciousness is the root, the cause, the origin, the condition of name-and-form."[10] Name-and-form is the translation of *nāmarūpa*, which means the combination of material form—here meaning the new body—with the mental faculties that (eventually) allow one to name experience. Yet another discourse speaks of this moment as the "descent into the womb" of the future embryo.[11]

Bhikkhu Bodhi summarizes it like this:

> It is the stream of consciousness coming from the preceding existence that functions as the nutriment consciousness by generating, at the moment of conception, the initial rebirth-consciousness, which in turn brings forth . . . name-and-form.[12]

The new life is influenced in both outer circumstances and inner disposition by the prior being's karma. Outwardly, the circumstances of the new being will be determined in some ways—though not necessarily in every way—by the being's prior karma, as outlined in the discourse cited above on the karmic causes for abundance and health. Inwardly, the character and spiritual temperament of the new being are influenced by the prior being's character development, as outlined in that discourse on the karmic cause for wisdom. In the story of the Buddha himself, it took many lifetimes for him to develop and perfect—to accumulate—all the wholesome qualities required to reach awakening under his own guidance. Collectively these qualities are known as the perfections (Pali: *pāramī*). In the Theravadan tradition they are ten in number: generosity, virtue, renunciation, wisdom, energy, patience, truthfulness, determination, loving-kindness, and equanimity. Similarly our journey to awakening may take many lifetimes, but we are advancing all the time, in every life, in which we conscientiously develop the perfections.

How long is the gap between a person's death and the conception moment of their next rebirth? The Buddha didn't answer this question directly, but there are hints in the Pali Discourses that the "being to be reborn" may refer to an interim form of existence that could last for an unspecified time.[13] The Theravadan Abhidhamma posits that there is not even a moment's gap between death and the next conception. Perhaps the Abhidhamma tenet was invented to support the view that consciousness cannot exist apart from a physical form—a view nowhere proclaimed by the Buddha. The Tibetan Book of the Dead says that the gap is typically around forty-nine days, although by tracking the deaths and subsequent rebirths of many Tibetan lamas, one can see a wide variation in this number.

Could the terms *death* and *rebirth* mean just the moment-to-moment passing away of a temporary identity (for example, "I am cold") and then rebecoming as a new identity in this life ("Now I am warm")? According to the Pali Canon, the answer is no. The discourses define death as "perishing, breakup, disappearance, mortality, death, completion of time, the breakup of the aggregates, the laying down of the carcass."[14] They describe birth (and hence rebirth) as beings' "being born, descent [into the womb], production, the manifestation of the aggregates, the obtaining of the sense bases."[15] Taken together, these passages clearly define birth as the taking up of a new physical body after a previous physical death.

REBIRTH AND LIBERATION

At first the idea of rebirth seems to offer the promise of some comfort: a continuation of our life that could offset to some degree our fear of death. Some Westerners criticize rebirth as just another religious invention that avoids the truth of death by substituting an imaginary ongoing existence, like the Heaven of Christian teachings. However, for those familiar with Buddhist teachings, the never-ending nature of the cycle of death and rebirth known as samsara is terrifying, not comforting. There is no security in the round of births, because it is hard to know whether one's next birth will be pleasant or extremely painful. Just looking around this planet, one sees a vast range of human experience, from great heights of comfort and pleasure to intense, unimaginable suffering.

Most of us don't know and can't choose where our next life will be or what it will be like. Our only protection comes from wholesome actions. That is why we are urged to do good actions now, because "goodness is the mainstay of beings in the hereafter." That is also why the final goal of Buddhist practice is nibbāna, the ultimate peace that offers the only complete freedom from the round of samsara.

11. THE END OF KARMA

Sitting quietly, doing nothing,
Spring comes, and the grass grows by itself.
—Zenrin Kushu[1]

IN EARLIER CHAPTERS we saw that each moment of experience consists only of arising and passing sense phenomena, constantly forming and dissolving. In the last two chapters we've seen how, despite the lack of any ongoing entity, patterns of action continue; each moment conditions the next in such a way that volitional formations repeat themselves. In the Buddhist view, this continuity extends even beyond death into rebirth. In this chapter we will explore the creation and the undoing of karmic patterns—how we become bound and how we become free.

At first glance, the concepts of not-self and karma might seem opposed or even contradictory. If there is no ongoing self, why do the results of my actions come back to me? Why don't they come to you? If there is no self, who is it that is affected by the results of karma?

In the Buddha's time, one of his disciples raised this question: "What self, then, will actions done by the not-self affect?"[2] The Buddha essentially told the monk that he hadn't been paying attention. Since you, no doubt, have been paying close attention, you will know that this is another of those questions that has no answer because it has been wrongly posed. In fact, not-self and karma need each other, both for us to understand the way things are and for us to stand any chance of liberation.

It is important to understand that the truth of not-self does not deny individuality. When you realize not-self in a transformative way, it does not mean that you merge with the cosmos and then live in a state of perpetual oneness with all things, with all personality washed away into a bland nothingness. Nisargadatta had a good explanation of this development:

> When the "I am myself" goes, the "I am all" comes. When the "I am all" goes, "I am" comes. When even "I am" goes, Reality alone is and in it every "I am" is preserved and glorified. Diversity without separateness is the ultimate the mind can touch.[3]

When we stop conceiving of ourselves as "I am something," then an experience of oneness may come. In the Buddhist view this is not essential, but it may happen. When the experience of oneness fades, there is still a sense of individuality ("I am"). When even that fades, there is only what is, and in that is still found every individual existence. The maturity of the insight into not-self is to see the uniqueness in individual existence but without the sense of separation created by concepts of self and other.

This recalls Dōgen Zenji's famous statement from the "Genjōkōan": "To learn Buddhism is to learn about the self. To learn about the self is to forget the self. To forget the self is to be enlightened by the ten thousand things."[4] The diversity of the ten thousand things does not go away. Each still expresses itself in its own way—the song of the robin, the croak of a bullfrog, the love of a mother for her sick child. This is the variety of life, the limitless creativity of nature, each of us manifesting our unique expression. In Buddhism this unique, vital aspect of each thing is called its suchness (Pali: *tathatā*) and is often contrasted with emptiness (*suññatā*), the absence of selfhood common to all things.

In karmic terms we would say that a being's suchness is at least partly the outcome of their past actions. So the teaching of not-self has to be paired with an understanding of karma to explain the incredible variety we see in beings. Equally, karma needs the understanding of not-self. Without it, individual transformation, much less liberation, would not be possible.

KARMIC PATTERNS AND THE CREATION OF SELF

In Buddhism, a sentient being is often described with the metaphor "mind stream." A stream is "a body of running water flowing on the earth."[5] It is bounded by banks, but the flowing water is what constitutes the stream. Like a river, a stream has a definable shape and location. The Mississippi River refers to one body of water and the Colorado River refers to another. The shape of any stream varies from moment to moment depending on rainfall, snowmelt, tributaries, and so on, but each stream can be named, or designated, in a meaningful way. These designations are useful and take on increasing importance as water becomes scarcer all over the world.

Although the name is fixed, when we stand on the bank and look into the body of a running stream, we see there is no constancy there at all. We may be looking at a fairly steady shape, but the actual makeup of the stream is always changing. We see the water in front of us for just a moment and then it passes by, replaced by a new swash that also then moves on. A fish swims past; a branch floats by; an eddy forms and is smoothed out. Nothing is fixed in a flowing stream but something is always there. It's an ongoing pattern of changing waters.

It is obvious why, for thousands of years, a stream has been used as an analogy for mind. The small portion of the stream we are looking at can be likened to the present moment. The past moment has already flowed downstream, and the future moment is still upstream. Nothing remains the same from one moment to the next, except the shape delineated by the banks, which we could say are analogous to the body. There is no enduring entity in the stream, just as there is no lasting self in the mind. Yet some streams are clear and fast, while others are slow and muddy. Each stream has its individual nature, its suchness. Once in place, the characteristics of a stream tend to continue, just as karmic formations tend to repeat, giving a sense of continuity to personality.

But unlike minds, streams don't form an identity around their personality. "I'm the mighty Mississippi, the longest river in the country! I'm so wide, I carry more cargo than any other river around!" What a bore the Mississippi would be if it thought like that. But we do. Our mind stream contains karmic patterns that repeat over and over. Some are beautiful, with qualities of compassion, generosity, and intelligence. Some are painful, with qualities of selfishness, rudeness, and confusion. Because we haven't deeply understood the truth of not-self, these repeating formations make us think we are something in an ongoing way, something fixed. We create a self-image based on these patterns. The more strongly we believe in the self-image, the more likely it is those patterns will arise again in the future, confirming the self-image. So our repeated actions—our habitual karma—strongly condition our personality view, and the personality view in turn reinforces the tendency to act in those same ways.

In short, we *identify* with our habitual actions of body, speech, and mind. This is an identification with the personality, which as we have seen is made only of impermanent volitional formations. Each time we identify, we become that person again—I'm the angry person or the helper, the addict or the moralist. A negative self-image is inherently painful and unsatisfactory, but even a positive self-image limits us: it restricts our choices ("I *should* do something generous, but I don't want to") or we suffer if others don't agree ("What do you mean I'm stingy?"). As the Chan master Zhaozhou said, "A clay buddha cannot cross water, a bronze buddha cannot get through a furnace, a wooden buddha cannot get through fire."[6] With entrenched patterns, we carry around this limiting sense of "I" over years or even a lifetime.

If we think of people we know well—or look closely at ourselves—we can see how sometimes a dominant pattern becomes the organizing principle for a person's whole life. We see lives organized around addiction, craving for attention, greed for money, ambition, need to control, fear, aggression, perfectionism, self-judgment, melancholy, or confusion. These identities are based on unwholesome qualities, but even wholesome qualities can become neurotic if the identification is strong—the compulsive helper, the strict moralist (perhaps the discipline expert in the monastery), or the overly generous person who has time for others but not for his family. One's whole life can be built around trying to satisfy these urges, which are of one's own making. The patterns have been formed through our own volitions and ultimately our own ignorance (in the technical Dharma sense). When entrenched, they feel very compelling and we lose touch with our freedom of choice. They bring suffering and are not easy to change.

This is the bondage of the past, bondage to our own choices, our own karma. As the Buddha described karma, translated here as *action*:

Action makes the world go round,
Action makes this generation turn.
Living beings are bound by action,
Like the chariot wheel by the pin.[7]

The point of the Buddha's teaching is for us to step out of these patterns of action and identification. He speaks of coming to the end of craving, which includes greed, aversion, and delusion; all unwholesome tendencies arise from these three roots. So *craving* is shorthand for all unwholesome tendencies of mind and thus is the basis for all unwholesome karmic patterns. Living beings are confined by karma, because these patterns shape our actions in compulsive ways that lead to suffering for ourselves and others. Dharma practice is to free the heart and mind from compulsive karmic habits. Given the power and tenacity of karma, a serious practitioner might ask, Is this possible? The Buddha's reply is unequivocal:

Abandon what is unwholesome. It is possible to abandon the unwholesome. If it were not possible, I would not ask you to do so. But because it is possible, I say, "Abandon the unwholesome."

Develop what is wholesome. It is possible to develop the wholesome. If it were not possible, I would not ask you to do so. But because it is possible, I say, "Develop the wholesome."[8]

USING KARMA TO CHANGE KARMA

To loosen the grip of mental habits, it can help to remember that there is no fixed self. If there were, if these habits were a part of "me," they would probably be unalterable. But because they aren't, they can be changed. How do we do this? We use the power of karma to change karma.

Suppose we are paying attention to our thoughts and feelings. We can do this while sitting still or engaged in daily activities. Something stimulates us and we notice a habitual reaction spring to life—desire or annoyance, anxiety or confusion. If we let the reaction pull us by the nose, we will soon find ourselves saying or doing something we'll regret later, simultaneously reinforcing this well-worn pattern. Habits compel us, by the power of reactive emotions, to act unskillfully.

Mindful attention helps us see that we have choices. When we recognize the unskillful nature of emotional reactivity, we can pause before we act, and in the pause, we can contemplate more skillful responses. We might, for example, refrain from saying or doing anything, or we may be able to say or do something helpful, something compassionate or loving. This kind of response is from wisdom, not from compulsion. We aren't being pushed into a habitual action by a strong emotion. Wisdom can discern the suffering in that choice and restrain us from acting upon it. Clear seeing has the power to transform a moment of compulsion into a moment of freedom. This is helpful, not only in the present moment but in future results as well. Whenever a karmic pattern is followed blindly, that pattern is reinforced. But when the unwholesome nature of the karmic reaction is seen and the pattern is not followed, the force of that habit is undermined and its karmic potency reduced.

TRANSFORMING OUR OWN HABIT PATTERNS

Working with reactive emotions in this way is a key part of Dharma practice. Sometimes clear seeing will be present—and we can heed the advice of wisdom and act skillfully. At other times it isn't present and we aren't able to do this. The old reaction will arise, and we'll act in the same old way, shouting with anger or withdrawing out of fear. There may be just enough mindfulness present for us to watch the reactive emotion and the unskillful act with some clarity, but not enough to slow its momentum. This can be discouraging; just when we think we have learned to prevent acting on this pattern, we fall into it again. At this point, you might lament, "I'm so tired of seeing my same old stuff again and again!" Trudy Goodman, founding teacher of Insight Los Angeles, once said in response to this quandary: "Well, whose stuff would you like to have?" Everyone's patterns are repetitive, including ours.

There is no shortcut. We have to see *this* pattern again and again until we learn how to relate to it. With each moment of clarity, the pattern loses some of its power over us. So the path to freedom from karmic habits is to see them clearly with wisdom and not to act on what is unskillful. Instead of following the old karma of the habit pattern, we can create new karma based on wholesome factors such as mindfulness, wisdom, renunciation, and compassion. Under the influence of wholesome karma, the old painful habit starts to fade away. It comes less frequently and with less power. In this approach, the reactive emotion doesn't need to be worked out, as some Western psychotherapies do, by revisiting past incidents, although psychotherapy may be helpful at an earlier stage. Rather the work of weakening the unwholesome reaction is done by mindfulness, wisdom, and compassion in the present moment.

It's hard to say how long this process will take or to mark exactly how far along we are, but we can trust that these habits are losing their grip. The Buddha put it this way:

> When a carpenter looks at the handle of his ax, he sees the impressions of his fingers and his thumb, but he does not know, "So much of the ax handle has worn away today, so much yesterday, so much earlier." But when it has worn away, he knows that it has worn away. So too when a practitioner dwells devoted to [meditative] development . . . he knows that [his taints] have worn away.[9]
>
> Or suppose, monks, an ocean-going boat rigged with ropes, having been exposed to the water for six months, has been dragged to the shore for the winter. Then the ropes that had been affected by wind and sun, when soaked by the monsoon rains, will easily go to waste and rot away. So too when a practitioner dwells devoted to [meditative] development, her fetters easily collapse and rot away.[10]

This is the path to freedom from past karma, which is one of the most binding forms of selfhood. The old karma of reactivity is replaced, moment after moment, by the new karma of the path. New patterns are created in the heart and mind based on wholesome factors: mindfulness, wisdom, and loving-kindness. The new volitional formations change our lives. We start to see that the path uses the law of karma—in fact, the path itself is a karmic unfolding.

KARMA IS OUR RUDDER

Where is the path leading? As Yogi Berra said, "If you don't know where you're going, you could end up somewhere else." The new volitional formations of the path—the eightfold path factors, the four divine abidings, the factors of enlightenment—start to change the course of the Old Mind River. That river has been flowing for a very long time into Lake Samsara, an Escher-like lake whose outflow channels back into its inflow, creating an endless recycling of currents. Now new intentions from Dharma practice start to flow into the old river like tributaries. They are tiny at first and their currents are weak. But as they grow stronger, the old flow gets weaker, and the tributaries start to dominate. They shift the channel of the river to an entirely new direction. It is now headed away from Lake Samsara and into the Nibbanic Ocean. That is the destination of this path.

If there were something fixed in the mind stream, it couldn't be redirected. The existing habits would be there forever. However, nothing about volitional formations is fixed, nothing about karma is fixed, and nothing about the self or personality is fixed. There is no solid core at the center of self—only an endlessly changing sequence of volitional formations arising and passing. Craving and ignorance, which lie at the very heart of suffering, are not fixed. This is the truth of not-self. In the beginning, we are bound by our volitional formations, and then we are transformed by the power of new volitions. We abandon what is unwholesome and the mind stream is turned into purity and freedom. The absence of a substantial self makes liberation possible.

The key to the transformative power of the path is the quality of volition, or intention (*cetanā*). In the beginning, the intention to be mindful seems to produce little result, but over time it generates a tremendous power. Anyone who has sat a week's silent retreat can testify to the cumulative power of continuous mindfulness. Our best intentions can't force insight or wisdom, but we can intend to pay attention, to inquire, and to care. The only real tool we have for lasting change is our intention. The Tibetans say, "Everything rests on the tip of motivation."

When I began Dharma practice, my life was chaotic. I was generally discontent and often miserable. What seems most alarming now is that I had no real understanding of why I was unhappy or how I could become happy. I felt adrift, at the mercy of forces beyond my control. Those forces felt as unpredictable as random winds, blowing sometimes hot and sometimes cold, sometimes north and sometimes west. Those winds sent me up into heaven and down into hell as they liked. To be sure, the winds of circumstance still blow around us, bringing alternating conditions of pleasure and pain, gain and loss, praise and blame, fame and dishonor. We are all afloat on a sea of changing conditions that are mostly beyond our control. What is different now is that I have a boat and a rudder and I have learned something about how to steer. The boat of course is the Buddhist path. The rudder is intention.

Intention, or karma, is our only reliable rudder in the vast ocean of uncontrollable events that we call life. As we follow the intentions of awareness, investigation, concentration, loving-kindness, compassion, and wisdom, we are heading for a harbor. And it is a safe harbor—for *harbor* is one of the synonyms the Buddha used for nibbāna—which is peaceful, the goal of the path. From a dialogue with Nisargadatta:

> Maharaj: "Your own will has been the backbone of your destiny."
> Questioner: "Surely karma interfered."
> Maharaj: "Karma shapes the circumstances [of your life], the attitudes are your own. Ultimately your character shapes your life, and you alone can shape your character."[11]

ENDING THE CYCLE OF BECOMING

Past karma may have shaped our present, but it is our will expressed now that sets our future course. Through Dharma practice we are shaping our character, which shapes our life. We can choose *how* we want to shape our life. If we aspire to ordinary worldly happiness, the way to that is through wholesome acts especially of generosity, virtue, and loving-kindness, which are the three bases of meritorious action (Pali: *puñña*).[12] If we aspire to liberation, which the Buddha called the highest happiness, these three bases are important but not sufficient. Generosity, virtue, and loving-kindness can still be done from a place of self. Wholesome acts can be used to support the construction of a more polished, beautiful self-image. Such acts can lead to happiness, but until we have seen through self, we are still creating new karma and continuing the rounds of becoming, or samsara. Tsoknyi Rinpoche warns his students, jokingly, about the risk of their becoming "masters of samsara," enjoying many worldly pleasures but turning away from the real work needed to become free.

The Buddha said that the true fruition of spiritual life is to end the cycle of becoming: "I attained the supreme security from bondage, nibbāna. The knowledge and vision arose in me: 'My deliverance is unshakable; this is my last birth; now there is no renewal of being.'"[13]

Sometimes the body is referred to as a "house," the home or abode of consciousness, sense impressions, and mind objects. Immediately after awakening, the Buddha spontaneously uttered this verse:

> Through many a birth I have wandered through Samsara
> Seeking but not finding the builder of this house.
> Painful is birth again and again.
> Housebuilder, you are seen!
> You will build no house again.
> All your rafters are broken.
> The ridgepole is shattered too.
> My mind has attained the Unconditioned
> And reached the very end of craving.[14]

The awakened being comes to the end of becoming. Such a one, the Buddha said, has also come to the end of karma. This is a provocative statement. The Buddha continued to live, act, and teach for forty-five years after his enlightenment. How is it that he had come to the end of karma? What does that mean? There are numerous stories in the discourses in which awakened beings still suffer the results of past karma: Angulimāla, the former killer, was stoned while on alms round, and Moggallāna, one of the Buddha's two chief disciples, was murdered. In both cases, the Buddha said these were karmic results due to their actions prior to awakening. But enlightened beings, he said, do not generate new karma from their actions. This is curious, but we may get some sense of its meaning by considering the Buddha's account of the night of his awakening as he sat under the bodhi tree near the city of Gaya in northern India.

THE BUDDHA'S AWAKENING

In one discourse, the Buddha relates the events of that night in some detail.[15] He began the night as an unenlightened bodhisattva, a being seeking to be awakened. In the early hours of the night the Bodhisattva directed his concentrated mind to remembering his own past lives. He saw many lives over great stretches of time, through a multitude of pleasant and painful situations. Later, in the middle hours of the night, the Bodhisattva investigated with his intuitive powers the deaths and rebirths of many other beings. He saw directly that those who had lived with good conduct were reborn in favorable circumstances, while those who had lived with harmful conduct were reborn in painful circumstances. This was his first recorded insight into the law of karma.

We might use our imagination here to wonder about the Bodhisattva's thought process between the early hours and the middle hours. In the early hours, he recollected his own past births, which evoked and recalled mixed experiences of pleasure and pain. Seeing all those lives, someone intent on ending suffering would surely want to know what it was that led to happiness or unhappiness in a given life. We can imagine that in the middle hours of the night he set out to find the answer to this question. His investigation revealed that one's conduct in the previous life gives rise to favorable or unfavorable circumstances in the next birth.

Now let's imagine a step further. By good conduct one can gain a birth that is generally happy. But it would have been clear to the Bodhisattva—who had long ago given up the vanity of youth, health, and life—that even a happy life is still subject to the suffering of aging, illness, and death. Wholesome acts can lead to a good birth, but they don't solve the problem of suffering entirely. We can imagine that at this point in the night, the Bodhisattva saw clearly the limitations of wholesome karma. It can lead to worldly happiness for some time, but one is still in the cycle of samsara, with one's future welfare beyond one's conscious choice. The Bodhisattva must have seen at this point that wholesome karma alone does not bring an end to becoming or suffering. Perhaps it was this revelation that spurred him on to the next and ultimate insight.

In the final hours of the night, the Bodhisattva directed his concentrated mind to the "destruction of the taints," those root unwholesome qualities of mind that bind us to suffering. He understood the taints as they actually are, their origin, the potential of their end, and the way to their end. He continues:

When I knew and saw thus, my mind was liberated from the taint of sensual desire, from the taint of becoming, and from the taint of ignorance. I directly knew: "Birth is destroyed, the holy life has been lived, what had to be has been done, there is no more coming to any state of being."[16]

The Buddha had reached the end of becoming and also the end of karma. In many discourses he describes the eightfold path as the way to the end of suffering and becoming. But how does one reach the end of karma? In a few discourses, the Buddha describes not just two types of karma (or *kamma*, in Pali)—wholesome and unwholesome—but four:

> There are these four kinds of kamma. . . . There is dark kamma with dark result; there is bright kamma with bright result; there is dark-and-bright kamma with dark-and-bright result; and there is kamma that is neither dark nor bright with neither-dark-nor-bright result, kamma that leads to the destruction of kamma.[17]

The Buddha then explains dark karma as killing living beings, taking what is not given, sexual misconduct, false speech, and indulgence in intoxicants.[18] These are unskillful actions because they cause harm and because the volition behind them involves some combination of greed, hatred, and delusion.

Bright karma is explained as conduct that abstains from these actions. We may recognize this description of bright karma as the five guidelines for ethical conduct for laypeople, commonly called the five precepts. Reflecting on the meaning of bright karma, I expand somewhat on this definition and summarize it for myself as equivalent to the bases of merit: generosity, virtue, and loving-kindness. This formulation of bright karma includes not just refraining from negative actions with negative intent but acting positively with positive intent, actions that express a caring, altruistic frame of mind.

The third type of karma, dark-and-bright karma, covers actions that mix ethical and unethical conduct, such as stealing for the benefit of someone in need.

Then there is the mysterious fourth type:

And what is kamma that is neither dark nor bright, with neither-dark-nor-bright result, kamma that leads to the destruction of kamma? Right view, right intention, right speech, right action, right livelihood, right effort, right mindfulness, and right concentration.[19]

This, of course, is the noble eightfold path.

THE PATH FACTORS AND THE PRACTICE OF NONDOING

Developing the eightfold path is action that leads to the end of karma. Let's look at these path factors in more detail to see what kind of action the Buddha is pointing to here.

Three of the eight factors are related to ethical conduct (*sīla*):

- Right speech: to refrain from speech that is untrue, malicious, harsh, or purposeless
- Right action: to refrain from killing living beings, taking what is not given, and sexual misconduct
- Right livelihood: to refrain from wrong livelihood, which for a layperson is defined as trading in weapons, living beings, meat, intoxicants, or poison[20]

Some of these are the same actions described as bright karma in the discourse above. Note that the definitions of these three factors are based on *not doing* unskillful actions.

The other five factors have to do with wisdom and meditation. In the wisdom section we have:

- Right view: to understand the four noble truths
- Right intention: intentions of renunciation, loving-kindness, and compassion

In the meditation section we have:

- Right effort: to guard against and abandon unwholesome states, to develop and maintain wholesome states
- Right mindfulness: to notice our experience of body, feeling tone, mind state, and Dharmic principles
- Right concentration: to abide in states of strong concentration called the jhānas

These five factors pertain to the purification of the mind. There is not a lot of *doing* here, with expressions like *understand*, *notice*, and *abide*. Right intention specifies the proper motivation for action but does not prescribe or proscribe any particular doing. The most active factor in the meditation section seems to be right effort. However, effort is needed only up to a certain stage of meditation. After a certain point of meditative refinement based on strong concentration, unwholesome states simply don't arise. Their absence is temporary, however, as they may return once concentration diminishes, but they are absent from the mind for some time. Meditation then takes on a quality we can call effortless.

> Eradicate exertion and no more suffering is produced.
> When exertion has been abandoned, there is the freedom of the effortless.[21]

As the practitioner develops the path factors, they are described more and more not as actions but as nonaction. These factors mature into a quality of stillness and nondoing. Ultimately the wise practice of nondoing leads to the end of karma and of suffering. We will look into this further in the next chapter on abiding.

This emphasis on nonaction sometimes gives Buddhism a reputation for quietism or passivity, even in the face of injustice. This, however, is a misunderstanding of the meaning of nondoing. Enlightened beings can act forcefully when action is needed. In his lifetime, the Buddha instructed kings on the proper ways to govern, and he intervened to stop a potential war. He established a monastic order with thousands of monks and nuns and enforced its many communal rules. In our day, the Dalai Lama has been a vigorous defender of human rights in Tibet and worldwide. The Vietnamese monk Thich Nhat Hanh was so active in peace work during the war in his country that both sides threatened his life. Activists from many countries have been involved in social, political, and environmental work in an avenue that has been termed "engaged Buddhism," including Nobel laureate Aung San Suu Kyi in Burma, A. T. Ariyaratne in Sri Lanka, Sulak Sivaraksa in Thailand, and Joanna Macy in the United States.

Nondoing does not mean that one no longer acts. The true significance of nondoing is that the actions of a fully enlightened being no longer come out of self-centeredness. The self has been seen through so thoroughly that I-making and mine-making have ceased to operate, so there is no longer an imaginary core that actions have to feed or protect. Without the burden of self, the mind is clear and the heart is open. When a situation presents itself, the response from the enlightened mind comes naturally and immediately, without premeditation. Wisdom and loving-kindness have become so well established that they are the intentions from which actions spring. Volition still operates but without reference to the false sense of self. It is the selfless, spontaneous nature of the action that takes it out of the field of karma leading to future results.

We might ask if this kind of action is possible for those not yet fully enlightened. Is it possible for you and me to act from a place of nondoing, free from self-centeredness? A similar question arises about the third noble truth, which says that the end of suffering is, in essence, in the end of craving. Does this truth refer only to the total and final end of suffering attained by a fully enlightened being who has reached the total and final end of craving? Or can it be understood as referring to a temporary end of suffering? Speaking pragmatically, it is useful to notice how a single episode of suffering can come to an end when one relinquishes the specific craving that has fueled it. So it is useful to contemplate the third noble truth as it applies moment by moment, even as we are still practicing toward the complete end of suffering.

Perhaps we can understand acting from a place of nondoing in a similar way. If we are momentarily free from the preoccupations of self-centeredness and the mind is rich with wisdom and loving-kindness, we can start to get a sense of the spontaneous nature of our response at that time. We can trust in the purity of our heart and in our wholesome intentions. We do not need to claim perfect purity or wisdom, just that we feel the strength of the wholesome qualities of mind that are present. We then notice how an action that comes in that mind state is trustworthy, blameless, and appropriate. This same principle was elaborated by the Taoist sage Lao Tzu:

> Therefore the Master
> acts without doing anything
> and teaches without saying anything.
> Practice non-doing,
> And everything will fall into place.[22]

We may not have reached the final end of karma, but such "nonacts" lead us in that direction.

In the next chapter we will explore qualities of the mind that is maturing in nondoing.

12. ABIDING IN EMPTINESS

At the still point of the turning world
. . . there the dance is.
. . . Except for the point, the still point,
There would be no dance, and there is only the dance.
The inner freedom from the practical desire,
The release from action and suffering.
—T. S. Eliot[1]

AS THE FACTORS of the path mature, there is less and less to do in meditation. Due to the strength of the concentrated mind, the afflictive emotions are largely held in abeyance and don't require much attention. Thought activity slows down. Even when thoughts arise, they are felt to come and go within a spacious field that is undisturbed by their appearance. One still knows what is present at the sense doors, which continue to function capably and efficiently, but there is no avoiding, grasping, lingering, or seeking to perpetuate what has arisen. Things come and go on their own and are seen with equanimity. There is a pervasive sense of stillness and peace.

If asked to describe the overall flavor of such an experience, the meditator might say that she is resting, but the attention is alert, neither dull nor sleepy. The peace of meditation is hard to find through other means. As Suzuki Roshi said to his Western students, "You know how to rest physically. You do not know how to rest mentally."[2] Meditation provides a reliable avenue to rest mentally.

A term often used in the Pali Discourses to describe meditative states of mind is *abiding*. One who is strongly concentrated is said to abide in the jhānas.[3] Jīvaka, the physician to King Bimbisāra of Magadha, described the Buddha as abiding in loving-kindness.[4] On more than one occasion, the Buddha remarked to his attendant Ānanda, "I often abide in emptiness" (Pali: *suññatāvihāra*).[5] Sāriputta used the same words in describing his meditation to the Buddha.[6] This phrase, abiding in emptiness, is an evocative description of meditation experience as the path factors mature.

The *Shorter Discourse on Emptiness*[7] offers a detailed approach to a meditation for abiding in emptiness. When I first discovered this discourse, I thought it would be philosophical in nature, but it's actually quite practical. The theme is how to simplify perceptions in meditation so there is less and less disturbance in the mind. The Buddha first encourages the meditator to let go of perceptions of the complicated nature of one's surroundings in order to attend to a simpler perception:

> [A] bhikkhu—not attending to the perception of village, not attending to the perception of people—attends to the singleness dependent on the perception of forest. His mind enters into that perception of forest and acquires confidence, steadiness, and decision. He understands thus: "Whatever disturbances there might be dependent on the perception of village [. . . or] people, those are not present here. There is present only this amount of disturbance, namely, the singleness dependent on the perception of forest.[8]

The Buddha points out that the meditator, who is in the forest, need not trouble himself thinking about what is not there—the nearby village or its people—and simply focus on the presence (nonemptiness) of his perception of the forest.

> Thus he regards it as empty of what is not there, but as to what remains there he understands that which is present thus: "This is present." This is his genuine, undistorted, pure descent into emptiness.[9]

What is there, he understands as "This is present." At the same time he regards the moment as empty of what is not there. This way of seeing might be summarized as, "What is, is. What is not, is not." This formulation, both simple and profound, points to meditative emptiness as a quality of mind that does not alter, deny, project onto, or elaborate upon the reality of what exists. Thanissaro Bhikkhu describes it in this way: "Emptiness is a mode of perception, a way of looking at experience. It adds nothing to and takes nothing away from the raw data of physical and mental events."[10] Abiding in emptiness is considered a deliverance of mind, because one is free from hindering or extraneous thoughts and emotions.

To abide in emptiness requires a high degree of mindfulness and meditative stabilization. Most of the time, our chaotic thoughts are reacting to the moment with likes and dislikes, leaping from past to future, and coloring the bare reality of the present with our many prejudices and opinions. This is conceptual proliferation (*papañca*). When we abide in emptiness, we halt the flood of this stream of thoughts. As Nāgārjuna said, "Emptiness stops proliferation."[11] Stopping this flow of reactivity allows us to see reality clearly.

In addition to thoughts, emotional habits and tendencies also prevent us from abiding in emptiness. For example, if our mind is strongly inclined toward fear, that mental habit will lead to our feeling unsafe much of the time. At those times, we have a mental projection onto the world that imagines it as a field full of dangers and threats, even though none may be present in that moment.

One summer in the early years of my practice, during a long retreat in England, around sundown I was doing standing meditation on the back lawn of the retreat center. For reasons I didn't understand, fear was arising in my mind. I was not equanimous with the fear; it was a struggle just to be present and feel it. At one point I opened my eyes, perhaps to find some relief from its unremitting pressure, and let in the experience of the garden, which at that moment was very beautiful. I was standing beside a fruit tree filled with blossoms. The grass and trees were bathed in the warm golden light that comes at the end of the day. The air was soft and enveloping in the way that only a midsummer English evening can offer. Mourning doves were cooing in the fields nearby. My senses were revealing a world that was sweet, inviting, and lovely. The difference between the reality I was actually in and the fear my mind had conjured up was startling. The thought came to mind, "It's really a scary world out there, isn't it?" and I had to laugh.

In the grip of emotional habits, we see the world through that colored glass. The projection keeps us from recognizing reality the way it actually is. For many of us in the West, the world has generally taken care of our needs for food, clothing, and shelter since the moment we were born. Perhaps we could just as well learn to perceive this world as supportive and nurturing. This perception engenders a quality of trust that can be very helpful in deepening our meditation and understanding.

The *Shorter Discourse on Emptiness* continues with instructions to the meditator on how to further simplify his perceptions and disturbances until he is liberated. Now the descent into emptiness is called supreme and unsurpassed. The meditation at the end of this chapter offers simplified guidance for abiding in emptiness.

GIVING NO ATTENTION TO SIGNS

In the next discourse in that text, the Buddha explains the essence of this abiding: "to enter and abide in emptiness internally by giving no attention to all signs."[12] *Sign* (Pali: *nimitta*) can mean a sense object (like the sight of a bird), something being perceived about an object (the bird's red wing), or the characteristic of an object by which we notice it (the bird's speed in flight). In all these cases it points to a sense experience that can become the focus of our attention. But the Buddha's instruction here for abiding in emptiness is *not* to give attention to any signs that appear. We can abide in emptiness, he teaches, by withdrawing our mental energy and attention away from sense objects.

Why is this important? Because every form of suffering arises from an overinvolved relationship with sense objects. When we examined the chain of dependent origination in chapter 5, we saw how attachment is born from the sequence contact-feeling-craving-clinging. That attachment, which we've also described as *selfing*, leads inevitably to suffering, whether subtle or gross. The root of suffering, then, is a kind of "overreaction" to the experience of sense contact. When we deliberately refrain from giving added attention to sense objects, we take away the ground that supports suffering.

When we stop focusing attention on signs, we acknowledge that sense doors and objects cannot bring lasting happiness. If we withdraw our fixation on signs during meditation, moment by moment, we turn away from constantly seeking gratification from sense objects. We make this shift not because sense objects are "bad" or unwholesome, but because we acknowledge their limitations—they cannot satisfy us deeply. We turn away from them out of wisdom. Letting go of the habit of looking for happiness in pleasurable sense experiences is a powerful act of renunciation. Shifting our attention this way is a karmic action that leads in only one direction: to the end of karma, or liberation. This practice has a powerful and onward-leading effect.

If you cease giving attention to sense objects during meditation, what would you then be aware of? That's best left to each meditator's own discovery, though we will revisit this question in the section on awareness. It does not, however, mean you've retreated from the world or into the oblivion of unawareness. In this same discourse, the Buddha points out that while abiding in emptiness, he was still able to meet and talk with people—monks, nuns, lay followers, kings, and kings' ministers. One time Ajahn Jumnien, a forest master from Thailand, was visiting Spirit Rock in California. Although he was in his sixties, he taught enthusiastically all day and didn't seem tired in the evening. Someone asked how he did this, and he replied, "I live in emptiness, so I don't get tired." Ajahn Jumnien had found that abiding described by the Buddha so that he could rest inwardly while still interacting with students and the world.

There are many references from modern masters to the importance of this approach. Ajahn Dun, another contemporary Thai master, said that the heart of Dharma practice is to not send the mind out toward objects. In fact he created an original formulation of the four noble truths based on this insight, although in a different order. The standard numbering is in parentheses. Ajahn Dun's formulation is this:

> The mind that goes out in order to satisfy its moods is the Cause of Suffering (II);
> The result that comes from the mind going out in order to satisfy its moods is Suffering (I);

The mind seeing the mind clearly is the Path Leading to the Cessation of Suffering (IV);

The result of the mind seeing the mind clearly is the Cessation of
Suffering (III).[13]

As we practice abiding in emptiness, we strengthen the mind's ability to see
clearly its own movements, because they stand out in strong contrast to the
underlying peace. When the mind sees clearly that its going out to sense objects
leads to suffering, wisdom arises and the insight itself leads to the end of that
tendency.

Ajahn Mun was yet another great forest monk in Thailand in the early twentieth century. Considered by many to be an arahant, he was largely responsible for
revitalizing the wandering style of forest ascetic practice, known as *thudong*, and
transmitting it to such renowned disciples as Ajahns Chah, Maha Boowa, and
Lee Dhammadaro. Ajahn Mun wandered in the forests practicing meditation
for over twenty years. In his day, Thailand was more than 60 percent covered in
virgin forest and there was ample room for monks to practice and still be close
to a village for requisite support.[14] (Forest cover in Thailand has now fallen to
about 13 percent, making it nearly impossible for that style of monastic life to be
maintained.)[15]

The only known written teaching from Ajahn Mun is a long poem called the
"Ballad of Liberation from the Aggregates." In it, he reinforces the theme of not
sending the mind out to objects.

> Not doubting that perceptions are right,
> The heart gets caught up in running back and forth.
> Perceptions grab hold of things outside
> And pull them in to fool the mind,
> Making it think in confusion
> And go out searching,
> Wandering astray.[16]

While the Buddha spoke in terms of signs, sense objects, and contact, Ajahn
Mun focuses on perception, the third aggregate, the faculty that recognizes or

names a thing. All four of these terms point to the mind's capacity to single something out from the overall field of experience, to isolate one aspect of experience. Once it has been apperceived, there is a ground for sending the mind out toward it, taking hold, and clinging.

> What connects the mind into the cycle [of Samsara]?
> The tricks of perception make it spin.
> Attached to its likes,
> Wandering till it's dizzy.[17]
> What gains release from the five aggregates?
> The heart and the heart alone.
> It doesn't grasp or get entangled.
> No perceptions can fool it into following along behind them.[18]

Perceptions occur as our six sense doors contact the inner and outer worlds. If we pick up a perception to dwell on an object, we become vulnerable to the changing fortunes of pleasure and pain, likes and dislikes, and so on. If we don't pick it up, there is no occasion for mental suffering.

What do I mean by "picking up" a perception? The next time you find yourself feeling upset, stop and notice what you're upset about. Then ask what recent contact brought this into your field of experience. It might have been a conversation, something you read, an action you or someone else took, a memory. Next, see if you can remember the moment of contact and locate the brief period of time in which you fastened on that contact, picking it out from the overall field of experience and holding it. Finally, notice how you dwelt on it, repeatedly sending your thoughts back to it. If we look in this way, we can see that we have created the upset around that contact. Once we know that the agitation, in this sense, is of our own making, we can try to refrain in the future from creating it again.

The purpose of this review is not to say that whatever happened in that contact was *fine* or *fair* or *should have* happened or *should be allowed* to continue. We may need to take direct action to rectify an injustice or communicate something important. But this investigation lets us discover that we have the power to choose whether or not we become upset and suffer over the contact. As Suzuki

Roshi said, "Nothing outside yourself can cause any trouble. You yourself make the waves in your mind."[19] The contact has happened. If we don't pick it up, the mind can continue to abide in emptiness, allowing the present moment to unfold as it will. If we choose out of craving to pick it up and dwell on it, we are adding something to the present situation that isn't required to be there. We have fallen back into self-centered doing. This disturbs the basic principle of meditative emptiness: Don't add to reality. What is, is. Let it be. What isn't, isn't. Don't create more.

Of course, living in the world, there are many occasions when we need to focus on a problem and devote some attention to its solution. At these times, we want to take care that our reflections and plans come from stillness and balance. Then even thinking can take place while resting in emptiness.

UNENTANGLED KNOWING

Abiding in emptiness, we see clearly what disturbs our meditation. It is the movement of our own heart and mind, born from greed, aversion, and delusion. Giving no attention to signs offers us a way to rest, find peace, and practice renunciation, and it also provides an excellent base for insight. We can see which actions lead to suffering and which ones lead to peace and happiness. It is this understanding that trains and finally frees the heart.

One of the greatest female teachers in Thailand in the last century was Upasika Kee Nanayon, who was born in 1901 and taught from 1945 until her death in 1978. Her title, *upāsikā*, means laywoman supporter. She was not able to fully ordain as a nun, restricted by the canonical law of her time, so she practiced and taught as a laywoman—an uphill path in a patriarchal Asian society. Her teachings are deep, direct, and strong. Here she describes leaving her town to move to the forest to practice meditation:

> I had never before lived in the forest. I thought it would be better to stay in the town, running a store and making enough money. But coming to the forest and living very simply, I came to feel light-hearted and free. Seeing nature all around me inspired me to explore inside my own mind.[20]

She advises us to train in a state of mind she calls "normalcy." I call it "natural-ness," a state of awareness that is relaxed and at peace with whatever is present. (I wish this state of naturalness were more normal in the world!)

> Once the mind can stay in a state of normalcy, you'll see mental fab-rications and preoccupations in their natural state of arising and dis-banding. The mind will be empty, neutral, and still—neither pleased nor displeased.[21]

Here she uses the description of an empty mind to indicate a mind that is not preoccupied with anything at all. It doesn't mean that nothing is present in the mind, but rather that nothing is stuck there. In the same colloquial manner, we could speak of this as abiding in emptiness. Her instructions on the central importance of not taking hold of objects are similar to those of the other teach-ers mentioned above:

> If mindfulness slips and the mind goes out giving meanings to things, latching onto things, troubles will arise. So you have to keep checking on this in every moment. There's nothing else that's so worth checking on.[22]

She points out that when we assign meaning to objects of mind, trouble begins. From the center created by self-concern, things feel important based on their ability to give us pleasure or pain. Once we assign a meaning on this basis, we give that thing power to exert sway over us. We impulsively respond to its calls of seduction, alarm, or anger, surrendering our peace and balance as we do. This is why the Buddha said, "Lust is a maker of measurement, hate is a maker of measurement, delusion is a maker of measurement."[23] When we operate from craving, everything that touches us gets graded on the scale from pleasure to pain. We desire the contacts that give the highest pleasure scores and fear most those with the highest pain scores. Delusion gives neutral experience a score of zero, and so we ignore it.

Abiding in a state of normalcy, abiding in emptiness, is summed up in this short passage:

An inward-staying
unentangled knowing,
All outward-going knowing
cast aside.[24]

"Unentangled knowing" is a lovely and evocative turn of phrase. It conveys the quality of alert awareness that is free of grasping and the inevitable tangles it creates. The Buddha often described the mind's ills as a tangle: "The world is smothered and enveloped by craving like a tangled ball of yarn."[25] At the beginning of the *Visuddhimagga*, there is an exchange[26] in which a celestial being asks a question of the Buddha, addressing him by his family name Gotama:

The inner tangle and the outer tangle—
This generation is entangled in a tangle.
And so I ask of Gotama this question:
Who succeeds in disentangling this tangle?[27]

The Buddha replies that one who is well established in virtue, concentration, and wisdom succeeds in disentangling the tangle. The *Visuddhimagga* goes on to explain that *tangle* is a term for the network of craving "in the sense of lacing together, like the network of branches in bamboo thickets."[28] It is easy to see how inner conflict comes from opposing desires, such as wanting to be liked and at the same time wanting to do exactly as one wishes. Outer conflicts arise from one person or group wanting something that another person or group opposes. In all these situations, the tangle persists until there is some letting go of desire.

Abiding in emptiness, we don't get caught in the tangle of craving. Upasika Kee advises us to be "inward-staying," not pulled out toward sense objects, but to attend inwardly, to the peace of resting unentangled or to noticing when the mind is pulled to something. Ajahn Amaro encapsulates this direction: "Rest in the natural peace and ease that is the natural peace and ease of mind and body. Then pay attention to whatever disturbs that peace."

Suzuki Roshi sums this up:

When you have something in your consciousness you do not have perfect composure. The best way towards perfect composure is to forget everything. . . . Then things will not stay in your mind so long. Things will come as they come and go as they go. Then eventually your clear, empty mind will last fairly long. So to have a firm conviction in the original emptiness of your mind is the most important thing in your practice.[29]

When we learn how to abide in emptiness, life becomes simple and straightforward. The heart is uncluttered, allowing its natural responses to come easily and accurately.

MEDITATION

Abiding in Emptiness

- Sit quietly and let your eyes remain open. Become aware of all the things in the room: table, desk, chairs, rug, lamps, art, books, and so on. Notice how many thoughts and emotions may arise based on these objects, any of which might cause a disturbance in the mind.
- Now let go of noticing all the objects in the room. Be aware only of the walls of the room and the space within them. Notice that many perceptions have faded along with the disturbances that could have arisen in association with them. The walls and space may still give rise to some thoughts and emotions, but they will be fewer.
- Now let go of your perceptions of the walls. Notice only the space. Now any disturbances that might have arisen from perceiving the walls have fallen away. The space may give rise to some thoughts and emotions, but they will be fewer. Abide with the simplicity of space.

At each step in the meditation, notice how the perceptions have become less intrusive and simpler. As the mind becomes empty of the more complicated perceptions, only simpler perceptions remain. This is a progression toward abiding in emptiness. For further guidance, please see Bhikkhu Anālayo's excellent commentary on the original discourse.[30]

13. CESSATION AND NIBBĀNA

There is always a possibility of understanding as long as we exist in the
utter darkness of the sky, as long as we live in emptiness.

—Suzuki Roshi[1]

TO ABIDE IN EMPTINESS takes a leap of faith. You have to leave behind the
familiar comforts of sense objects and the old habits of thinking, liking, and
disliking. You set off on a wide sea with just *intention* as your rudder, and you
don't know what will come next. You can try paddling hard and kicking, but
that only sends you in circles. Relaxing with awareness helps but does not bring
complete security. The maps are encouraging, but so much of the vastness seems
uncharted—and yet you have committed to the journey. You need to maintain
your effort but without striving hard for a result. In such a moment, you have to
trust in the journey—and you have to trust in emptiness enough to surrender to
it. This expresses a deep faith in the unfolding.

A celestial being asked the Buddha how he crossed the flood of existence,
meaning how he attained liberation. He replied, "I crossed the flood by not tarrying and not hurrying. When I tarried, I sank, and when I hurried, I was swept
away."[2] Abiding in emptiness has this quality of not tarrying and not hurrying.

At this point in meditation, we are less interested in the objects of the six
senses. We have seen that "picking up" perceptions leads to trouble. In the spirit

of renunciation, we let go of those pleasures that don't ultimately satisfy. We are not sending the mind out through the sense doors; we are resting as far as possible in a state of naturalness, empty and still. Through this meditation, we express our faith, and that faith leads *beyond*.

TRANSCENDING SUFFERING

As we begin to abide in emptiness it's natural to ask, Where does the meditation go from here? What further steps might bring about the release the Buddha pointed to? The more we know about the journey, the more faith we'll have. The Buddha spoke of the stages that lead up to liberation. In a famous discourse called *Discourse on Proximate Cause*, he spelled out twelve steps leading from suffering to liberation. The linkage is similar in structure to the chain of dependent origination, which begins with ignorance, moves through craving, and ends in suffering. This new chain begins with suffering and then lists the wholesome states that bring the mind to release. After suffering, the next link in the chain to liberation is faith. It is from investigating our own suffering that we find the faith needed to go beyond it. Because this sequence describes a way to overcome suffering, it has become known as the chain of transcendent dependent origination. Here are some key links:

> With concentration as proximate cause, knowing and seeing things as they really are comes to be. With knowing and seeing things as they are as proximate cause, disenchantment comes to be. With disenchantment as proximate cause, dispassion comes to be. With dispassion as proximate cause, liberation comes to be.[3]

We've talked before about how stability of mind, or concentration, is needed for a meditator to know and see things as they really are (Pali: *yathābhūta ñāṇadassana*). What is revealed when we see things as they are is their impermanent, selfless nature, which makes them incapable of giving lasting satisfaction. Knowing their unsatisfactory nature, we lose our fascination with the conditioned realm of sense objects. This loss of fascination is known as disenchantment (Pali: *nibbidā*). This is the first of three key factors we'll focus on in this chapter. As the discourse states, disenchantment leads to dispassion (Pali: *virāga*), the second key factor. A third key factor not cited in this passage appears in many other discourses: cessation (Pali: *nirodha*). The Buddha was once asked to express the Dharma in brief. He replied, "When you know that a teaching leads exclusively to disenchantment, to dispassion, to cessation, to peace, to enlightenment, to nibbāna, then you should recognize this as the Dhamma."[4]

These factors combine to lead to liberation (Pali: *vimutti*). We'll now examine these terms in more detail.

DISENCHANTMENT

Disenchantment with the world of the senses should not be confused with cynicism or withdrawal. It simply means "being freed from illusion."[5] Thus, in the *Discourse on Proximate Cause*, disenchantment follows directly from knowing and seeing things as they are. We are no longer *enchanted* by the false promises of sense objects, which for years we had hoped might offer lasting happiness. Since *bewitch* is a synonym for *enchant*, we might now say, as Lorenz Hart did, that we are "bewitched, bothered, and bewildered no more." The seductive spell has been broken, freeing us to find a wise relationship to the sense world, one we are already exploring through the practice of abiding in emptiness and not giving attention to signs.

Disenchantment is a source of strength and happiness, not of doubt or pessimism. It supports the movement toward renunciation, which is not a painful moral obligation but a wise action that lightens the burden of the heart. As the Buddha said, a wise person gives up a lesser form of happiness to find a greater one.[6]

The Limitations of Sense Pleasures

At least three forms of happiness are greater than pleasant sense experiences. The first is the happiness of virtuous conduct, which we described in chapter 9 as the bliss of blamelessness. The second is the happiness of a mind temporarily free of afflictive emotions, which is accomplished through the unification of mind (*samādhi*). The Buddha said that as a bodhisattva, when he discovered the great pleasures of a concentrated mind, he lost all interest in sensuality.[7] The third is the happiness of liberation, the unshakable peace of mind the Buddha called the highest happiness.[8] When we practice for greater freedom and discover these more satisfying kinds of happiness, the central appeal of sense pleasures begins to fade.

It is not that sense pleasures are wrong or should be condemned for those of us living a lay life. In fact the availability of these pleasures is often a key motivation for choosing to live as a layperson. If one is truly uninterested in all sense pleasures, then the monastic life has much to recommend it. However, if we choose to live as lay practitioners and want to penetrate to the depth of the Buddhist path, we need to explore the power of renunciation in both our meditations and our lifestyle. We should constantly evaluate our relationship to sense pleasures to be sure they are not excessively consuming our time, energy, and money. For most of us, these resources are valuable and limited commodities that could be directed to Dharma practice, study, and reflection.

There tends to be a connection between sense pleasures and wealth. When people have money, they spend much of it on pleasurable sense experiences: a bigger home, a newer car, better food and drink, prettier clothes, and so on. The Buddha gave excellent advice on the wise use of wealth for a layperson that also applies to sense pleasures. He began by praising laypersons who gain wealth in an ethical way and share it with others. This aligns with his frequent emphasis on ethical conduct (*sīla*) and generosity (*dāna*). The Buddha went on to praise those who "use that wealth without being tied to it, infatuated with it, and blindly absorbed in it, seeing the danger in it and understanding the escape."[9]

We lay practitioners can also apply this principle to sense pleasures, aware of their danger as well as how to be balanced in relation to them. The danger is that sense pleasures condition the mind to constantly want more, strengthening lust and greed. The wisdom in relation to them is to exercise enough restraint that the habit of wanting does not build up. Moderation in sense pleasures is essential for realizing the depths of insight the path offers.

DISPASSION

As we become less enchanted by the false promise of sense objects, the wellsprings of craving start to dry up. The Pali word for dispassion, *virāga*, means "without lust" or "without attachment." It points to a state of mind in which lust and craving are absent, at least temporarily. In other Pali usages, *virāga* has the sense of "fading away," as color starts to fade from a shirt that has been washed many times. So the meaning of this term as dispassion also carries the connotation of something fading away, in this case craving. We might say that dispassion is simply the maturing of disenchantment. The conditioned habits of mind, based on greed, aversion, and delusion, start to wither as we realize that those habits are directed toward sense objects that are only going to change, rendering moot their delivery of pleasure or pain. At a certain point on the path, all desire for sense objects is extinguished through wisdom.

Dispassion should not be confused with an unfeeling or uncaring attitude. When we are no longer compelled by self-centered passions, the heart becomes lighter and more open to the feelings of others. There is more space in the mind for the divine abidings of loving-kindness, compassion, and appreciative joy to flourish. In fact dispassion is close in spirit to equanimity, the fourth divine abiding, which is a necessary foundation for the other three. Without the balance of mind offered by equanimity, it is difficult to truly care about the welfare of others. Without equanimity, the other divine abidings easily tip over into what are called their near enemies: qualities that masquerade as the divine abidings but are actually unwholesome imitators. We might think of the near enemy as the neurotic, ego-based version of the true divine abiding. Below is a table of the four divine abidings and their "near enemies"—states which may superficially seem similar, but which in fact are very different.

DIVINE ABIDING	NEAR ENEMY
Loving-kindness	Attached affection
Compassion	Grief from being overwhelmed with suffering
Appreciative joy	Self-centered exuberance
Equanimity	Indifference, absence of caring

CESSATION

As dispassion strengthens, we have less and less inclination to self-centered action. What would be the point? Any gratification would be, after all, fleeting.

In our practice, it feels like something is stopping. We may resist this sense at first, because it is new and not yet trustworthy. But it is a key step in the journey to liberation, known as cessation (*nirodha*) or ending. In a number of discourses, the Buddha pairs the term *cessation* with dispassion. In response to a bhikkhu named Mālunkyāputta, the Buddha states once again that sense contact—framed here as the five aggregates—is unsatisfying and suggests he direct his attention elsewhere:

> Whatever exists of form, feeling, perception, formations, and consciousness, she sees those states as impermanent, as unsatisfactory, as disintegrating, as empty, as not self. She turns her mind away from those states and directs it to the deathless element thus: "This is peaceful, this is sublime, namely the stilling of all formations, the relinquishing of all attachments, the destruction of craving, dispassion, cessation, nibbāna."[10]

In this passage, the Buddha describes sense contact first as unsatisfying in ways we are already familiar with. Then he instructs the practitioner to direct her attention away from sense contact and to the deathless element, a synonym for nibbāna. This guidance may be fine for one who has realized the deathless, but what if we haven't had a personal experience of this unconditioned state? The Buddha offers the terms *peaceful, sublime, still,* and so on to help us approach the deathless element, to help guide us there. He is speaking like an air traffic controller guiding a pilot toward a runway that she can't quite see because of cloud cover. We'll look at these descriptors in more detail in a moment. First, though, you might want to know what the landing strip looks like.

WHAT IS NIBBĀNA?

Even more than *not-self* and *emptiness, nibbāna* is the most mysterious term in Buddhism and the hardest to describe—akin to the opening of the *Tao Te Ching,* "The Tao that can be spoken of is not the eternal Tao."[11] Many commentators have explained that it is impossible to define nibbāna through concepts, because words discriminate while the nature of nibbāna transcends dualities. The Buddha himself said it is "profound, hard to see and hard to understand, . . . unattainable by mere reasoning."[12] A few teachers have claimed that nibbāna means nothing more than the mind free of craving. But in a clear reference to nibbāna, a passage in one discourse states, "There is an unborn, unbecome, unmade, unconditioned" that gives the possibility of release from what is born, become, made, and conditioned.[13] In other words, what is referred to as nibbāna has a reality beyond the simple absence of craving. This reality, which some would say is ontological, is the basis for liberation. It is "to be experienced by the wise."[14]

Many Buddhist teachers agree that nibbāna refers to a latent element within human experience that can be discovered and experienced. It is unconditioned in the sense that it is not subject to arising and passing based on other, prior conditions. The direct realization of this unconditioned element has the power to end craving and suffering. This is the goal of the Buddha's teaching and of our practice. We will take nibbāna to mean both this latent unconditioned element *and* the end of suffering, which is the goal of the path.

In the discourse above, the stilling of all formations (Pali: *sabba sankhāra samatho*) is the explicit invitation to nondoing. All willful formations now come to calm. The relinquishing of all attachments is the invitation to let go of anything that is being grasped. The destruction of craving is the end, at least temporarily, of greed, aversion, and delusion. Then come dispassion, cessation, nibbāna. This is the direct trajectory to the goal.

WHAT CEASES?

What is meant by cessation? It has to do with the end of craving, as pointed to in the third noble truth: the cessation of craving (*taṇhā nirodha*) is the cessation of suffering (*dukkha nirodha*). In this context, cessation means the destruction of craving. However, cessation is also used in the discourses in other important ways.

As we discussed in chapter 11, the discourses often say that one who is fully liberated is not born again. For such a one, after death there is "no renewal of being." This is sometimes referred to as the cessation of being (*bhava nirodha*), which could also be translated as the "cessation of existence" or the "cessation of becoming." I will use these translations interchangeably. In the discourses of the historical Buddha, when craving ceases fully and suffering ceases fully, then becoming in the round of samsara comes to an end as well. In this way, the cessation of craving and the cessation of being point to the same outcome.

Cessation also figures prominently in the chain of dependent origination. When ignorance is ended (*avijjā nirodha*), all the other links are eventually ended too. These links include craving and becoming as well as another interesting factor: consciousness, here understood as the six types of sense consciousness. The complete cessation of being can only come after the death of the liberated individual, but the cessation of consciousness (*viññāṇa nirodha*) can occur during this life and is a significant experience in meditation.

CESSATION OF CONSCIOUSNESS

What would it mean for consciousness to end temporarily while we are still alive? During deep sleep, fainting, and general anesthesia, we are not conscious of anything external for a while, as far as we know. Even if there is a thin thread of consciousness, it isn't of much interest to a practitioner, because it is not transformative. What is of interest is when cessation of sense consciousness is preceded by a relaxed yet alert attention characterized by equanimity and dispassion. In the *Discourse on Proximate Cause* and the *Discourse to Mālunkyāputta*, this is precisely the description of the state of mind that immediately precedes enlightenment, or the realization of nibbāna.

Abiding in emptiness, the meditator does not give attention to signs. When disenchantment and dispassion are strong and formations are stilled, there is a palpable lack of interest in sense contact. When one loses interest in sense contact, one also loses interest in sense consciousness. The loss of interest in sense consciousness can bring sense consciousness to a temporary end. This can be unexpected, since we generally assume that sense contact will continue as long as we are awake. What we discover is that sense contact is fueled by interest or appetite. When appetite is withdrawn, contact and consciousness can end, for a time.

In one discourse, the Buddha encourages practitioners to discover this:

That sphere should be known where the eye ceases and the perception of form fades away . . . where the ear ceases and the perception of sound fades away . . . where the nose ceases and the perception of smell fades away . . . where the tongue ceases and the perception of taste fades away . . . where the body ceases and the perception of sensations fades away. That sphere should be known where the mind ceases and the perception of mental phenomena fades away. That sphere should be known.[15]

When asked by other monks to explain this statement further, Ānanda said that the Buddha was referring to the cessation of the six sense bases. Later, the Buddha confirmed this.

NIBBĀNA

Many meditators report experiences of cessation. Following a very alert, still, equanimous mind, moments may come in which all sense consciousness completely ceases and falls away. Without sense consciousness, there is no experience of sense objects. The six senses cease to manifest anything, so there is no sense of a body or even of mind states. Wholesome states like mindfulness, concentration, disenchantment, and dispassion become irrelevant; in fact they are nonexistent, as are all mundane mind states. What is being realized in this moment is only the unconditioned element, nibbāna, which is not of the six senses and cannot be known by the six sense consciousnesses. This is a moment of enlightenment. The great Zen master Dōgen referred to this experience as "dropping off body and mind."[16]

It is impossible to say what precipitates such a moment of awakening to the unconditioned. Certainly the mind must have been developed through right effort, so the factors of concentration, wisdom, disenchantment, and dispassion are strong. But once those factors have been brought to maturity, nothing more can be done by effort. We simply abide with patience and mindfulness and without expectation. The breakthrough to nibbāna comes as grace.

When asked to describe the inner experience of an enlightenment moment, meditators respond in different ways. Based on a compilation of such accounts, enlightenment experiences are described as having no awareness present at all or having the presence of an awareness that is not based in the six senses. I once asked Mingyur Rinpoche, and he said he also has heard it described in these ways.[17]

ENLIGHTENMENT MOMENT WITHOUT AWARENESS

In the Theravadan world, the most influential teacher of the past sixty years was Mahasi Sayadaw of Burma. His meditation teachings were rooted in the *Visuddhimagga*, which outlines a clear experiential sequence leading to enlightenment. In the view of Mahasi Sayadaw, no awareness at all is present in an enlightenment moment when sense consciousness ceases. A number of Westerners who practiced in this system described a period of meditation with strong equanimity during which they were keenly aware of objects coming and going, moment after moment. The next thing they knew, sense consciousness was returning after having been absent for an indeterminate period of time. They reported a "gap" in experience.

This report might be describing an authentic enlightenment experience, but it's difficult to be sure, for the student or for the teacher. A gap in experience is not enough to verify that what took place was enlightenment. Other causes could be falling asleep or an imbalance of energy and concentration. A teacher who knows the meditator's recent practice history might make a reasonable surmise as to its validity, but even so, the teacher might not communicate about this directly with the student. So it's up to the student to assess his own experience. That assessment could take months or years and should be based on the particulars of the experience and its associated insights, as well as on the wholesome effects in the student's life and practice going forward.

A valid enlightenment experience is ultimately indescribable, but often the most fruitful appraisal of such an experience comes in the moments when sense consciousness is just returning after its absence. Because no mental activity or perception takes place in the direct experience of nibbāna, it is impossible to store up an adequate description or image of that experience. But when sense consciousness has just returned, it is as though the two kinds of moments rub up against each other—one is unconditioned and the next is conditioned. Then perhaps a sense of the unconditioned can come through in the aroma that lingers. This is as close as the conceptual mind can come to the unconditioned.

ENLIGHTENMENT MOMENT WITH AWARENESS

In the other type of enlightenment account, some awareness is present during the experience. This account is from a Western meditator:

> It was in the middle of a long retreat. I had been following the breath at the abdomen for three weeks with continuous noting: "in, out, touching." In one sitting there was a deep sense of calm, followed by the grasping of that calm. Immediately and without any effort on my part the note arose: "grasping." I wondered with great curiosity: "What knew that?" Then there was an abrupt transition. A subtle vibration of unmoving peace stood out from the background. The foreground fell away: there were no mental formations, and no consciousness of the body or physical senses. But some kind of awareness continued. Because perception wasn't operating it's impossible to say what was being known. But some unshakable peace was revealed which had been there all along, totally uncaused.[18]

In this account, sense consciousness ceased, though some awareness continued. Reports similar to this can be found in the Thai forest tradition. This is Ajahn Maha Boowa's description of his own enlightenment, abridged for readability:

> At this point the mind was empty and the awareness was prominent. It fully comprehended form, feeling, perception, formations, and consciousness. It fully let go of them. All that was left was awareness. Why is it that the mind is completely empty? A realization appeared: *"If there is a point or a center of the knower anywhere, that is the essence of a level of being."* But I was simply bewildered. I let more than three months pass by in vain.
>
> When the time came for me to know, I was contemplating just the mind. Mindfulness and wisdom kept making contact with that awareness, examining it back and forth. However radiant or splendid it might be, there was still [ignorance] (*avijjā*) within it. Mindfulness and wisdom realized that that state of mind should

simply be let go. Then the mind, mindfulness and wisdom became impartial and impassive. *That moment was when the cosmos in the mind over which [ignorance] held sway trembled and quaked.* [Ignorance] was thrown down from its throne on the heart. In its place the pure mind appeared.[19]

He concludes with a boxing metaphor:

The middle way, the truth of the path, was declared absolute winner, while the truth of the origin of [suffering] was knocked out and carried off on a stretcher, with no way of reviving ever again.[20]

The origin of suffering being knocked out and not revived describes the end of craving and thus the end of suffering. In this passage Ajahn Maha Boowa is essentially relating his moment of full liberation, or arahantship. It is an unusual thing for such a teacher to talk about. I appreciate his willingness to share this level of detail. The "pure mind" in his account indicates some kind of awareness at the key moment.

The presence of some awareness at the moment of realizing nibbāna, even without a functioning sense consciousness, suggests that such awareness could be an aspect of nibbāna itself. We will return to this question in part 3 on awareness.

SUDDEN AWAKENING, GRADUAL CULTIVATION

Sometimes the first experience of enlightenment is so strong that craving and suffering are permanently ended. It seems the Buddha's enlightenment was like that. For most of us, though, the first direct realization of nibbāna, though a valid enlightenment moment, is not strong enough to end all craving. This was the case for the Buddha's first enlightened disciple. After the Buddha gave his first discourse on the four noble truths, one of the five ascetics listening gained a direct insight into the unconditioned: "There arose in the Venerable Kondañña the dust-free, stainless vision of the Dhamma: 'Whatever is subject to origination is also subject to cessation.'"[21] The Buddha renamed him Añña Kondañña: Kondañña Who Has Understood.

This description of Koṇḍañña's enlightenment is a stock phrase that appears throughout the Pali Discourses to indicate stream-entry, the first moment of directly realizing nibbāna. It may sound like no more than an insight into impermanence, but the key part of the phrase is the "dust-free, stainless vision of the Dhamma." Dhamma is often used as a synonym for nibbāna, and it is used here in that way. Such a one has seen the ultimate truth. However, this insight, which happened quite suddenly, was not the end of Koṇḍañña's path.

The thirteenth-century Korean Zen master Chinul was asked whether sudden awakening meant the end of the journey. He said it was true for a few who had greatly developed the path in previous lives, but for most of us, a sudden awakening has to be followed by more work.

Although he has awakened to the fact that his original nature is no different from that of the Buddhas, the beginningless habit-energies are extremely difficult to remove suddenly and so he must continue to cultivate while relying on this awakening. Through this gradual permeation, his endeavors reach completion. . . . Hence it is called gradual cultivation.[22]

Chinul termed this "sudden awakening, gradual cultivation." This is the correct path for most of us. Sudden awakening removes all doubt and shows us the way, while gradual cultivation is required to reach the final end of suffering. Koṇḍañña had to keep practicing for about two more weeks before he reached full liberation. Most of us need longer.

The experience of stream-entry marks a significant maturing in the course of one's Dharma practice. It is the natural outcome of the growing insight into not-self, the abandoning of self-centered striving, and the development of trust in mindful awareness. In the maturity of abiding, the three factors of disenchantment, dispassion, and cessation build and lead to the direct realization of Nibbana. Now the dharma doors are wide open for greater cultivation. Two avenues present themselves at this point for further investigation: the nature of phenomena and the nature of awareness itself. These are the subjects of the next two parts of the book.

PART II:
PHENOMENA

14. A LUMP OF FOAM

Every existence is a flashing into the vast phenomenal world.
—Suzuki Roshi[1]

SO FAR WE HAVE EXPLORED emptiness primarily as it relates to the notion of a self. We have investigated what is real in our experience and discovered the selfless, changing, and unsatisfying nature of the sense bases and aggregates. We have taken for granted the existence of these components, but we have not yet explored in detail *in what way* they exist. The Dalai Lama puts it this way: "The essential nature of things is not in question. But it is important to clarify the manner in which things exist."[2]

In this section of the book—on phenomena—we will return to the objects of the six senses to investigate the question, In what way do these objects, these phenomena, exist? At this point we are less interested in the specific properties of objects, such as whether the breath is long or short, whether a sensation is aching or stabbing, or whether a mood is of annoyance or impatience. We are more interested in the object's cycle of existence: its process of arising, persisting, and passing away. When the thing is, *how* is it existing? Is it substantial, solid, stable, lasting, graspable? Or is it insubstantial, light, disintegrating, fleeting, tenuous?

We've seen that we mistakenly give a sense of stability and permanence to our body and inner life through the idea of an ongoing self. We've also noticed that we project onto the world around us an assumption of permanence and solidity. We are not saying whether these are true or false; we're only noticing the assumptions we carry. Concepts, it turns out, play a key role in creating this assumed stability. We look outside and see a tree. By naming it "tree," we have a fixed, unchanging concept of what it is. If we walk up and touch it, the trunk feels hard and solid, further confirming the sense of its stability. We take for granted that it exists outside and independent of us. From childhood on, everyone around us has talked and acted as though the physical world is solid and stable. Perhaps the exceptions were science teachers who told us that matter is mostly empty space, but that didn't seem to affect their way of being in the world or make them any happier.

Where science primarily treats the physical world as something that exists independent of us, Buddhism does not. In the Buddhist approach, the domain for appraising the physical world is through our direct experience. Totality in Buddhism means the eye and sights, the ear and sounds, the nose and smells, the tongue and tastes, the body and sensations, and the mind and mental phenomena. By investigating the world through our direct experience, we can find the wisdom we need to come to the end of suffering. Investigating the world through the physical sciences leads to many useful inventions but not necessarily to the end of suffering.

So instead of conceptualizing "tree" as an object independent and outside of us, we are more interested in noticing our *sight* or *touch* or *smell* of the tree, and then how we relate to those direct experiences through the mental factors of perception, feeling tone, craving, grasping, and becoming. This is an extension of meditation practices we are already familiar with. We want to investigate the *objects* of the six senses, both inner and outer, to see how they exist. We will explore them in the order of sounds, smells, tastes, sensations, thoughts and mind states, and sights. We're not doing this just out of intellectual curiosity or to create some new technology, but to learn about suffering and its end, in order to benefit ourselves and others.

SOUNDS

It may be helpful at this point to review the instructions for meditating on sounds at the end of chapter 3. Once you've connected to the sounds around you, begin to notice the ways in which they manifest. In paying attention to a sound, can you notice it in the moment it arises? If you don't notice its beginning, start paying attention to it as soon as you do notice. Then investigate its stage of persisting. Does it stay exactly the same, or does it change in pitch or volume or location? Is it just one sound, like the ring of a bell that slowly fades, or is it the repetition of similar sounds, like a woodpecker tapping on a tree? With each sound you are able to discern, notice its duration. Is there any sound that lasts long enough to be *grasped*, or are the sounds more like musical notes: as soon as you perceive one, it's already ending and the next is arising? With each sound you notice, pay clear attention to its ending. In one moment, something audible can be heard, and in the next moment, nothing. Can you detect this transition? Continue meditating in this way, noticing how various sounds arise, persist, and pass away.

This meditation gives a clear sense of the insubstantiality of sounds. Most pass quickly, and it's difficult to take hold of them. When we pay attention, we can usually discern the end of each sound. Many are momentary and end as soon as they are noticed. It is rare for a single sound to last very long. Some, like those from traffic or a chainsaw, seem to be ongoing, but as we pay closer attention, we hear that even those sounds are changing moment to moment. It's seldom possible to find anything steady or fixed to land on in the field of sounds. Sound is mostly in flux, fleeting and insubstantial. This absence of anything concrete to hold on to is the sign of their emptiness. There is nothing solid in sounds.

SMELLS AND TASTES

We'll consider these two senses together, because they are so similar. We'll use the term *smell* to describe our inner experience and the words *odor*, *scent*, or *fragrance* to describe the external cause of the smell. Often it is not possible to detect any smell or taste in the present moment of experience, so we'll need to explore these senses when they visit us. This is often at mealtimes. Next time you are preparing or being served a meal, pay attention first to any smells that arise. Investigate the smells in the way we did with sounds. Can you notice the first moment of contact, the first moment you experience that you are smelling something? How long does it last? Does it stay constant or change from moment to moment in either strength or fragrance? As you pay attention to a smell, does it remain as clear as it was at first? Due to a phenomenon called habituation, the smell from a scent weakens after ongoing exposure to it, although the smell sense recovers quickly when the scent is taken away.[3] Notice the ending of the smell, which could come from habituation, moving away from the odor, or a change to the source of the odor.

Investigate taste in a similar way. When you are eating, notice the first taste you experience after putting a bite of food into your mouth. Does the taste change if you let the food stay on your tongue? Does it change as you chew the food? Stay with the experience of taste as you continue to chew and then swallow the food. As the taste changes, does it change just in intensity or does the flavor also change? How long does a single taste continue? Can you notice the moment that taste ends?

Exploring in this way, you're likely to find that smells and tastes are even less substantial than sounds. These are subtle experiences, ephemeral, fleeting, and hard to pin down. Still, from the amount of money consumers spend every year on pleasant smells and tastes, these two senses seem to exert a significant influence on us. Worldwide, the perfume industry brings in $29 billion a year,[4] and restaurants bring in $2.1 trillion a year.[5] Despite our sometimes obsessive relationship to them, tastes and smells, like sounds, are characterized by emptiness, by a lack of solidity, by their ungraspable nature.

SENSATIONS

The investigation of sensations, or the sense of touch, brings us into the direct experience of our body. We usually take the body for granted as though it were an independent object in the world in much the same way we take a tree for granted. If we reflect for a moment, however, we realize we only know the body by experiencing it as an object of the five physical senses. We know its existence in the same way we know all physical objects: because we can see it, hear it, smell it, taste it, and touch it. It is curious that the physical sense doors (eye, ear, nose, tongue, tactile system) are both parts of the body *and* the ways by which the body is known.

As for specific senses, the sounds, smells, and tastes of the body are not generally highly charged experiences. They are usually not all that pleasant, but we have learned to live with them. (Some bodily sounds, like speech and song, are more highly charged, but those are really volitional formations, not simply body. They acquire their impact not as pure sound but through the merging of sound with thoughts and emotions.) The strongest physical senses in general are sight and touch, and we know the body primarily through these two senses. We will explore sight last, so for now let's consider how we know the body through the sense of touch, that is, through sensations. Here the sense of touch is not limited to contact with the skin but includes all the ways in which bodily sensations are felt in the skin, muscles, organs, tissues, joints, bones, and so on.

Touch is a potent sense field that includes a wide range of pleasure and pain. Sensations can affect us strongly, and we often have strong feelings about them. The pleasures of sensuality may be the most compelling force drawing us back into existence: the Buddha called them "the bridge."[6] Strong physical pain, on the other hand, is one of the most stressful experiences a person can have. With this great range of power, delight, mystery, and misery, could the sense field of touch also be empty?

THE EMPTINESS OF MATTER

In a discourse called *A Lump of Foam*, the Buddha addresses this question directly using the schema of the five aggregates. As noted, the body is included in the first aggregate, called material form (*rūpa*). Here is the beginning of that discourse. Blessed One (Pali: *Bhagavā*) is another appellation for the Buddha.

> On one occasion the Blessed One was dwelling at Ayojjhā on the bank of the river Ganges. There the Blessed One addressed the bhikkhus thus:
>
> "Bhikkhus, suppose that this river Ganges was carrying along a great lump of foam. A person with good sight would inspect it, ponder it, and carefully investigate it, and it would appear to him to be void, hollow, insubstantial. For what substance could there be in a lump of foam? So too, bhikkhus, whatever kind of material

form there is, a practitioner inspects it, ponders it, and carefully investigates it, and it would appear to him to be void, hollow, insubstantial. For what substance could there be in material form?"[7]

Since material form includes the body and all five kinds of physical sense objects, this declaration from the Buddha is fairly radical. Let's see if it aligns with what we have discussed so far. The key to this passage is in the words translated as void, hollow, and insubstantial. In the original Pali they are *ritta*, *tuccha*, and *asāra*, respectively. These terms warrant a little scrutiny.

The Pali word *ritta* (void) is often used in the sense of "being devoid of." The Pali Text Society's *Pali-English Dictionary* (hereafter abbreviated as *PTS Dictionary*) defines it as "devoid, empty, free, rid (of)."[8] The word *tuccha* (hollow) is often combined with *ritta*. The *PTS Dictionary* gives its meaning as "empty, vain, deserted."[9] Bhikkhu Bodhi commented that in the discourses, this word is sometimes paired with the word for man as *tuccha purisa* to mean a hollow, empty, or superficial man. The Pali term *asāra* (insubstantial) is defined in the *PTS Dictionary* as an adjective meaning "worthless, vain, idle" or as a noun meaning "that which is not substance."[10] Finally the Pali term used twice in the discourse for "substance" is *sāro*—the noun that is the root of *asāra*.

This discourse does not use the terms *suñña* and *suññatā*, which we have heretofore used to translate *empty* and *emptiness*. Nonetheless, all the terms used here have a similar, almost synonymous, meaning. The voidness, hollowness, and insubstantiality that the Buddha points to here are essentially the same as the emptiness we have been discussing in this chapter. So the Buddha is indeed declaring that the body and all material form are as void, hollow, and insubstantial as a lump of foam floating down a river. Can this be true? Let's consider it from three different perspectives.

We know that eventually all matter decays and fades away. We see this every day with food left out of the fridge and plants taken out of the soil. Scientists tell us that even the Earth will eventually burn up when our sun dies. (Interestingly, the Buddha predicted this 2,500 years ago!)[11] We can also see this decay in the bodies of humans and animals.

During a retreat at Spirit Rock a few years ago, I was giving a talk one evening when we heard from outside a loud cry like the wail of a baby in pain.

Some staff members left to investigate it. After the talk I went outside with a few retreatants to find our staff standing beside the dead body of a deer lying on the ground. Someone mentioned they had seen two large dogs running away. It is not unusual for dogs in a pack to kill deer in the countryside near the retreat center, but we had never seen it on the Spirit Rock land. We stood in a circle and chanted verses on loving-kindness for the deer. A staff member called the local Humane Society, who said they would pick up the carcass the next day. Our caretakers placed the deer in a cart and drove it to the parking area for pickup.

The Humane Society, who no doubt had more pressing issues to deal with, never came, and the deer remained by the parking lot where we could all observe it over the next two weeks. Every night the scavengers of the land—vultures, crows, raccoons, insects—picked over the body, and every day a little more of it disappeared. After about ten days, all that was left was some fur and bones. Most of the deer had vanished, like a lump of foam breaking apart.

A second perspective on the emptiness of matter comes from the Dalai Lama. Some years ago he gave a teaching at an outdoor amphitheater in the Bay Area. There must have been a hundred monks and nuns on the stage with him, and an audience of a few thousand spread out in seats and on the grass. The atmosphere was festive, like a Buddhist Woodstock. As His Holiness explained the connection of suffering to emptiness, he began to talk about the unsatisfactory nature of conditioned things (Pali: *sankhāra dukkha*). He said that people often misunderstand the teaching of impermanence to mean that things last for a time and then come to an end. He explained that in fact, things are constantly breaking up and falling apart, moment after moment. Every moment of experience is disintegrating right now. There is no duration for a conditioned thing. Matter is like a lump of foam.

Thirdly, we can explore this in our meditation practice by looking closely at the direct experience of physical sensations, as we did with sounds, smells, and tastes. When we glance at the body quickly and superficially, it can appear to be a solid, unchanging mass. There is skin, flesh, and bones, and they seem quite solid. We've seen pictures of what's under the hood—the organs and joints, and so forth—and they too look solid. The body feels hefty, massive, weighty. It all appears substantial.

But when we investigate the body with mindfulness, a different perception comes through. The Buddha frequently advised, "One thing, if developed and cultivated, leads to great benefit, to security from bondage, to a pleasant dwelling in this very life, to the realization of the fruit of liberation. What is that one thing? Mindfulness directed to the body."[12] When we pay close attention to sensations in the body, we see that nothing can be more intimate with the body than our own awareness of it, felt from within. No anatomy text or photograph or lover's touch can reveal the truth about the body as well as our own direct experience of it.

It may be helpful to review the meditation instructions on bodily sensations at the end of chapter 2. When we first pay attention to sensations, the weightiness of the body seems to reinforce the sense of a stable, solid mass. But what we perceive of the body through touch is only the result of our perceiving many individual sensations arising in different parts of the body. To understand sensations more precisely, we need to investigate in detail these particular sensations and the way they manifest. Consider the following exploration.

Choose a sensation in the body that is apparent but not overwhelming, because it's difficult at first to be mindful of an intense sensation. The one you select could be the pressure where the buttocks rest on the chair, or the contact of the feet with the floor, or some tension in the back from sitting straight, or the touch of the palms wherever they are resting. Let that one sensation be felt thoroughly with mindful attention, without judging or trying to change the experience. Let your awareness pervade the entire area of the sensation.

Now that the attention has drawn close to the sensation, notice the bare physical experience. What is being sensed? Is it tingling, itching, pressing, warm, cool, aching, light, heavy, relaxed, contracted, tight, stabbing, or something else? As you keep feeling that particular sensation, notice whether it stays the same or changes in some way. Does it shift location? Does it grow stronger or weaker? Is there any sort of rhythmic, pulsing quality to it? If so, how long is a cycle in the rhythm? Does the sensation fade away completely at some point?

If there is *anything* graspable in the world, it should be our own body. But a close investigation reveals that no sensation in the body is stable and enduring. As we found with the senses of sound, smell, and taste, the sense of touch is also characterized by moment-to-moment change. This insight is at the heart of the body-centered meditations taught by U Ba Khin and his disciples, including

S. N. Goenka. Even sensations are not substantial. Like all form, sensations are empty, like a lump of foam.

ALL FORM TREMBLES

A celestial being named Subrahmā was one of the Buddha's followers. Subrahmā explained his understanding to another celestial being, who was still attached to material things:

> Having seen form's flaw, its chronic trembling,
> The wise one takes no delight in form.[13]

All form trembles with impermanence, with momentary change, with emptiness. We might think this is an unfortunate situation—no stability in the whole physical world. But the universe we are in, with its lack of solidity, has one immense benefit: it allows us to be liberated.

A bhikkhu once asked the Buddha if there is material form anywhere that is permanent and stable. The Buddha scooped up a little bit of soil in his fingernail and replied:

> There is not even this much form that is permanent, stable, eternal, not subject to change. If there was this much form that was permanent, stable, eternal, not subject to change, this living of the holy life for the complete destruction of suffering could not be discerned. But because there is not even this much form that is permanent, stable, eternal, not subject to change, this living of the holy life for the complete destruction of suffering is discerned.[14]

THOUGHTS AND STATES OF MIND

Having discussed emptiness in four of the six kinds of sense objects, let us now consider mental phenomena—thoughts and states of mind, including moods, emotions, mental states, and meditative factors of mind. This category, also called *mind objects*, covers the same range as the middle three aggregates of feeling, perception, and volitional formations. The *Lump of Foam* discourse also describes these three aggregates. First is feeling:

> Suppose, bhikkhus, that in the autumn, when it is raining and big raindrops are falling, a water bubble arises and bursts on the surface of the water. A person with good sight would inspect it, ponder it, and carefully investigate it, and it would appear to her to be void, hollow, insubstantial. For what substance could there be in a water bubble? So too, bhikkhus, whatever kind of feeling there is, a practitioner inspects it, ponders it, and carefully investigates it, and it would be appear to her to be void, hollow, insubstantial. For what substance could there be in feeling?[15]

The Buddha then introduces two more potent images to show the insubstantial nature of the next two aggregates. "Suppose, bhikkhus, that in the last month of the hot season, at high noon, a shimmering mirage appears." The mirage is, of course, an analogy for perception. Next, volitional formations are compared to the trunk of a plantain tree: "Suppose, bhikkhus, that a person would enter a forest, cut down a plantain tree, and uncoil its trunk." The plantain, a member of the banana family, grows on a tree that fruits once and then dies. Its trunk has no true wood or solid core but consists of tightly rolled vegetation.

Thus feeling, perception, and formations are said to be like a water bubble, a mirage, and a plantain trunk—void, hollow, and insubstantial. Objects of mind, the discourse is saying, are all empty.

We can verify this from direct observation. You might like to review the meditation instructions for emotions at the end of chapter 2. In chapter 5, we saw that thoughts have significant power to shape our decisions, actions, and view of the world. We also saw that a single thought, in its momentary arising and passing, is light and fleeting. We give thoughts power by taking hold of them, but when we just let them come and go, their existence is so ephemeral they're barely there. This light, fleeting, insubstantial quality is the sign of the emptiness of thoughts.

Moods and emotions are also hard to pin down. As we discussed in chapter 4, they are cloudlike by nature. Sometimes it's difficult to know what emotion is present or whether an emotion is even there. As objects of *mind*, moods and emotions are even less substantial than sounds and sensations, which have a physical presence. When a strong emotion is felt as a sensation in the body, it seems to have more substance, but that is the physical sensation. When we tune in to the *mental* aspect of the emotion, we can again see its cloudlike nature, subtle and hard to locate or grasp. What we often end up holding on to instead is the *idea* behind the emotion: she hurt me, or I'm angry at him, or I want this or that. Once we turn it into a concept, we can carry it around for a long time. But the direct experience of the emotion as a mental object is ephemeral and hard to hold.

If even our strongest emotions are cloudlike and ungraspable, how much more so are meditative states, which are also in the aggregate of volitional formations. Qualities like mindfulness, concentration, wisdom, peace, and equanimity are much more subtle than our usual emotions—so much so that they are easily overlooked. A mature sense of discrimination is needed to discern which ones are present or absent. An attempt to grasp one of these states often destroys it. These factors when well established may be less fleeting than most emotions, but their relative endurance doesn't change their fundamental nature, which is insubstantial and ungraspable.

15. THE MAGIC SHOW

The bodhisattva Avalokiteshvara, while practicing deeply the perfection
of wisdom, perceived that all five aggregates are empty and was saved
from all suffering and distress.

—Heart Sutra

IN THE PREVIOUS chapter, we saw the emptiness of the four physical senses
of sound, smell, taste, and sensation, as well as the emptiness of feeling, perception, and volitional formations. Now we will examine the sense of sight (the last
aspect of form) and the aggregate of consciousness.

SIGHT

Sight is the predominant physical sense for humans and for many animals.
Throughout our evolution, sight has been the main sense we've employed to
locate food and detect threats. Because of our reliance on this sense, it is hard for
us to perceive it as empty. The world looks stable and solid. Of course, the objects
within it change, but the visual field itself seems steady and reliable, always there,
and therefore not subject to change. This steadiness gives us the belief that the
material world is stable and ongoing. Is that true, or is there emptiness in this
sense base as well?

We can get glimmers of the emptiness of sight through direct experience. In certain conditions, we can see the visual field pixelate, or break up into small discrete patches of form and color, like the granular pixels on a computer screen. Given that the retina is made up of discrete rods and cones, we may be seeing more "accurately" when we observe pixelation. Seeing the fragmentation of the visual field destroys the sense of its continuity and undermines the assumption of stability.

Another common experience is the way the visual field changes when we put on glasses. The moment before, we may have thought that we were seeing the physical world just as it is, but as soon as we put on glasses, a different world appears. Were we ever seeing the world as it truly is? What else might be revealed if we put on even more powerful glasses, or glasses that can see infrared or ultraviolet radiation? Perhaps the physical world we are seeing is not the actual physical world. We will consider this further below.

We have become so accustomed to the idea of a stable world we see that we give it a kind of ultimacy of being: the physical world exists first and foremost, it existed before us, we came into it at birth, and when we die it will continue without us. Put another way, our culture generally believes that matter is the basic ground for being. It existed first and everything else can be explained on the basis of it. This is the basic tenet of a worldview known as *materialism*. Western science has tended to adopt this view without seriously asking if there might be another view to consider.

CONSCIOUSNESS

Like most Eastern systems, Buddhism does not hold to a materialist view, the philosophy that physical matter is all there is. The Buddha criticized this view[1] and identified physical matter, space, *and* mind as fundamental constituents of reality.[2] He used the word *consciousness* (*viññāṇa*) to represent mind in this context. Describing how a being takes birth, he said that consciousness deriving from the previous life must "descend into" the mother's womb at the time of conception for a being to be born.[3] In Buddhist cosmology, there are realms of beings that have only mental qualities, with no physical aspect, such as a body, at all.[4]

MIND AND MATTER ARE LINKED

All of the Buddha's discourses that shed light on the relationship between material form and consciousness[5] employ a variant of dependent origination. Starting at the last link of the chain, these discourses trace suffering back to feeling, which arises from contact, which arises from name-and-form (*nāmarūpa*). And how does name-and-form come to be? It arises from consciousness (*viññāṇa*). Then the question is posed, "When *what* exists does consciousness come to be? By what is consciousness conditioned?"[6] In the standard scheme of dependent origination, the response is that consciousness arises based on volitional formations. In these discourses, however, the reply is, "When there is name-and-form, consciousness comes to be; consciousness has name-and-form as its condition."[7]

We have reversed track and are now going back up the ladder of the links. Consciousness conditions name-and-form, and name-and-form conditions consciousness. This is circular. To make sense of it, we need to consider the import of these two links. Consciousness, or knowing, is the basic characteristic of mind. Its function is to know sense experience. Name-and-form conjoins the naming faculty and physical matter, including the body. Consciousness and name-and-form are now said to be mutually dependent. The Buddha's disciple Sāriputta explains:

> Just as two sheaves of reeds might stand leaning against each other, so too, with name-and-form as condition, consciousness [comes to be]; with consciousness as condition, name-and-form [comes to be]. If, friend, one were to remove one of those sheaves of reeds, the other would fall, and if one were to remove the other sheaf, the first would fall.[8]

Mind and matter are both linked in our experience. We cannot say one is more critical than the other.

Why does this series differ from the standard version of dependent origination, which traces the links further back from consciousness to volitional formations and ultimately to ignorance? The answer lies in an almost parenthetical expression the Buddha offered in one discourse, "Thus far is the sphere of understanding . . . as far as can be discerned in this life, namely to name-and-form together with consciousness."⁹ The phrase "in this life" is key. To bring in volitional formations and ignorance involves tracing the analysis back to the rebirth prior to this one, since it was the force of volitional formations rooted in ignorance at the time of the previous death that led to this rebirth. In this life, the chain can only be traced to the mutual dependence of consciousness and name-and-form. We'll now consider further the relationship between consciousness and the world of form, especially visible forms.

THE MAGIC SHOW

In the *Lump of Foam* discourse, the mental aggregates of feeling, perception, and formations were compared to a water bubble, a mirage, and a plantain trunk. The discourse then goes on to discuss the aggregate of consciousness.

> Suppose, bhikkhus, that a magician would display a magical illusion at a crossroads. A person with good sight would inspect it, ponder it, and carefully investigate it, and it would appear to him to be void, hollow, insubstantial. For what substance could there be in a magical illusion? So too, bhikkhus, whatever kind of consciousness there is, a practitioner inspects it, ponders it, and carefully investigates it, and it would appear to him to be void, hollow, insubstantial. For what substance could there be in consciousness?¹⁰

The Buddha is saying that what is revealed through consciousness is not different from a magic show. Note that what is revealed through consciousness is our entire human experience of body and mind. How does this work in the sense of sight?

We see an object, like the wall of the room you're sitting in, and take it as a solid physical reality. But if we reflect on how that sight comes to be, we'll question that assumption. The sight arises because reflected light from the wall comes into the eye and lands on the retina, which generates a nerve signal and sends it to the brain. The brain does its neuronal work and—presto!—a millisecond later the image of a wall appears in our consciousness. This is a miracle! How does neuronal activity, which is a physical process, manage to generate an appearance in consciousness, which is a mental activity? In short: *no one knows.* Scientists don't know how this transition happens. (As long as they consider mind to be a byproduct of matter, I suspect they never will.) Most scientists believe that the brain generates consciousness, despite the lack of evidence for this view, but some suspect that the brain is a receptor for consciousness, not its originator.[11]

As we consider the chain from light to eye to brain to conscious image, we realize that the image cannot be identical to the physical wall. Light from the wall has been filtered through the sense door of the eye and processed by the neurons in the brain to generate in consciousness an *image* of the wall. The wall may exist on its own, but our image has been constructed by our sense door, nervous system, brain, and mind. Is the image faithful to the wall? Who knows! We can have no idea what the relationship is between the physical wall and the image we've constructed, because the only way we can know the wall is through our senses. We cannot apperceive the original wall itself. But we forget this.

A WORLD OF ILLUSION

We walk around thinking that we live in the real, physical world, but we don't. This is the illusion (Skt: *māyā*). We live in a representation of the world generated by our senses, brain, and consciousness. Everything we see is an appearance in consciousness, a production conditioned and limited by our sense doors and consciousness. This is the magic show. To say that it is an illusion is not to say that nothing exists. It is to say that we have misunderstood the way in which things exist. The things of our human experience—the totality that Buddhism is interested in—exist as appearances in consciousness. The appearances are not solid. They are void, hollow, and insubstantial, like a magic show.

We can see this in other ways as well. When we examine the visual field, what we actually see are not objects but raw combinations of shape and color. When I was first exposed to the idea of emptiness, I became interested in the question of where color resides. I would look at a blue book jacket and ask the question, "Where is blue?" I couldn't say that blue was in the book cover itself. An object that appears blue is reflecting that light to our eyes, which means that it is absorbing the other colors of the spectrum. So the blue book cover was, in fact, every color except blue. The blue, I realized, only existed in my experience of seeing. It was not an attribute of the book itself. Color is an interior experience. We can't actually know if what we call blue is the same color as what someone else calls blue. After a few meetings when the Spirit Rock design committee was selecting blue, green, and gray paints for some new buildings, we each became convinced that no one else sees colors the way we do.

Most of us have long assumed that the physical world provides an ultimate kind of ground to our life and experience, but we have to question that. If the physical world we see, including the earth, sun, and stars, is an appearance in consciousness, we have to ask, Does consciousness have a ground? Does consciousness rest upon something else? Clearly it does not rest upon the physical ground of the earth. This body rests upon that ground, but consciousness does not. In zero gravity the body loses its ground, but consciousness doesn't. In the domain of Buddhism, our experience of earth is an appearance in consciousness, not the other way round. The Buddha pointed to this in his famous comment, "It is in this fathom-long body endowed with perception and mind that I proclaim the world, the origin of the world, the cessation of the world, and the way leading to the cessation of the world."[12] The body and perception create the world as an appearance in mind. So there is no floor to consciousness, with one possible exception: nibbāna may be the ground for consciousness. We will discuss this further in part 3 on awareness.

A STAR AT DAWN

In the Buddhist tradition many images of insubstantial things have been used to convey the emptiness of phenomena. In the *Lump of Foam* discourse, the Buddha used the images of a mass of foam, a water bubble, a mirage, a plantain trunk, and a magic show. Another beautiful image is that of a rainbow, which appears vividly in the sky but is only a play of light. Nothing multicolored is there, only plain drops of water.

I once went into retreat for six weeks to study Nāgārjuna's key work on emptiness, *Fundamental Verses on the Middle Way* (Skt: *Mūlamadhyamakakārikā*). One day shortly before dawn, I dreamed I was standing in front of a full-length mirror looking at my reflection. I asked a question that in waking life had been on my mind for some days: "So why is emptiness important?" The image in the mirror replied, "Because it means that you don't exist." That answer woke me up! "I" don't exist in the way that I think of myself, as an ongoing solid entity. And it was striking that the reply came from the image in the mirror. In Buddhism, a reflection in water or a mirror is used as a symbol for the insubstantial, empty nature of what is seen, because a reflection is ungraspable. The dream spoke in a way that was, at the same time, logical and symbolic. It told me that, like all appearances, I don't exist in a solid way, and the wisdom had come from an image made only of light.

A famous stanza in the *Diamond Sutra*, a text from early Mahayana Buddhism, puts it like this:

> Thus shall you think of all this fleeting world:
> A star at dawn, a bubble in a stream,
> A flash of lightning in a summer cloud,
> A flickering lamp, a phantom, and a dream.[13]

We could fall into a philosophical rapture about the profound beauty of this vision, but it is important to remember that the reason to understand emptiness is not philosophical but practical: to free ourselves from craving and clinging to what is in fact ungraspable. The Buddha says this clearly in a verse from the *Dhammapada*:

> Knowing this body is like foam,
> Fully awake to its mirage-like nature,
> Cutting off Māra's flowers,
> One goes unseen by the King of Death.[14]

To cut off Māra's flowers is to abandon the unwholesome mind states of greed, aversion, and delusion. One who does so goes beyond death to the deathless state, nibbāna.

EMPTY IN TWO WAYS

We understand now that a being is empty in two ways. First, there is no central core that we can call a self. This is the insight we explored in part 1, on self. And second, the constituents that do exist—that is, the sense bases and aggregates— are themselves void, hollow, and insubstantial. This is the emptiness of phenomena. So we are "twice empty"—empty of self and made from empty pieces. Each brings to light a different facet of our emptiness. We need to understand both to penetrate our situation.

Like insights into not-self, insights into the emptiness of the world can be unsettling. One year we were exploring this topic in a group of senior students at Spirit Rock. After the class one of the students shared her reflections.

> It's spooky. I would look at everything, like this Japanese lamp that I love, and I'd see that it's just an appearance. Where that took me is that we're all appearances. When I went from an object to say it's an appearance, to a person and say they're an appearance—it made my hair stand on end! But it's true! And it makes you both more compassionate and more vulnerable. When I look at my friend Mary, I see that she is changing all the time. When you start thinking like this, you have to be more compassionate because we're all in the same boat, and we're all so fragile.[15]

A MAGICAL DISPLAY

We also hear of the emptiness of phenomena from the perspective of awakened consciousness. In chapter 13 we quoted a meditator's account of stream-entry in which the six senses were absent. This is a continuation of that account:

> Normal consciousness started to return, but I could still feel something of that other presence. The profound sense of peace and stillness was continuing. I was so shocked that I immediately opened my eyes and saw the room I was sitting in. The visual field was reduced to two dimensions and all the contents—not objects—were bleed-

ing down and running like watercolors off a paper. It was unmistakably obvious that the visual contents were completely insubstantial and empty. The entire outer world was held in this still awareness, like a painting on a canvas.[16]

From reports like these, we know that the truth of the emptiness of phenomena can be known directly and nonconceptually through meditative insight. This is the most liberating way of understanding emptiness. I think that the Buddha saw the world in this way and that all his teachings came from this view. It takes a great stability of mind, or we could say tranquility (Pali: *samatha*), to be able to sustain such seeing. Why? Because the peace of the unconditioned is so subtle. Other vibrations, especially those of greed, hatred, and delusion, are much grosser and stronger and thus easier to feel. The mind has to be well purified, at least temporarily, to perceive the unconditioned.

Everything that comes into our human experience is an appearance in consciousness. Speaking of sense impressions, Tsoknyi Rinpoche says, "Nothing that appears has any real existence whatsoever." Here, *real* is a synonym for *substantial*. Another teacher expressed this as "Things exist, but they don't really exist." Tibetan Buddhists use the phrase "magical display" to mean the immense variety of appearances in the phenomenal world, all characterized by emptiness and yet following their own lawful natures. Never departing from emptiness, birds know how to sing and flowers know how to bloom.

Isn't this amazing?

16. THE MIDDLE WAY

From true emptiness, the wondrous being appears.

—Suzuki Roshi[1]

THE MIDDLE WAY, a key term in Buddhism, can be described in several ways. In his first discourse, on the four noble truths, the Buddha declared the eightfold path to be the middle way between indulging in sense pleasures and self-mortification, both of which he said are ignoble and unbeneficial. We've discussed the eightfold path as the karma that leads to the end of karma and as the way of nondoing. Hence the middle way can also be seen as the way between inactivity and egoic striving.

BETWEEN EXISTENCE AND NONEXISTENCE

Perhaps the most philosophical expression of the middle way comes in a discourse to a monk named Kaccānagotta (whom the Buddha calls Kaccāna), who asked the Buddha about right view, the first element of the eightfold path. The Buddha replied:

This world, Kaccāna, for the most part depends upon a duality—upon the notion of existence and the notion of non-existence. But for one who sees the origin of the world as it really is with correct wisdom, there is no notion of non-existence in regard to the world. And for one who sees the cessation of the world as it really is with correct wisdom, there is no notion of existence in regard to the world. . . .

"All exists": Kaccāna, this is one extreme. "All does not exist": this is the second extreme. Without veering towards either of these extremes, the Tathāgata teaches the Dhamma by the middle.[2]

Then the Buddha recited the twelve links of dependent origination, showing how they arise based on ignorance and how the cessation of ignorance leads to the cessation of the others. In other words, the middle way between existence and nonexistence is the way that things arise through dependent origination and also the way they can cease.

Here the "notion of existence" is understood as the belief in a solid, permanent existence, a doctrine known then as eternalism. The "notion of non-existence" is understood as the belief that nothing exists, a doctrine known as annihilationism. Although these might sound like stark philosophical views that no one would subscribe to today, we still find instances of them in our modern world. The modern eternalist imagines an afterlife in pleasant circumstances in which the self goes on forever, like a heavenly birth that has no death; while the modern annihilationist is blinded by nihilism, the cynical view that nothing matters and nothing is worth doing. Tsoknyi Rinpoche calls this cynical view "one-legged emptiness": everything else is worthless but I am supremely important.

On a more immediate level, most of us have a subconscious assumption about the solidity and permanence of things. Though it is not a clearly formed view of eternalism, it is the basis for us to continue with craving and grasping. The subconscious assumption that our actions don't have consequences, while not an explicit theory of annihilationism, permits us to avoid reflecting on the implications of the law of karma. These theories in their unconscious forms continue to exert great sway in our lives.

The great Buddhist philosopher Nāgārjuna used the *Discourse to Kaccāna* as the foundation for his key work, *Fundamental Verses on the Middle Way*. The tradition based on his analysis, called Madhyamaka, or middle way, is still a major lineage in Tibetan Buddhism, especially within the Gelug school—and one with which the Dalai Lama feels a strong philosophical affinity.

THE SEEMING PARADOX IN EMPTINESS

The middle way points to a mode of being that is somewhere between existing solidly and not existing at all. As we saw in the previous chapter, this is the way in which things exist in the domain of human experience: "Things exist, but they don't really exist." This kind of language lends itself to paradox, since one could say, with equal validity, "Yes, that exists" and "No, it doesn't really exist." For the sake of brevity or poetry or because of absent-mindedness, one might omit the qualifier "really," and the statement would come out, "No, it doesn't exist." Then the person speaking would believe both statements to be true—"Yes, it exists" and "No, it doesn't exist"—because the speaker understands the qualifier to be implicit in the second statement. Unfortunately, the listener may not be in on the joke, at least in the beginning.

For about two thousand years, an entire dynasty of lineages has been built upon paradox using this linguistic sleight of hand, beginning with Nāgārjuna and the Perfection of Wisdom (Skt: *Prajñāpāramitā*) texts and running all the way through Chan and Zen. One example is the *Heart Sutra*, a short text within the Perfection of Wisdom family, so named because it is considered to be the heart or essence of wisdom. It is the source of the famous statement "Form is emptiness and emptiness is form." Less often quoted is the following line, which says, "The same is true for feeling, perception, volitional formations, and consciousness," thus including all five aggregates. The text goes on:

[1]   In emptiness there is no form, no feeling, no perception, no volitional formations, no consciousness;

[2]   No eye, no ear, no nose, no tongue, no body, no mind; no sight, no sound, no smell, no taste, no touch, no mind object;

[3]   No element of eye and so on until no element of mind consciousness;

[4]   No ignorance and no cessation of ignorance, and so on until no old age and death and no cessation of old age and death;

[5]   No suffering, no origin of suffering, no cessation of suffering, no path;

[6]   No wisdom and no attainment.[3]

What is fascinating and arresting about this passage is the way it juxtaposes the entire foundational teachings of the Buddha with the negation of every one of them. Listed and then categorically denied are the five aggregates (line 1) and the six internal and six external sense bases (line 2). Line 3 lists and negates the eighteen elements of sense contact. For example, eye contact is composed of the eye, a sight, and eye consciousness. The phrase "and so on until" indicates an elision to be filled in by the listener's knowledge of the basic teachings, here ranging through all six kinds of sense contact. Line 4 declares and denies the twelve links of dependent origination, beginning with ignorance and running through old age and death, which in this series is the shorthand for all types of suffering. This line negates not only the arising of the links but also their ending. Line 5 lists and negates the four noble truths. Line 6 denies the wisdom that leads to enlightenment as well as the view that enlightenment is any kind of attainment. This entire series could be regarded as shocking, if not downright heretical, for an orthodox Buddhist.

Some ambiguity is added by the passage's first words: "In emptiness there is no . . ." What is the text saying here? Does this mean that what is sought is a state of being of such total vacancy and blankness that all of these experiences are cut off and not arising? We discussed a state like this in chapter 13 when we noted that an enlightenment experience is sometimes described as the cessation of consciousness. Is this the emptiness being described here? In short: no, it isn't. It cannot be meant in this way, because the earlier lines of the text just equated emptiness with all five aggregates, which are present in every ordinary moment of experience. The heart of the perfection that is wisdom is not reserved for a special esoteric experience, even a valid enlightenment experience.

I first confronted the *Heart Sutra* in some depth when, as a young practitioner, I attended a seven-day *sesshin* (meditation retreat) led by a Rinzai Zen master. Three times a day, at mealtimes, we chanted the sutra in Japanese to the rhythmic beat of a small drum. I still hear those deep rumbling syllables when I think of that retreat. We also had the English text at hand. Having been schooled in the fundamental teachings, I was puzzled by their denial in this respected sutra. It took me quite some reflection and later study to be able to make sense of the *Heart Sutra*. I needed first to examine the power of words and concepts to shape our view of reality.

CONCEPTS AND REALITY

As we saw in the last two chapters, all sense contacts, which are the core constituents of human experience, are characterized by their frail, fleeting, ungraspable nature. If we look closely, we have to say that there is something there, but that something appears only for a moment. As the Dalai Lama said about the unsatisfactoriness of conditioned things (Pali: *sankhāra dukkha*), all sense experience is disintegrating moment by moment. A sense impression comes into being and then vanishes. As Suzuki Roshi put it, "Everything is in flowing change. Nothing exists but momentarily in its present form and color. One thing flows into another and cannot be grasped."[4] What comes is present so briefly it can be hardly be called a thing at all. If we look closely, we can see that it never actually exists substantially enough to be called an "object." It is just a fleeting, flimsy flash. In the words of Nāgārjuna, "That to which language refers is denied, because an object experienced by the mind is denied."[5]

And yet—something is there, or was there, is here now, and is gone. In fact all manner of things—trees, walls, birds, humans, consciousness, desire, love, confusion, perceptions, opinions, and so on—appear and pass. From the dawn of humankind, if not before, we have been compelled to give names to the appearances. This is the function of name-and-form (*nāmarūpa*). The names are just convenient designations so we can communicate with one another about the appearances. But after countless repetitions over time, the names have taken on a life of their own. The designation, simply an invented concept, becomes static and unchanging. The more we live in the world of concepts, the more we forget that what the name points to is just a momentary flashing into sense experience. We take the static concept as real and forget the changing reality. Thus "my friend" should be constant to me, while in fact my friend is constantly changing. This is the tension between conventional designation and the fleeting nature of the underlying reality.

THE TWO TRUTHS

In the Buddhist tradition, two ways of looking at phenomena are delineated, conventional truth and ultimate truth, also known as the two truths. Conventional truth is based on naming appearances. It is verbal and conceptual, and because of the static nature of concepts, conventional truth necessarily treats appearances as though they are ongoing objects. These designations are extremely useful for our survival as a species, for societal organization, and for the comforts of life. The conceptual realm has its own laws and associated truths. Laws of physics, biology, and chemistry, for example, govern the behavior of and interactions among "objects," and we ignore them at our peril. The problem is that conventional truth can obscure our seeing the reality of things, which is the ultimate truth of their emptiness. The Sanskrit term for "conventional" is *saṁvṛti*, which literally means "all-concealing." It is not the concepts that obscure; it is the belief we give to the concepts that creates the sense of permanence and solidity. We need to remember that the name is just something we've invented because it is useful. There is no actual conflict between the two truths. They're just different ways of looking and speaking.

In the passage above, the *Heart Sutra* is pointing out that the terms of Buddhist doctrines are also concepts; they are not reality itself. When one is in touch with the underlying reality of things, one doesn't have to label it as "eye" or "sight" or "consciousness." The thing is what it is before our label. When we examine it closely, we do not find a solid thing but only a temporary flashing into being. When we see the emptiness of things, we do not see a substantial eye or sight or consciousness. We feel only the reality of the momentary flash. This is seeing clearly the empty nature of things. We might now understand line 1 of the Heart Sutra as saying, "In emptiness, there is *no concept of* form," or feeling, and so on.

HUINENG

Another example of paradox can be found in the story of Huineng, the Sixth Ancestor of Chan (Chinese Zen) Buddhism. Born in 638 C.E. to a poor family in the south of China, he had an awakening when he overheard someone recite a Buddhist text. Still in his teens, he set out to join the monastery of Hongren, the

Fifth Ancestor. Hongren acknowledged Huineng's insight but could not outwardly recognize the young man because the other monks would condemn his poverty and lack of formal education. So the master set up a competition and announced that the person who wrote the best verse expressing his understanding would be appointed his dharma heir. Shenxiu, an instructor in the monastery, posted this poem:

> Our body is the bodhi tree,
> Our mind a mirror bright.
> Carefully we wipe them hour by hour
> And let no dust alight.[6]

The master told Shenxiu that this was a useful verse for meditators but that it did not express the deepest understanding. Two days later Huineng gave his reply, anonymously:

> Bodhi doesn't have a tree,
> Nor stand of mirror bright.
> From the first not a thing exists,
> So where could dust alight?[7]

The master gave Huineng his robe and bowl, symbols of Dharma transmission, naming him the Sixth Ancestor. He then told him to flee into the mountains and hide for a while before teaching, to avoid harm stemming from the jealousy of the other monks. Huineng did so and later became one of the greatest figures in the history of Chan. His teachings are recorded in a work known as the *Platform Sutra*.

Shenxiu's line "Carefully we wipe them hour by hour" is a useful meditation instruction as it encourages the practitioner to keep the mind free from the afflictive forces of greed, hatred, and delusion. This is a necessary foundation for insight to arise. However, this advice is still in the realm of meditative effort that has not yet ripened into profound wisdom. "From the first not a thing exists" is Huineng's rejoinder from a place of deeper insight. This statement shows Huineng's realization of the emptiness of all things, an insight confirmed by Hongren with the Dharma transmission. Huineng's line is reminiscent of Nāgārjuna's statement "That to which language refers is denied."

Here we again encounter the seeming paradox between the conventional and ultimate truths. To say "not a thing exists" could be taken in two ways, of which one is wrong while the other is right. (1) The wrong way: As the Buddha said to Kaccāna, "All does not exist" is an extreme to be avoided. As the statement of an annihilationist, this would be condemned as wrong view. The right view of the middle way includes conventional truth, in which things *can* be said to exist, at least in a way. (2) The right way: On the other hand, when Huineng says "not a thing exists," he means that things do not exist in a substantial way. Now the statement is considered right view—some would say, the highest kind of right view.

This is the heart of the paradox one finds over and over in Nāgārjuna and in the Perfection of Wisdom texts. When a phrase like "nothing exists" occurs, one has to figure out whether the statement is the wrong view of the nihilist or a right view expressing the ultimate truth of emptiness. Similarly, when the opposite is stated, "a thing exists," one needs to decide whether this is the wrong view of an eternalist or a right view expressing a conventional truth. The context will usually give clues to help you determine this, but sometimes it's hard to be sure. Some schools of Zen use koans to clarify a practitioner's understanding of the two truths. Huineng had this advice on training through questions and answers:

> If in questioning you, someone asks about being, answer with non-being. If he asks about non-being, answer with being. If she asks about the ordinary person, answer in terms of the sage. If she asks about the sage, answer in terms of the ordinary person. By this method of opposites mutually related there arises the understanding of the Middle Way. For every question that you are asked, respond in terms of its opposite.[8]

If you've ever felt confused by Zen, this might be why.

THE NOBLE TRUTHS ARE CONCEPTS

We need to return now to the proclamation in the *Heart Sutra* that in emptiness, there are no four noble truths. In other words, the noble truths are just concepts. Really? Does suffering not exist substantially? Nor the end of suffering? But suffering and the end of suffering are the entire basis of the Buddha's teachings! And the path is the way through! Is the *Heart Sutra* denying all of that?

Of course it isn't. The *Heart Sutra* is embedded in many Buddhist schools, all of whom share the vision of leading from suffering to its end. But to see the noble truths as concepts is to see them in the realm of conventional truth, and this insight has some wonderful implications.

The first obvious implication is that the four noble truths are truths. They work. Like the laws of science, they explain with great practicality the domain for which they were invented, in this case the liberation of the human heart. To see them as conventional truth is to acknowledge their effectiveness as the supreme tools for liberation. To know that they are not reality itself points us to the right direction. Nāgārjuna put it this way:

> The Dharma taught by the Buddha relies on two truths:
> The conventional truths of the world and an ultimate truth.
> Those who do not understand how they differ
> Do not understand the profound teaching of the Buddha.
> Without using conventional truth, the ultimate truth cannot be
> disclosed.
> Without understanding the ultimate truth, Nirvana cannot be
> attained.[9]

Ultimate truth cannot be pointed to without using conventional language—and so sometimes students get impatient with conceptual teachings, wanting only to meditate and have some direct experience for themselves. Of course meditation is necessary, but some conceptual understanding is usually helpful first. Tsoknyi Rinpoche explained it with an analogy. If you come in from the garden and your hands are dirty, first you have to scrub them with soap until they are all lathered up. Are they clean now? No. Next you have to rinse them under running water.

The soap has loosened the dirt, and now the running water removes both the soap and the dirt. Dharma concepts are like soap. When we begin Dharma practice, we still have lots of worldly concepts and attachments. Dharma concepts scrub those away. Once those are loosened, then we rinse away both the worldly concepts and the Dharma concepts in the direct experience of meditation and clear seeing. Then there is just the bare reality known free from concepts.

The second implication of seeing the noble truths as concepts is that they were created by someone, in this case Gotama Buddha. Acknowledging them as concepts takes them out of the realm of ultimate truth and relieves us as practitioners from having to defend them. Throughout human history, religious ideologies have led to so much conflict and war. In Buddhism no doctrine represents an absolute truth that we need to fight about. All Buddhist teachings are simply tools for those who find them useful.

Seeing the noble truths as concepts reminds us that they are not even to be attached to inwardly. In one famous discourse, the Buddha compares his teachings to a raft built in order to cross a body of water, journeying from the near shore, which is dangerous and fearsome, to the further shore, which is safe and protected. Once someone has crossed the water on the raft, she doesn't need to carry the raft any longer. She can put it down and go on her way, unburdened. Thus, "the Dhamma is similar to a raft, being for the purpose of crossing over, not for the purpose of grasping."[10]

This same attitude applies to any kind of verbal formulation, view, or opinion. The Buddha was explicit on this point: "The wise one does not adhere to dogma."[11] In another discourse he puts views into a wise perspective: "Examining all views, but not grasping them, and searching for the truth, I found inner peace."[12] It is not the view that is important but the inner peace that can be discovered. Then he points out the consequences of grasping views: "For one who is free from views there are no ties; but those who grasp after views and philosophical opinions, they wander about in the world annoying people."[13]

The third implication is that we understand even the first noble truth to be conceptual. In pointing out that suffering is not substantial, the *Heart Sutra* places it too in the territory of the fleeting. However pervasive suffering may seem in one's life or in the world, nothing in it is fixed. If it were a fixed attribute of our being, it could never be removed. Once we know its empty nature, we know that it can be undone: "All that is subject to arising is subject to cessation." Moreover, the noble truths tell us how this happens. Suffering arises due to craving. Suffering ceases due to the noble eightfold path.

CAUSALITY IN BUDDHISM

Cause and effect is central in all the principal teachings of the Buddha. The four noble truths are structured as suffering and its cause and the end of suffering and its cause. The law of karma says that certain kinds of acts lead to certain kinds of results. Dependent origination, possibly the most profound insight in the Buddha's teachings, is expressed as twelve causal links.

Why did the Buddha emphasize causality at every turn, making it the crucial point of all his deepest teachings? The first answer has to do with the emptiness of both self and phenomena. If there is no ongoing self at the center of experience who controls things by free will, then that central causal mechanism falls away. If things aren't happening because of "my" agency, what is making them happen? Seeing the emptiness of self requires that we account for outcomes in some other way. Second, if phenomena aren't solid and permanent but instead are arising and passing, what makes them arise and pass? If these phenomena that arise and pass are conditioned, by what are they conditioned? They are conditioned by prior phenomena. And what do they condition? They condition future phenomena. There is only an unbroken flow of past causes and conditions leading to present effects, which in turn become the causes and conditions for future effects.

The longest book in the Theravadan Abhidhamma is the *Patthāna*, or Book of Conditional Relations, which totals 2,500 pages in the Burmese edition. It details twenty-four laws of conditionality, called *paccaya*, that govern the interactions among all existent things of mind and matter, describing in great detail how things come to be. Bhikkhu Bodhi says that the *Patthāna* is "probably the most important work in the Abhidhamma" and "one of the truly monumental products of the human mind, astounding in its breadth of vision, its rigorous consistency, and its painstaking attention to detail."[14]

For all its amazing complexity, the whole *Patthāna* is built on this basic principle of dependent arising as enunciated by the Buddha:

When this exists, that comes to be;
With the arising of this, that arises.
When this does not exist, that does not come to be.
With the cessation of this, that ceases.[15]

This is a very profound statement. Its depth could be overlooked because of its simplicity. The Buddha is reported to have said, "One who sees dependent arising sees the Dhamma; one who sees the Dhamma sees dependent arising."[16] According to this principle, no conditioned thing exists from the first. Everything that arises depends on underlying causes and conditions; it would not exist without them. All conditioned phenomena lack inherent self-existence. This is a statement of their intrinsic emptiness. To say that something is dependently arisen is to say that it is empty. In the words of Nāgārjuna, "Whatever is dependently arisen, that is explained to be emptiness."[17] This is the heart of the understanding of the middle way.

The Buddha's teaching of the middle way is an understanding of the way things are. It does not veer into a belief in either solid existence or complete nonexistence. Things are seen to exist only fleetingly and in dependence on other things. Their very fleeting and dependent existence is the basis for their (imminent) nonexistence, as their underlying causes cease. Their dependently arisen nature is the sign of the emptiness of all phenomena.

PART III:

AWARENESS

17. THE NATURE OF AWARENESS

That everything is included within your mind is the essence of mind. To
experience this is to have religious feeling.
—Suzuki Roshi[1]

WHEN WE BEGIN training ourselves to pay attention, the emphasis—in this
book and in meditation instructions generally—is on being mindful of all
appearances: breath, body, sounds, thoughts, emotions, feeling tone, intention,
craving, clinging, and so on. We develop a familiarity with all the elements of
our experience in order to understand their empty nature and to develop greater
ease in relating with them. This proves to be enormously helpful in reducing the
suffering in life and coming to greater happiness.

After achieving a certain degree of skill working with phenomena, people
often have a question that points their meditation in a different direction. The
question can take different forms: Is this all there is? Why am I watching these
things? What is the constant here? What is mindfulness really? This questioning usually arises unprompted and can feel both startling and urgent. Coaxed by
the question, the meditator may get a sense of a different approach, or a teacher
might suggest a new direction. In either case, the meditator might discover
another way to look at his or her experience. This new vision suggests that all
the phenomena have been like beads on a string, each set right next to another,

arising and passing ceaselessly moment after moment, bead after bead after bead. Seeing this is engaging and freeing, but what are all these beads of momentary experience set on? What is the string? What holds them together?

Through this inquiry, the meditator might realize that it is *awareness* that is present moment after moment with each bead, as it appears. It is awareness that holds all the varied beads of experience. This awareness seems always to be there. Even its flavor seems consistent over time, especially when the afflictive emotions are not so active. What is this factor we're starting to call awareness? Is it truly ongoing? Can it become the next focus for our meditation? How would we do that? Is awareness empty too? These are the questions we'll explore in part 3, on awareness.

AWARENESS: THE FIELD OF CONSCIOUSNESS

Our first discovery of awareness in meditation can be quite exciting. We may have been observing objects for a long time but never quite noticed the observing faculty itself. Once we see it, it's hard to believe we missed it all this time. It now seems so obvious. D. H. Lawrence compared this to someone sitting by a fire outside at night and being so entranced by the things illuminated that they forget to notice the beauty and mystery of the firelight. Awareness is the light at the heart of sentient life.

Why have we not been meditating on awareness directly? Because awareness is subtle. It seems it is there all the time, so we can't mark it by its coming and going, as we would other subtle phenomena like calm or equanimity. We can keep asking, "Am I aware right now?" and the answer keeps coming back, "Yes." But it isn't easy to locate awareness. There is no Pali word that is typically translated as awareness, so we can't rely on the Buddha's direct teachings here. Still, *awareness* is an evocative word in English that different Buddhist schools have found to be a helpful pointer in both meditation and understanding. Awareness seems very close to consciousness (*viññāṇa*) in that it holds sense experience, but perhaps there is also mindfulness (*sati*) since it seems somewhat intelligent. As a way to explore awareness, we'll start by looking at its similarities with consciousness.

We've seen that the Pali term *viññāṇa* usually refers to one of six kinds of consciousness corresponding to the six senses: eye consciousness, ear consciousness, and so on. Consciousness in this usage means the *knowing* of an individual sense object: sight, sound, and so forth. If the sense organ is functioning, then in our immediate experience the consciousness of the object arises together with the object; the meeting of the three is contact. When the object ceases, the knowing of it also ceases. Consciousness in this usage is clearly an impermanent, conditioned phenomenon.

The English word *awareness* has a slightly different sense. It includes the knowing of sense objects, since they are what make up our experience, but in English the term isn't so tied to just one sense organ at a time. There is for some the intuition of a faculty that is more pervasive and perhaps more fundamental than sense consciousness. We might say that all the objects of sense consciousness are arising and passing within a broad field of knowing, the way individual clouds come and go in a blue sky. The Buddha didn't explicitly describe such a dimension, so perhaps we are overinterpreting here, but some of the Pali Discourses do seem to hint at such a thing. At any rate, let us use as a working definition of awareness "the broad field or space of consciousness within which individual objects are known." This provides, we might say, an alternate vantage point for looking at our experience. The meditation at the end of this chapter offers an experiential way to connect to this sense of awareness.

Awareness is present at any point in the broad field to which you direct your attention. It does not seem to be entirely dependent on the presence of an object. This reminds us of the Buddha's advice for abiding in emptiness: give no attention to signs. Without fixating on any of the signs, can we sense the awareness clearly enough that we can pay attention to that? Then we are not sending the mind out toward anything but are abiding in that "inward-staying, unentangled knowing" that Upasika Kee spoke about. By shifting our attention from a sense object to the knowing of it, we are taking a step back. We are not attached to or entangled in the object, but we are still aware of it. We are neither cut off nor disconnected.

All objects of the phenomenal world appear and disappear in the big empty space of awareness or, we could say, in the empty space of mind—what Suzuki

Roshi called "big mind."[2] When we see in this way, there is a greater sense of spaciousness and ease because we are not fixated on or grasping after objects. But there is still a focus for attention, a thing to come back to again and again, which is the awareness itself. So we can also call this practice the awareness of awareness. It is subtle; awareness is not quite locatable. It is not an object that can be taken hold of; awareness is what holds objects. Your right hand can hold a stick, but it can't hold itself. As Wei Wu Wei put it, "What we are looking for is what is looking."[3]

Ajahn Sumedho likened it to our eyes:

> Just like the question "Can you see your own eyes?" Nobody can see their own eyes. I can see your eyes but I can't see my eyes. I'm sitting right here, I've got two eyes and I can't see them. But you can see my eyes. Looking in a mirror I can see a reflection, but that's not my eyes, it's a reflection of my eyes. But there's no need for me to see my eyes because I can see! It's ridiculous, isn't it? If I started saying "Why can't I see my own eyes?" you'd think "Ajahn Sumedho's really weird, isn't he!"[4]

Awareness can't be grasped, but we know it's there. As Ajahn Chah said, "You're riding on a horse and asking, 'Where's the horse?'"[5] Don't search too hard. We know awareness by its functioning, its activity of revealing sense objects. If you lose touch with it, just ask, "Am I aware right now?" Then stay with whatever you notice about the awareness. Over time, as this practice becomes more familiar, it will be easier to notice awareness itself.

Awareness is not a thing that can be taken hold of—and we have to ask if it is in fact a *thing* at all. We might rather say that awareness is the *activity* of knowing what arises—not a noun but a verb. Awareness is the knowing. It is a functioning: a revealing, an illuminating of what appears. Awareness is *aware-ing*.

WHAT IS DOING THE KNOWING?

Joseph Goldstein sometimes gives meditation instruction in the passive voice. Instead of telling students to observe sensations in the body, he phrases it

"Sensations are being known." This helps reduce the sense of a separate observer, usually imagined to be in the head looking down at the rest of the body. When following an instruction given in the passive voice, we are more likely to have a direct experience of sensations being where they are, with no separate watcher. This is like the Buddha's instruction to Bāhiya from chapter 7, "In what is sensed, let there be just the sensed."

We can apply this passive phrasing to many situations in life. If you rub your hand along your cheek, you might say, "The cheek is being rubbed." If you strike a bell with a stick, you could say, "The bell is being struck." If you cut a piece of paper with a pair of scissors, you could say, "The paper is being cut." For each passive construction, something unspecified is performing the action. If you ask, "By what is this act being done?" the answers are simple. The cheek is rubbed by the hand. The bell is struck by the stick. The paper is cut by the scissors. In each case, there is an agent doing the act.

Now direct your attention to the body and notice, "Sensations are being known." Spend a few moments in touch with this experience, retaining the passive voice. Then ask the question, "Known by what?" If sensations are being known, what is the agent doing the knowing?

Before answering, notice if there is a shift in the quality of your attention when you ask this. You've been paying attention to sensations in the body, and now you ask what it is they are known by. If there is a shift in your attention, does it lead to a shift in mood, thoughts, or perceptions? We'll come back to this investigation a little later.

One possible response to the question "Known by what?" is to say that the sensations are being known *by awareness*. However, awareness doesn't point to a thing, to an actor. Awareness is the *activity* of knowing, so as I've said awareness seems to be a verb. It is the act of knowing itself; awareness is not the agent carrying out the knowing.

If you don't know the answer to these questions from direct experience, consider two possible responses. One is to say the question is not valid. There is no noun carrying out the action. Awareness is happening, knowing sensations is happening, but *there's nothing else there*. No agent is behind the knowing. Perhaps knowing how this happens is not important to you. We've already spent some time looking at a version of this view: there is nothing beyond the five aggregates except nibbāna, and in this view, nibbāna doesn't have any quality of knowing.

Another possible response is to admit that *known by what?* might be a valid question but you don't know the answer. This leaves you free to further investigate this question in the context of meditative practice.

In my experience, even the meditative asking of this question—irrespective of whether the question yields answers—often brings about some effect, like a widening of attention, a sense of spaciousness, a release from any present fixation, an inner stillness characterized by keen interest, or a highlighting of the mystery of awareness. A genuine inquiry with sincere interest has its own rewards. This inquiry can also lead us to further and deeper insight.

THAT WHICH KNOWS

We don't yet know what knows, so we'll continue our search. We human beings are made up of a body and a mind. The body is not doing the knowing; too many things are known that are not physical. So let's try the mind. What do we mean by mind? Our mental nature includes mental objects like thoughts and emotions, but those are things being known. They aren't doing the knowing. Perhaps another aspect of mental nature is doing the knowing. Let's review the Buddha's teachings to see how he described "mind" and if he ever used a word signifying "that which knows."

There are three Pali words that can be translated as "mind." The first and most common is *citta*, which might arguably be best translated as "psyche." In the Buddha's teaching on the four foundations of mindfulness, *citta* is the third. The Buddha instructs his disciples to contemplate the mind in the mind, or the mind as mind, observing dispassionately if there is lust, hatred, delusion, or their absences; if it is contracted or not, concentrated or not, and so on. Thus, he describes *citta* in terms of what influences or molds it: These traits are objects or attributes of mind. The way the Buddha uses the word *citta* throughout the discourses, it is a conventional designation, not a thing that fundamentally is. So *citta* cannot mean "that which knows."*

---

* The Abhidhamma uses the term *citta* differently. There it is viewed as an ultimate, but this Abhidhamma usage corresponds more to the way the term *viññāṇa* is used in the discourses as the fifth aggregate.

The second Pali term is *mano*. In the *Discourse on Totality*,[6] *mano* is the word for mind in the sequence "eye and sights, ear and sounds, nose and smells, tongue and tastes, body and sensations, mind and mind objects." *Mano* here designates the sixth internal sense base, the organ that takes in mental objects like thoughts and emotions, as the eye takes in sights. *Knowing* mental objects is *manoviññāna*, mind consciousness. Perhaps *mano* should be translated as "mind organ." Since *mano* receives only mental objects, it is not qualified to be "that which knows" all categories of sense experience.

The third Pali term to consider is *viññāṇa*, or consciousness. This term usually denotes the six classes of mental faculty that cognize the six kinds of sense experience. In this way, sense consciousness is close to "that which knows." But as with our word *awareness*, we have come to see the activity of knowing as a verb. Consciousness *is* the knowing, just as awareness is. They are exactly alike in this way. So consciousness is also a verb, in this sense. It therefore cannot be the noun doing the knowing, or "that which knows."

None of these three terms—*citta*, *mano*, and *viññāṇa*—is quite what we're looking for. We'll have to keep looking. In many schools of Buddhism, the word used for this agent is "mind": "Mind is that which knows." Let's provisionally adopt this and see where it takes us. We're not the first to try to find it.

Bodhidharma was the Indian master who brought Buddhism to China in the fifth century C.E. He is revered as the First Ancestor of Chan Buddhism. Legend has it that Bodhidharma spent nine years in a cave, not speaking to anyone. Finally, a student named Huike so desperately wanted instruction that he cut off his left arm and tossed it into the cave to prove his sincerity, yelling:

> Huike: "My mind is not at peace! I beg you, Master, pacify it!"
> Bodhidharma: "Bring me your mind and I will pacify it."
> Huike: "I have searched for this mind but I have never been able to find it."
> Bodhidharma: "There, I have pacified your mind."

With this, Huike is said to have awakened.[7]

Searching, with or without finding—the inquiry itself—can lead to great insight. This was pointed to by Lama Shabkar, a great Tibetan practitioner of the eighteenth century.

> Now come up close and listen. When you look carefully, you won't find the merest speck of real mind you can put your finger on and say, "This is it!" And not finding anything is an incredible find. Friends! To start with, mind doesn't emerge from anything. It's primordially empty; there's nothing there to hold on to. It isn't anywhere; it has no shape or color.[8]

Awareness is the broad field of knowing, and here *mind* is that which knows. The two are intimately related. Awareness occurs as the result of mind's functioning. Wherever mind is, awareness is there too. They are coterminous; they occupy the same territory. Awareness is the *activity* of knowing; mind is the *thing* that does the knowing. They are not synonymous but they share many attributes.

THE NATURE OF MIND

You can approach mind by looking at your *experience* of awareness. Does it have shape or color? Size? Boundary or limit? As you sit with the sense of awareness, is there anything *fixed* within it or is everything coming and going? We've explored this before and are pretty confident that the sense objects within awareness are impermanent—all are coming and going. The field of awareness does not have anything in it that is fixed, or stuck. There is no unchanging object there. Therefore, awareness is fundamentally empty, and it is this basic emptiness that creates the space for phenomena to arise and depart. And even as phenomena come and go, awareness is never completely filled up. There is always room for the next thing to arise. Awareness's emptiness allows all things to come into being.

If awareness is fundamentally empty, then so is mind. That which knows is even harder to discover than the knowing. We find nothing fixed in the things being known or in that which is knowing them. As they are coterminous, we can talk about the empty space of mind as well as the empty space of awareness.

To see the empty nature of mind is liberating. If nothing is there from the beginning, anything that has come in can be taken out. It's like a room full of furniture. Originally the room is empty. The furniture is brought in piece by piece. The person living there knows that anything they brought into the room can also be taken out—chairs, beds, tables, and so on. Similarly anything brought into the mind by prior causes and conditions can be taken out—afflictive emotions, karmic patterns, all kinds of suffering. Nothing is stuck. This empty nature is the direct route to freedom. Once we know it, it is only a question of doing the work. As Suzuki Roshi put it, "People who know the state of emptiness will always be able to dissolve their problems by constancy."[9] Constancy here means continuing with our practice of right effort. Once we know the peace of an empty mind, we only need to keep letting go of the sources of suffering.

The field of awareness, like vast space, is intrinsically empty. The emptiness of space allows physical objects to arise within it. But unlike physical space, the field of awareness has another power. It is "intrinsically knowing." Its basic activity is to know, to know things. Physical space accommodates objects, but it doesn't know them. The space of awareness accommodates objects and knows them. Each phenomenon is known in awareness as soon as it arises. In fact, we can't completely separate the object from the knowing of it. The object and the knowing arise as one experience with two aspects, like seeing the roundness and the yellowness of a gold coin. Awareness is always knowing; it cannot not know.

The Buddha pointed to the accommodating power of space in the advice he gave his son, Rahula, when the boy was about seven:

> Rahula, develop meditation that is like space, for when you develop meditation that is like space, arisen agreeable and disagreeable contacts will not invade your mind and remain. Just as space is not established anywhere, so too, Rahula, develop meditation that is like space.[10]

In describing space as not established anywhere, the Buddha is pointing to its emptiness.

Awareness is empty, and mind is unfindable, but we cannot say that mind doesn't exist. It functions unceasingly; its function is knowing. This capacity of knowing is native to us; it isn't manufactured. The objects that mind reveals are shown as they are, subject to the limits of our senses. And awareness is like a clear mirror; when an object appears, it is reflected accurately.

THE UNION OF EMPTINESS AND COGNIZANCE

As we investigate the empty openness of awareness and its knowing activity, we see that the two aren't separate. Space allows things to arise, and as soon as they arise, they are known. It's almost as though the empty space of awareness does the knowing. Joseph Goldstein calls this "the cognizing power of emptiness."

We can say that this field of awareness is an indivisible unity of emptiness and knowing, or emptiness and cognizance. Because of its function of *illuminating* what arises, the "knowing quality" might also be called luminosity or radiance. This doesn't mean that if we close our eyes, we are going to see a bright light because we are aware, or that a bright light is the proof we are being *really* aware. Rather, it's that this intrinsic knowing is always present to shine a light on whatever arises. Because of it, we know the objects of our experience. Ajahn Buddhadasa said that we should call it "emptiness," but because of its *knowing* property we call it "mind."[11]

Mind is the indivisible unity of emptiness and cognizance. It does not obstruct any arising, and it knows phenomena immediately with a mirrorlike accuracy. This describes not just your mind or my mind but the mind of all sentient beings. As we will see, this mind has breathtaking qualities.

MEDITATION

Big Sky Mind

We might ask how we can meditate from this vantage point and whether we can meditate directly on the faculty of awareness. To explore this, we can practice a meditation called Big Sky Mind.

- Sit still and let your eyes gently close. Begin by paying attention to all the sounds around you, noticing how the range of sounds evokes in you the sense of space. Let the attention become wide and open so that all the sounds are simply coming and going within the wide space of awareness, which is like a big empty sky.
- After a few minutes, extend your attention to include body sensations. Sensations throughout the body can be felt as glimmers in the darkness of the night sky, arising and changing in the open space of awareness.
- Next, include thoughts and images. Thoughts and images are like clouds drifting through the sky, all within the empty space of awareness.
- When all these appearances have been noticed within the space of awareness, direct your attention to the *knowing* itself, which extends throughout the whole wide, empty space. Awareness is like the sky. It's wide and empty. To see if it's like that, look directly at the nature of your own awareness.

18. WOMB OF THE BUDDHAS

The Perfection of Wisdom is limitlessly open and inexhaustibly rich in its power to awaken, heal, liberate, and enlighten.

—Prajñāpāramitā Sutra[1]

IN THE LAST chapter's meditation on Big Sky Mind, we began to use awareness itself as the focus for attention. Now that we have considered awareness more systematically, we understand mind to be the indivisible unity of emptiness and cognizance. The meditation at the end of this chapter offers an opportunity to begin to explore this for yourself.

RESPONSIVENESS

Meditators often report that seeing the union of emptiness and awareness brings presence, interest, ease, and a relaxation that comes from not being fixated on any of the things that are being known. There may be pain in the back or a few wandering thoughts, but these are simply passing clouds in the vast space of knowing. There is no need to grasp them, first because the objects are so clearly fleeting, and second because no grasping would change the basic space of awareness we are attending to. The lack of motivation to grasp, or even to crave, brings a sense of lightness and relief to the heart, and a sense of freedom opens up.

When the heart is freed from its burden of self-concern, many wonderful qualities can come forth.

The avenue to these beautiful qualities is seeing the unity of emptiness and cognizance. The arising of these qualities isn't random or accidental. They arise to the degree we see this unity. This capacity for wholesome qualities is another basic aspect of the nature of the mind. There is emptiness, there is awareness, and there is this manifestation of beautiful states through what we can call the mind's *responsiveness*. Responsiveness is an intrinsic part of the mind, but it cannot function freely when dense reactive formations like greed, hatred, and ignorance are present. When emptiness is seen thoroughly in a moment, that moment is empty of self, which means it is empty of grasping. Thus, seeing the unity of emptiness and cognizance means that the moment is free from grasping or fixation. That is when the beautiful qualities of mind can come forth.

In a continuation of the passage quoted in the last chapter, Lama Shabkar states, "Mind's nature is vivid as a flawless piece of crystal: intrinsically empty, naturally radiant, ceaselessly responsive."[2] Radiance here is a synonym for cognizance.

In Tibetan, the term for this responsive nature can be translated literally as "unobstructed compassionate activity." Whether it is the wisdom that frees us or the love that lets us care for others, this responsive quality of mind leads to healing, connection, and liberation, all aspects of compassionate activity. Seeing emptiness and cognizance opens the door to this responsiveness.

Some Mahayana teachers understand the quality of responsiveness in a more limited way, referring only to the ability of cognizance to respond by illuminating appearances. We will meet this kind of understanding again in a passage from the Pali Discourses a little later.

WOMB OF THE TATHĀGATAS

Now we see all three aspects of mind together—emptiness, radiance, and responsiveness. All are united and form the nature of this mind, "that which knows," fundamental and intrinsic to all sentient life. Together they provide the capabilities for a sentient being to become enlightened, or even to become a fully self-awakened buddha, as Siddhattha Gotama did. Because of their intrinsic power to liberate, this union of emptiness, cognizance, and responsiveness is called in Sanskrit *tathāgata garbha*. *Tathāgata* is the term Gotama Buddha most often used when referring to himself. Some scholars say it means, literally, "one who has thus come," or "one who has thus gone." For our purposes, it can be said to be synonymous with the term *buddha*. The word *garbha* signifies womb or embryo. All buddhas, indeed all awakened beings, can be said to be born out of these three intrinsic facets of mind—emptiness, radiance, and responsiveness—that make up *tathāgata garbha*.

This beautiful phrase can be conveyed in English in a few ways. Literally we could call it "the womb of the tathāgatas" or "womb of the buddhas." When the term was first translated into English, early in the twentieth century, it was rendered as "buddha nature." It has also been described as the "nature of mind," the most basic qualities of sentience present in all beings. We might also call it our "threefold nature." I will use these terms synonymously.

These three aspects of the nature of mind are often explained in this way: The *essence* is emptiness, the *nature* is cognizance or radiance, and the *function* is responsiveness or compassionate activity.

Meditators are encouraged to *recognize* this empty, radiant, and responsive nature of mind in as many moments as possible. Recognition brings this fundamentally pure nature actively into the moment and over time establishes it as our normal way of being. As it becomes the norm, defilements and afflictive emotions are gradually weakened and eventually eliminated, leaving only the peace and wholesome qualities of our basic nature. This approach to practice does not involve wrestling with the defilements or countering them with antidotes so much as letting them evaporate in the radiance of emptiness, as clouds dissolve in the light of the sun. When one trusts that one's fundamental nature is pure, one inclines toward nondoing, allowing this basic nature to effect the purification.

Other paths not based on this threefold nature, such as insight meditation on objects, reach a similar point when the qualities of mindfulness, concentration, and wisdom are strongly developed. Then the meditator simply trusts these wholesome qualities to continue to grow, and these qualities do the work of purification and liberation. Hence, the same flavors of trust and nondoing are found through insight meditation as well.

GOTAMA BUDDHA AND THE WOMB
OF THE BUDDHAS

The concept of this threefold nature as the womb of the buddhas has had a powerful influence on practice and theory in many Buddhist schools for nearly two thousand years. The question naturally arises whether the Buddha himself taught this notion. A thorough review of the Pali Discourses shows that it seems not to have been explicitly taught by the Buddha. However, a careful and impartial reading reveals passages that point to this understanding. One famous passage discusses the radiance of the mind:

> Luminous is this mind, O monks, but it is obscured by visiting defilements. An uninstructed ordinary person does not understand this as it really is, so for them there is no development of mind.
> Luminous is this mind, O monks, and it is freed from visiting defilements. An instructed noble disciple understands this as it really is, so for them there is development of mind.[3]

The Pali term here for luminous is *pabhasarram*, which could also be translated as "radiant." The passage does not say that radiance is an *intrinsic* factor of mind, and some commentators explain it as a conditioned state of concentration resulting in bright light. In either case the passage points to a connection between the purity of mind and a quality of brightness. Thus it aligns well with the understanding of the threefold nature of mind. It even suggests a direction for a meditation practice based on seeing the nature of a mind free from defilements.

In another discourse, the Buddha uses the same term to point to a more obviously transcendent way of seeing. A questioner asks the Buddha about the physical elements of the world, considered to be earth, water, fire, and air: "Where do the four material elements cease without remainder?"—inquiring about a spiritual understanding that goes beyond this world and its suffering.

The Buddha replies that this is the wrong question and begins by stating what the correct question is: "Where do earth, water, fire, and air find no footing? Where are name-and-form completely destroyed?" The Buddha is not so interested in escaping from the world of form, as the original question suggests, but rather in finding a way to be free within it. It is our grasping that gives the elements their solidity or footing. How do we live within form so as not to grasp at it? We recall that name-and-form is a primary part of the psychological mechanism that leads to the sense of the duality of self and other. How can the sense of duality be overcome? The Buddha then replies to his own question:

> Where consciousness is signless, boundless, luminous all around,
> That is where earth, water, fire, and air find no footing,
> There name-and-form are wholly destroyed.
> With the cessation of consciousness, this is all destroyed.[4]

As an experiential pointer to the unconditioned, this is one of the deepest, most significant passages in all of the Pali Discourses. The term translated here as consciousness is *viññāṇa*, the term we've seen used for the six types of sense consciousness that know the six sense objects. When consciousness is described here as "signless, boundless, luminous," it is clear that *viññāṇa* is being used in a broader way. Now it refers to a kind of knowing that is not primarily concerned with knowing the sense objects. The material elements including the body are a key part of ordinary experience, but those elements find no footing in the consciousness described here. The whole apparatus of naming forms is undermined.

The emphasis in the Buddha's reply is on the qualities of consciousness itself, not the objects it reveals. Where consciousness is described as signless, it has no specific characteristics or marks. We cannot take a conceptual hold of something without a sign. This is a clear pointing to its emptiness, or lack of substance, the first aspect of the threefold nature of mind. The Buddha goes on to describe this consciousness as boundless, indicating that its nature is like space, without any form or edge. Both these descriptions align well with the way we have used awareness: the broad field of consciousness not limited to a single sense door. Finally, this consciousness is luminous all around, wherever we turn, illuminating all sense objects as they arise. There is not a single point in the whole space of awareness that isn't characterized by cognizance. So here in one brief line, the Buddha eloquently points to the same three aspects of the nature of mind that later schools elaborated: emptiness, cognizance, and responsiveness (in the more limited sense of illuminating what appears).

By describing consciousness in such experiential terms, the Buddha is essentially laying out a meditation practice and path. If we can realize, moment after moment, this signless, boundless, luminous consciousness, the elements will cease to find footing and duality will be seen through. The phrase in the final line, the "cessation of consciousness," is shorthand for nibbāna. The word *consciousness* here refers to the six types of sense consciousness, which temporarily cease at the moment of enlightenment. Possibly some awareness continues even when sense consciousness stops, but any continuing awareness is likely to be signless, boundless, and luminous. So perhaps there is a direct link between the consciousness described in this passage, nibbāna, and *tathāgata garbha*. This linkage will be the theme of the next chapter.

THE PITFALLS OF LANGUAGE

There is a potential misunderstanding when *tathāgata garbha* is translated as "buddha nature." The language suggests that everyone has a nature that is the same as the Buddha's enlightened nature—that since we all have buddha nature, we are all buddhas. This is misleading. "Having buddha nature" is not the same as being a buddha. While a great Zen master like Dōgen might say that we are already enlightened because he truly sees the nonseparation of samsara and nirvana, for most of us a statement like this is a simplistic misrepresentation that confuses conventional and ultimate understanding. On the ultimate level, perhaps there is no distinction between buddhas and ordinary beings. All of us are formed of the five aggregates, for example. But on the conventional level, there are many valid distinctions. All share the union of emptiness and cognizance, but for some there is still suffering and for others there is not.

It's sometimes said, "There is one nature but two paths." One path leads to nirvana, the other remains in samsara. The key is whether one activates the implicit liberating qualities through seeing the nature of mind to be empty, aware, and responsive. One who sees this is said to *recognize* buddha nature and therefore might be on a path to becoming awakened. When one does not recognize one's buddha nature and isn't developing a path, one is therefore perpetuating greed, aversion, and delusion and ensuring continuation in samsara. It is not correct to speak from an ultimate point of view when one's mind is not truly free of distinctions—and one does not need to have in mind the concept of buddha nature in order to activate the path to buddhahood. Followers of other schools who understand emptiness, cognizance, and responsiveness are also activating this path.

There is the risk in even speaking "about buddha nature" that it comes to be taken as a "thing" that exists in the same way that sense objects, for instance, exist. Partly this may be an outcome of the way we have learned to relate to nouns in Western languages. The reification of buddha nature arises from misunderstanding its complete emptiness. It may be more helpful to consider it as a capacity within us that has great potential. *Garbha* can also mean "embryo," so *tathāgata garbha* can point to the notion that the *potential* for awakening is in us without necessarily declaring that something exists like an intrinsic nature. Because the mind's tendency to reify is strongly conditioned, as revealed by our persistent perceptions of permanence and self, it is helpful to reflect often on the complete emptiness of *tathāgata garbha*—even as we continue to use the term.

Another misunderstanding that arises around the concept of buddha nature concerns the nature of compassion. Some claim that since compassion is an intrinsic part of responsiveness, compassion is permanent. Responsiveness, however, hinges on the recognition of empty knowing. Without the recognition of emptiness and awareness, the beautiful qualities, including compassion, do not manifest. In addition, responsiveness points to the potential for many wholesome qualities to arise, not just compassion. These include love, wisdom, joy, equanimity, and gratitude. A beautiful quality arises *in response* to current experience. Around someone who is suffering, compassion is the natural response. Around someone who is truly happy, appreciative joy is the natural response. There isn't one specific quality that is fixed in the heart.

MEDITATION

The Unity of Emptiness and Cognizance

- Sit quietly. Your eyes can be open or closed, as you like. Begin by paying attention to the space that surrounds you. If your eyes are open, let the visual field provide a sense of the broad space of awareness in all directions. If your eyes are closed, let the presence of sounds lead to that perception of space. If there are no sounds, notice the extent of the silence. Sit for a minute just noticing the sense of vast space that extends around you in all directions.

- Now ask, *Am I aware right now?* It should be easy to say yes. Sit and feel the awareness.

- Now ask, *Is awareness everywhere within this big space?* Don't think about an answer; just feel the extent of the awareness you are in touch with. Does awareness reveal appearances throughout the space wherever they arise? Even if nothing is appearing in some parts of the space, is awareness present to notice that? Is there any area in this space that is blocked off to awareness? Is there any point that awareness can't touch? Stay with this until you feel that awareness pervades the whole space.

- Now ask, *Can the space actually be separated from the awareness?* Or, *Can space and awareness be seen as a unity?* The space is empty. The awareness is knowing. Are they in any way separate? Can I see the two together? This is the unity of emptiness and cognizance. Stay with this sense.

- Now ask, *Can I see this union at one glance? Can I look for a moment and see emptiness and awareness together?* This is the purpose of this meditation. If you are not able to see the two joined with one glance, go back to the reflections above and rediscover this sense of unity. Then look again with a glance to see the union.

- Now notice how it feels to see in this way. There's emptiness and there's knowing, together. What is this experience like? If an emotion comes—whether frustration, confusion, or pride—just allow it to come without fixating on it or trying to change it. Then it will also go. Return to seeing the union of emptiness and awareness. Notice again how it feels. You can repeat this process for as long as you like.

19. SUNLIGHT IN EMPTY SPACE

The field of boundless emptiness is what exists from the very
beginning. The deep source, transparent down to the bottom,
can radiantly shine and can respond unencumbered to each speck
of dust without becoming its partner.
—Zen Master Hongzhi[1]

WHEN IT IS said that buddha nature is an intrinsic part of sentient beings,
the implication is that it is there from the beginning and present in every
moment. It is not subject to arising and passing and is not considered to be
an ordinary conditioned thing. It is taken to be fundamental in a way that
sense objects are not; they come and go and are known to this nature. They
may obscure it but they do not alter it. In this way, the nature of the mind is
something like the *ground* for a sentient being, in relation to which all other
things take their places. Circumstances come and go according to their own
conditioned nature; the ground endures. Turning our attention toward this
intrinsic nature can become the path.

This sounds very much like the way nibbāna is described in the Pali
Discourses—as "everlasting";[2] "no coming, no going, no staying, no ceas-
ing, no arising";[3] the "ground" of the eightfold path;[4] "unaging";[5] "deathless";[6] and "unconditioned."[7] At one point, Sāriputta urges Anuruddha in
meditation, "Turn your attention to the Deathless."[8]

In all the Pali Discourses, only nibbāna is described in these terms. Can we take buddha nature as a synonym for the deathless element, nibbāna? Is the union of emptiness and cognizance to be considered what is most fundamentally real?

Most Pali scholars wouldn't hesitate to consider emptiness a fundamental aspect of nibbāna. Ajahn Buddhadasa quotes a saying famous in Thailand, *Nibbānam paramam sunnam*, or "Nibbāna is the supreme emptiness."[9] A well-known Pali commentary states, "The attainment of fruition [nibbāna] is called emptiness. . . . Nibbāna is called emptiness because it is empty of lust, etc."[10]

There is, however, no such agreement on whether cognizance is an aspect of nibbāna. Orthodox Theravadins and strict followers of Nāgārjuna are adamant that it is not so. Their primary term for cognizance, *viññāṇa*, or consciousness, one of the five aggregates, is always considered to be conditioned and therefore impermanent. In fact, all Buddhist schools agree that the six classes of sense consciousness are impermanent and conditioned.

We have seen earlier that awareness, which we've defined simply as the broad expanse of consciousness, has basically the same nature as consciousness and must obey the same laws. Therefore awareness should also be considered as impermanent and conditioned.

CONSCIOUSNESS AND BUDDHA NATURE

But what about mind, "that which knows"? When described as buddha nature, mind is considered to be ongoing and not subject to impermanence. Are these two views—the impermanent nature of consciousness and the ongoing nature of mind—completely in conflict? Must one adhere to one school and reject the other? This has, for the most part, been the case for more than two millennia of Buddhist debates. The Madhyamaka school, founded by Nāgārjuna, has long been critical of the Yogācāra doctrine of buddha nature. Within the Theravadan tradition, orthodox followers of the Abhidhamma and *Visuddhimagga*, commonly found in Burma and Sri Lanka, regard the teaching on buddha nature to be heresy. On the other hand, many teachers in the Thai Forest tradition echo views similar to buddha nature, though they don't use that term.

This is a passage from a dharma talk by Ajahn Maha Boowa, a disciple of Ajahn Mun, who was the founder of the modern Thai Forest lineage:

Although all phenomena without exception fall under the laws of the three characteristics—impermanence, unsatisfactoriness, and not-self—the true nature of the mind doesn't fall under these laws. ... The natural power of the mind itself is that it *knows and does not die*. This deathlessness is something that lies beyond disintegration."[11]

In his book *One Dharma*, Joseph Goldstein tells of his own struggle to resolve the dilemma posed by these opposing views. He'd been a longtime practitioner of insight meditation as taught by the great Burmese master Mahasi Sayadaw. "From this Burmese perspective the practice of meditation leads to a freedom that transcends even awareness itself. Anything less than that is still to be caught on the wheel of life and death." But as he began to practice with Nyoshul Khen Rinpoche, a Dzogchen master, he was taught that "the union of awareness and emptiness is the very nature of the liberated mind." He found both teachings to be inspiring and compelling. Goldstein recounts that the question of which was right "plagued me mercilessly."[12]

He resolved the dilemma for himself by acknowledging that he simply didn't know, and that he could embrace the meditation tools from both traditions simply as skillful means. He found great strengths and powerful techniques in both schools, and he didn't have to have a view about the ultimate nature of things in order to meditate effectively. Once he accepted that he didn't actually know the answer, he could continue to investigate the question without being bound to either view. This attitude has been very helpful to me also in meditation practice and has brought a healthy dose of humility around my own views and opinions.

As I have continued to investigate this question, it has seemed to me that there may be a way to reconcile the two different views. Some years ago, I was teaching a class at Spirit Rock for experienced meditators. We were exploring the topic of consciousness and the nature of mind from the perspectives of different schools, but I couldn't quite find the words to express an intuitive understanding I was forming of their relationship. After the class, I went to bed and slept well. Just as I was waking the next morning, an image came to mind. I'd like to introduce it with a brief preamble.

A THOUGHT EXPERIMENT

Let us try a thought experiment around the topic of consciousness and the unconditioned.

Imagine you are on the edge of our solar system—somewhere around the orbit of Pluto, for instance. You're comfortable in a space suit that allows you to see out. Your back is to the sun, and suppose you are looking into a part of space where there are no stars. (This is not easy to find in actual space, but this is the beauty of a thought experiment.) What do you see?

There is only black, isn't there? The sun is behind you and no stars are in front of you. It's all black. Is it the kind of black that comes from something colored black by a crayon or a paint? Or is it the kind of black that comes from a complete absence of light? It's the latter, isn't it? No light is striking your eyes. But is there light in front of you? Yes! The whole expanse of space that you're looking into is filled with light from the sun, which is behind you. (We'll say that your shadow is negligibly small.) So the empty space before you is completely pervaded by the sunlight, although you can't see it.

Now imagine that a meteor zips by in front of you. It comes from below, from the direction of your feet, and quickly zooms past, in the direction of your head. Do you see it? You do, don't you? Why? Because the meteor catches the sunlight and reflects it back into your eyes. The impression doesn't last long because the meteor has flown by so quickly, but you do see it. In fact, it is a startling burst of light in an otherwise dark and empty space. Then it is gone, but the sunlight continues to pervade the empty space, ready for the next object to come and be illuminated.

This scene is an analogy for consciousness and the unconditioned. The sunlight pervading empty space stands for the union of emptiness and cognizance, or we could say radiance. The ever-present luminosity is like the unconditioned in its unchanging steadiness. The meteor that is briefly illuminated is an analogy for the consciousness of objects. The illumination takes place only when an object appears and is very fleeting. Flash! And then it's gone. Consciousness arises only momentarily, dependent on an object.

The sunlight in space is ongoing, while the illumination of the meteor is temporary. The cognizant nature of mind continues, while sense consciousness is a brief flashing. What is interesting, and what the analogy highlights, is that the two are made of the same stuff, light. One light is unreflected and invisible—this is the empty nature, unconditioned. The other light is reflected and visible—this is consciousness in its conditioned state. So consciousness, and by extension awareness, partake of the unchanging, unconditioned nature but are themselves conditioned arisings. This suggests that awareness is what we might call a bridge to the unconditioned, a bridge to nibbāna. This has a number of interesting implications for meditation practice that we will explore in the next chapter. For now, it's enough to say that becoming aware of awareness is a valid path to enlightenment.

OTHER IMAGES OF SUNLIGHT IN SPACE

In describing consciousness to some monks, the Buddha also used the image of sunlight. In his example, sunlight was entering a room and passing through without striking anything. Here is the teaching:

> "Suppose, bhikkhus, there was a house or a hall with a peaked roof with windows on the northern, southern, and eastern sides. When the sun rises and a beam of light enters through a window, where would it become established?"
> "On the western wall, venerable sir."
> "If there were no western wall, where would it become established?"
> "On the earth, venerable sir."
> "If there were no earth, where would it become established?"
> "On the water, venerable sir."
> "If there were no water, where would it become established?"
> "It would not become established anywhere, venerable sir."

The Buddha concludes by saying that this is an analogy for consciousness not being established anywhere, leading to the end of suffering.[13] Notice that in this analogy, for consciousness to be unestablished does not require that the sunlight cease from shining, only that it does not land anywhere. The sunlight then pervades the empty space.

We find a similar analogy involving sunlight in space from Saint John of the Cross around 1585 in his classic treatise *Dark Night of the Soul.*

[W]e shall here set down a similitude referring to common and natural light. We observe that a ray of sunlight which enters through the window is the less clearly visible according as it is the purer and freer from specks, and the more of such specks and motes there are in the air, the brighter is the light to the eye. The reason is that it is not the light itself that is seen; the light is but the means whereby the other things that it strikes are seen, and then it is also seen itself, through its reflection in them; were it not for this, neither it nor they would have been seen. Thus if the ray of sunlight entered through the window of one room and passed out through another on the other side, traversing the room, and if it met nothing on the way, or if there were no specks in the air for it to strike, the room would have no more light than before, neither would the ray of light be visible. . . .

Now this is precisely what this Divine ray of contemplation does in the soul. . . . [B]y thus leaving it empty and in darkness, it purges and illumines it with Divine spiritual light, although the soul thinks not that it has this light, but believes itself to be in darkness, even as we have said of the ray of light, which although it be in the midst of the room, yet, if it be pure and meet nothing on its path, is not visible.[14]

What Saint John calls the soul, we could hear as *citta. Citta* is generally unaware of the Divine spiritual light (we could hear as "buddha nature"), but for one who attends to it, that light pervades the person's being, carrying out the work of purification (we might say through nondoing).

Two other terms are used for nibbāna in the Pali Discourses—"the unborn"[15] and "the unmanifest."[16] The three sunlight analogies convey well this aspect of the radiant nature: before an object appears, the light is invisible, unborn, and unmanifest. Once an object appears, the light is born and manifest. The object is then "born" in consciousness.

THE SACRED IN EVERYDAY LIFE

The image of sunlight also gives us a way to connect what is transcendent to what appears here and now through the senses. In the orthodox Theravadan view, there is the conditioned world of the six senses, on the one hand, and the unconditioned element of nibbāna, on the other. In the most traditional view, there is a stark divide between the two realms. A practitioner must completely leave behind the former in order to realize the latter. In such a view, ultimate reality can never come into the realm of the ordinary.

When we understand the mind as inherently pure in its union of emptiness and cognizance, then all that appears within the mind is held in, or touched by, this purity. The mundane is only revealed through the functioning of the transcendent and cannot be separate from it. The temporary light of consciousness is identical in nature to the stable radiance of buddha nature. The transcendent is never apart from the world. This way of seeing represents a philosophical shift in Buddhism that began with the dawning of the Mahayana. It provides a clear avenue to bring the sacred into everyday life.

Understanding the unconditioned as the ground for the sense world gives us a new way to think about nibbāna. Originally we might have conceived of nibbāna as the supreme peace characterized by the absence of any appearance, since appearances might disturb the peace. Now we can understand it as the *context* for *all* appearances. In this way it is like silence. We could take silence to be the absence of all sounds, in which case it might rarely be perceived since the world is usually a little noisy. Or silence could be understood as the vast context in which all sounds appear and disappear, in which case it can be perceived in any moment when we turn our attention to it. Space can similarly be seen as the absence of any physical object, or as the context in which all physical objects come and go. The latter understanding allows us to experience a great deal of space even in a crowded situation.

In a dialogue with a Brahmin, the Buddha pointed to this latter sense of nibbāna as the ultimate context for things. The Brahmin commented on the five physical senses (eye, ear, nose, tongue, body), noting that they all have different domains and so do not overlap. He then asked, "What is their resort?" That is, if they do not touch, where do the five sense faculties come together? What is their context?

> Buddha: "Mind (*mano*) is their resort."
> Brahmin: "But, good Gotama, what is mind's resort?"
> Buddha: "Mind's resort is mindfulness."
> Brahmin: "What is the resort of mindfulness?"
> Buddha: "The resort of mindfulness is liberation."
> Brahmin: "What is the resort of liberation?"
> Buddha: "The resort of liberation is nibbāna."
> Brahmin: "What is the resort of nibbāna?"
> Buddha: "This question goes too far, Brahmin. No answer can encompass it."[17]

So the Buddha described the context of the successive stages as the five senses, mind, mindfulness (which, in this usage, might be translated as awareness), liberation, and nibbāna. No resort or context can be given for nibbāna.

This idea of nibbāna as context appears again in another discourse:

> Arising from contact are all things; . . .
> Yielding deliverance as their essence are all things;
> Merging in the Deathless are all things;
> Terminating in Nibbāna are all things.[18]

Once we have discovered nibbāna as the context of all sense appearances, it is never far away. This will be helpful in the meditations we'll explore in the next chapter.

20. AWARE OF AWARENESS

Great Perfection is the inherent nature of reality.
—Dudjom Lingpa[1]

IN SOME WAYS, the meditation on awareness is the simplest of all meditations. Just notice awareness. This instruction is direct, immediate, and accessible. You can do it at any time, in any posture. It doesn't require quiet surroundings or a meditation cushion. You could do it all day long if you like. Some instructions for this kind of meditation are at the end of this chapter.

The instructions at the end of the chapter are simple—but despite their simplicity, they are not easy practices to maintain. Awareness is a subtle phenomenon and does not always hold the attention easily. A friend who was practicing in Burma was assigned the blue *kasina* as an object for developing strong concentration. With kasinas, you visualize a colored disk, or just a color, as the sole focus of your meditation. My friend was instructed to visualize the color blue. All day long as he meditated, he tried to see just the color blue, again and again and again. It's hard to sustain, because blue is a subtle focus—and awareness itself can be even more subtle.

And yet, in a sense, meditation on awareness is a very natural practice. What could be closer to us than awareness? What could be more ever-present? What could be more obvious? It is like what Suzuki Roshi said about Zen meditation: "This practice started from beginningless time, and it will continue into an endless future. Strictly speaking, for a human being there is no other practice than this practice."[2] This is not to say that other meditation techniques are less important or helpful, only that awareness is at the very center of sentient life. Whether our attention is directed to awareness itself or we use awareness to know objects, the essence of meditation is the same: awareness.

THE PURE SPACE OF KNOWING

Ajahn Jumnien explains the meditation on awareness like this:

> The best way to develop a great awareness (*mahāsati*) is to rest your attention within that knowing space of consciousness, in the pure space of knowing. If you understand and can rest in this pure knowing, that is the place of the deathless. From this pure consciousness that's unmoved by what arises, then you see the phenomena of the world which all have the nature to arise and pass away. Phenomena show their dharmas of impermanence, and this other is the dharma of the deathless.[3]

Ajahn Jumnien's instruction brings together a few elements of the meditation on awareness. The first is that this meditation is a style of mindfulness; in fact it is a "great mindfulness" (*mahāsati*). We have been using awareness as a near-synonym for consciousness (*viññāṇa*), but in English the word *awareness* also has connotations of intelligence that are more associated with mindfulness (*sati*) than with consciousness. The term *awareness* may slide between these two meanings of consciousness and mindfulness, and that ambiguity can be evocative in a helpful way for the meditator. As we practice being aware of awareness, perhaps what we are doing should be called "mindfulness of consciousness." This phrasing might best align with the Pali Discourses, since consciousness, as one of the five aggregates, is a proper subject for mindfulness, as described in the fourth foundation in the *Satipatthāna Sutta*. We are now trying to notice in an intelligent way the field of sense consciousness. As there is no Pali term that is generally translated as awareness, we can use the ambiguity in the English word and speak of being "aware of awareness."

The second key element in Ajahn Jumnien's instruction is to *rest* our attention. We are not trying to send the attention out toward changing objects, though they will of course continue to be known. Instead, the attention becomes rather still. This stillness is a sign of concentration (*samādhi*) and an aspect of the perception of emptiness. There is no chasing after or taking hold of sense objects.

Where does the attention rest? It is not on the breath or body or any other sense object. The attention rests "in the pure space of knowing." *Knowing* is another English word that has multiple meanings in Buddhism. Here it refers to the simplest kind of knowing, that is, the knowing of objects, or sense consciousness. It is striking that Ajahn Jumnien calls this a "pure space." We saw in the last chapter that consciousness, like awareness, provides a bridge to the unconditioned. This bridge is clearly indicated by the cognizant aspect of buddha nature. When we attend to knowing, we are at the borderline of buddha nature.

Consciousness is pure because the simple, mirrorlike illumination of what arises is free from the stains of greed, hatred, and delusion. Those afflictive reactions are born *in response to* the conscious experience of objects, but the knowing itself is prior to and free from those influences. What makes awareness of awareness such a powerful meditation is that it reveals a dimension within us that is already free. If we place our attention on awareness, we are connecting with that purity and are less likely to be drawn into entangling relationships with passing appearances.

Another way to describe the purity of awareness is to say that it is not stained by wanting. Consciousness has no motivation, stated or ulterior. It is not aiming to achieve anything. It simply functions to reveal things in a completely impartial way. This lack of motive is like nibbāna, which is desireless and aimless. Nibbāna is not trying to get anywhere. As we tune in to the dimension of awareness, we suffuse our being with the purity of desirelessness.

The third key part of the instruction is Ajahn Jumnien's statement that the pure knowing is "the place of the deathless." This aligns well with our understanding that cognizance is an ongoing part of buddha nature, not subject to arising and passing. Many Pali Discourses tell us that mindfulness inclines the mind to nibbāna. But by placing our attention on knowing, we are not simply inclining toward the unconditioned. We are leaning on the door.

REFUGE IN REALITY

As we attend again and again to this pure space of knowing, our being starts to take root in the deathless. The purity of buddha nature, free from afflictive formations, starts to become the baseline of our experience. We don't have to do anything to cause it to be that way. It is the very nature of our mind. As we recognize cognizance, we must also continue to see emptiness, the essence of buddha nature. Then we start to intuit what Ajahn Buddhadasa was pointing to:

> This emptiness is self-existent; nothing can touch it, concoct it, or improve it. [This] is the eternal state, for it knows neither birth nor death.[4]

Self-existent here means only that it was not produced by prior causes; of course there is no enduring *thing* within the emptiness. As we rest in the empty knowing, we see all the changing phenomena come and go. We do not need to follow them, because we are anchoring beyond change. This resting feels like a big relief and is deeply satisfying in a way that pleasurable sense experiences are not. Its peace leads to a great unburdening of the heart. We have found a reliable refuge—the most reliable refuge. And what are we taking refuge in? In things just the way they are: the empty cognizance illuminating appearances. We are "taking the fundamental nature of reality as the unsurpassable, ultimate refuge."[5]

We don't seek to make appearances go away, nor do we imagine that we will discover awareness as a destination apart from appearances. In ordinary states of mind, appearances are inseparable from awareness; the only exception being those moments of enlightenment that are characterized by the cessation of sense consciousness. Otherwise, phenomena are always being revealed by awareness. The more deeply we understand the emptiness of phenomena—their fleeting, insubstantial nature—the less we are bothered by them. In Ajahn Jumnien's phrasing, we remain "unmoved by what arises." Tulku Urgyen Rinpoche, a great Dzogchen master of the past century, put it like this:

> Because all the appearances are ultimately empty and will vanish completely, we really don't have to worry about them or analyze them too much. They're really just a magical display, just like when demons conjure up some magic to fool you.[6]

When we take refuge in the deathless, the passing show loses its power to disturb us. This is the growth in equanimity that is the hallmark of spiritual development.

Sayadaw U Pandita, one of the foremost recent masters of vipassana meditation, was a Burmese master skilled in the "noting practice" of Mahasi Sayadaw. The practitioner focuses attention on psychophysical phenomena by observing them and noting "seeing, seeing," "hearing, hearing," and so forth. During a silent retreat, U Pandita was meeting with a student who was complaining, in a mild way, of some of the mental and physical hardships she was experiencing. The Sayadaw responded, "What do you want, different objects to note?" The Sayadaw wanted the student to understand that mindfulness, like buddha nature, does not care what objects the sense consciousness reveals. What is important is the awareness or mindfulness itself.

How complete this equanimity can become is revealed in a short account of the Sixteenth Karmapa, head of the Kagyu school of Tibetan Buddhism, when he was dying in a hospital in Chicago. His students and supporters were saddened by his declining health, but each time they visited, to his doctors' astonishment, the Karmapa mustered his waning energy to sit up and smile, so his students wouldn't worry. He reassured one visitor, who seemed especially concerned about his death, "Don't worry—nothing happens." After years—or lifetimes—of meditation on the nature of mind, his being was completely integrated with the deathless.

HOW TO PRACTICE BEING AWARE OF AWARENESS

As I've said, meditation on awareness is (on the one hand) a simple practice: Look toward awareness, see with a glance the union of emptiness and awareness, then rest there—and repeat as necessary. Let's examine each of the steps in this instruction in a little more detail.

LOOK TOWARD AWARENESS

The first step in this meditation is to look toward awareness. The more you experiment with this instruction, the more puzzling you might find it. How am I supposed to look toward awareness? Awareness is everywhere and is not specifically located anywhere. Yet any time we are asked, we know with certainty that we are aware, that awareness is present. Here are a few skillful means that might be helpful in practicing the perception of awareness.

The first is the meditation introduced in chapter 17 on Big Sky Mind. If you practice this consistently for a period of time, you will gain a good facility in directing your attention toward awareness. One of the lines of the meditation suggests this in a powerful way: "Awareness is like the sky. It's wide and empty. To see if it's like that, look directly at the nature of your own awareness."

The second approach comes out of the writings of Douglas Harding, a British philosopher who explored the mystery of consciousness and selflessness. In his book *On Having No Head*, he describes an insight that came to him as he was exploring the question "What am I?" In one moment his thinking stopped, and past and future fell away. There was no longer any sense of self. As he explored what *was* present, he found "khaki trouserlegs terminating downwards in a pair of brown shoes, khaki sleeves terminating sideways in a pair of pink hands, and a khaki shirtfront terminating upwards in—absolutely nothing whatever! Certainly not in a head."[7] The space where a head should have been was instead a vast emptiness that held the world.

We can use Harding's description as a way to look toward awareness. Start by directing your attention outward toward physical objects, then turn it instead to look directly into your head. What do you find? Can you get a sense of the empty knowing that Harding discovered?

A variant of Harding's question begins with open eyes and noticing the visual field. Then ask the question, "Who is looking?" The question inclines one's look backward—not toward the outer objects that are being looked at but to the inner subject doing the looking. As we know from the teaching on not-self, there is no one who is doing the looking, only eye consciousness. So the question can often open up an empty space in which things are seen without a seer, emptiness and awareness joined.

Harding's question could also be phrased as "Who am I?" This was a favorite approach of Ramana Maharshi, the Indian Vedanta master who lived from 1879 until the mid-twentieth century. The question is asked not to provoke thought or find a conceptual answer, but to still the mind through sincere inquiry into the nature of the self. Many people who ask themselves this question repeatedly and wholeheartedly in a meditative environment find that it suspends the assumptions of selfhood and drops them directly into a clear perception of the empty nature of awareness.

SEE THE UNITY OF EMPTINESS AND AWARENESS

After turning toward awareness, the second step is to see the unity of emptiness and awareness in a single glance. This perception might not come easily when you begin this meditation, but it becomes much easier with practice. When I first began this practice, it was easy to see awareness, but I had to reflect to be sure I was also seeing emptiness. I used a few different questions and responses to become confident about the perception of emptiness: "Is there a self who is being aware? No, so the awareness is empty of someone who is looking. Is there a sense of space in the awareness? Yes, so that awareness is empty in the same way that space is empty. Am I seeing impermanence? Yes, so I am in touch with one of the characteristics of emptiness. Are the objects of awareness solid? No, they are just fleeting appearances, so there is emptiness in what is seen."

After reflecting along these lines many times, I became convinced that awareness was always joined with a thoroughgoing emptiness that embraced both the inner subject and the outer objects. It was not enough to answer the questions theoretically, and it was not helpful to think about them. I had to feel the truth of the emptiness directly, over and over, until eventually it became easy to perceive the union of emptiness and awareness. Those were my questions—you may wish to find your own questions to support seeing this unity.

These kinds of reflections and questions are preliminary tools to facilitate the perception of the unity at a single glance. The meditation on awareness doesn't really begin until you can see this with one look, because the meditation needs to be nonconceptual. To root our being in awareness, we have to let go of our attachment to the thinking mind. This doesn't mean thoughts will never arise, but we have to renounce hopping happily aboard the thought train as our refuge or our path.

STAY THERE

The third step in this meditation, after perceiving the unity of emptiness and awareness, is to rest there, "in the pure space of knowing," as Ajahn Jumnien describes it. To stay or to rest means we give up any kind of purposeful effort. We don't try to see awareness or emptiness or the unity. We don't try to direct our attention or control the experience or suppress thinking. We just let things be the way they are. In other words, we simply abide in emptiness as we learned to do in chapter 12.

In the beginning, this time of resting might not last long. Thoughts, memories, sensations, or sounds come along, capture our attention, and can lead to lengthy periods of distraction. Don't be discouraged—this is to be expected. When you took the breath as the focus of our first meditation, you probably were able to notice only two or three breaths before getting lost in thinking. So, too, when awareness becomes your focus, resting in the empty space of knowing may be just a brief experience at first before you become distracted. At this stage of meditation, let go of purposeful effort and don't even try to prolong the duration of this nondistracted awareness. Tulku Urgyen Rinpoche recommends that we simply aim for "short moments, many times." However brief a time you are able to rest in the empty space of knowing, remember that for those brief moments you are close to buddha nature, close to the unconditioned, close to nibbāna. With practice, the duration will lengthen by itself. But that is not under our control, so there's no need to be concerned about it.

When you notice that your attention has wandered away from the immediate experience and become captivated by thoughts or reactive emotions, simply begin the three-step meditation again. Turn your attention to awareness, notice the unity of awareness and emptiness, and rest there. As your skill in this meditation develops, you'll find that when thoughts and emotions arise in this empty space of knowing, you won't be carried away by them. They arise, are experienced, and pass away on their own. We don't need to make them go away, because that would be acting from aversion. As awareness grows stronger, we find that awareness has the power to know even potentially "sticky" phenomena, like moments of aversion, without being moved. Then the duration of the nondistracted knowing will naturally extend itself, without any effort on our part.

BENEFITS OF THIS PRACTICE

Being aware of awareness and its empty nature is a powerful practice. It can become one's primary meditation, because there are so many aspects of wisdom and skillful means embedded in it. Here is a list of ten benefits I've received from this practice.

1. Practicing with awareness, we take the *nature of reality* as our ultimate refuge. We understand that our basic nature of empty awareness is pure and ever-present. We can touch it and feel our freedom immediately. The activity of awareness ceaselessly reveals each appearance. The unity of awareness and appearances is fundamentally how things are. We trust in that, and it becomes a source of great faith. From Patrul Rinpoche, a great Tibetan sage of the nineteenth century:

   Don't prolong the past,
   Don't invite the future,
   Don't alter your innate wakefulness,
   Don't fear appearances.
   Apart from that, there's not a damned thing![8]

2. Coming back again and again to the empty nature of knowing highlights what is at the very heart of Dharma practice. After practicing this way for some time, I realized that I was tuning in to one basic choice-point

in each moment: *Is there freedom or is there grasping?* When there is freedom, there is no grasping. This is the meaning of the Buddha's third noble truth: the end of suffering is in the end of craving. When there is grasping, there is no freedom. Grasping creates the sense of a self, so in that moment one is not seeing the emptiness of self. The Buddha summarized his teaching: "Nothing whatsoever is to be clung to. One who has heard this has heard all the teachings. One who has practiced this has practiced all the teachings."[9] To see empty knowing over and over requires that we let go of grasping and selfing. This is the result of being aware of awareness. This is abiding in the unentangled knowing that Upasika Kee pointed to.

3. This practice gives us another way to view the path to awakening. The Buddhist path can be seen as a gradual accumulation of many wholesome moments of effort, as pointed to in the Buddha's advice: "Don't disregard what is good, thinking, 'It won't come to anything.' By the gradual falling of rain drops, a water jar is filled."[10] But the path can also be seen as *moments of the unconditioned nature peeking through the layers of obscuration* until the obscurations are worn down and that nature is uncovered in its fullness. Here we do not so much focus on generating wholesome states; rather we trust that they will shine through when we recognize the capacity of our inherent nature.

4. When the mind is very calm, awareness offers a skillful and reliable focus. When the environment is quiet and mind and body are both calm, objects can be hard to find. If we are relying on objects for deepening our meditation, we may feel adrift at such times. But awareness is always present as a reliable focus in times of calm or agitation. A student once asked Kalu Rinpoche why he should focus on awareness rather than the breath in meditation. Rinpoche replied, "Because there is no breath in the bardo." When phenomena are faint or absent, awareness is still a refuge.

5. Being aware of awareness is an excellent practice to strengthen the quality of nondoing. This practice highlights both the role of effort—returning

to awareness after being distracted—and noneffort—resting after recognizing the union of emptiness and awareness. It shows the need for both effort and letting go of effort, and it gives clear instructions when to apply each. When you're distracted, make an effort. When you're not distracted, don't make an effort.

6. We cannot recognize the empty nature when we are straining. When we don't strain, it can appear more easily. This is the way it was put by Angelus Silesius, a seventeenth-century Christian mystic and poet:

> God is a pure no-thing,
> concealed in now and here:
> the less you reach for him,
> the more he will appear.[11]

7. It provides an avenue for devotion, a quality that is recognized as central in many spiritual traditions. Devotion is a great support for humility and for opening the heart to what is noble and transcendent. The Buddha knew how important it is to have veneration and respect in our life and practice. Just after his enlightenment, he reflected on this:

> It is painful to dwell without reverence and deference. . . . However, in this world . . . I do not see another ascetic or brahmin more accomplished in virtue, concentration, wisdom, or liberation than myself whom I could honor, respect, and dwell in dependence on. Let me then honor, respect, and dwell in dependence only on this Dhamma to which I have become fully enlightened.[12]

We are fortunate that many beings are alive today who are well developed in virtue, concentration, wisdom, and liberation. We can develop respect and devotion for people with these qualities. The historical examples of the Buddha and many great sages can also inspire us. And like the Buddha, we can revere the Dhamma that leads to liberation. As a single image of that Dhamma, empty awareness itself can have a strong devotional appeal.

8. Through this practice, we get a clear direction of where nibbāna may be found. As we tune in to empty awareness, we are linking to buddha nature, which is of the same unconditioned nature as nibbāna.

9. This meditation reveals the primacy of awareness throughout the meditative path. Mindfulness can take many different objects, but it is the *mindfulness (or awareness) itself* and not the object that is most important.

10. The most liberating view is not conceptual. Abiding in empty knowing is key, and it requires neither thoughts nor concepts nor philosophical views. As the Buddha said, "Seeing all views and not grasping them, I found inner peace."[13] Understanding the truth of things is the most beneficial view, and that ultimately relies on experience, not concepts. The same can be said of the four noble truths, which are equated with right view.

Being aware of awareness is a powerful approach, but it should not be considered as the only or the best meditation technique. There are times when it is extremely helpful and times when it is less so. In my experience, it's most efficacious when concentration (*samādhi*) and attention are stable. Then, when we turn toward awareness, our vision can see its union with emptiness, and our attention is steady enough to rest there for a while. When concentration is weak and one is easily distracted, it can be more helpful to focus on a simple object like breath or body to collect the attention. No one technique is always the best practice. What is best is what's suited to your body and mind in a given moment. As a general rule, when distracted, focus on a simple object to collect the attention. When the attention is collected, move to a more open approach like choiceless attention or being aware of awareness.

MEDITATION

Four Meditations on Awareness

You might like first to review the meditation at the end of chapter 18 on the unity of emptiness and cognizance. Here are four variations on this theme arranged in order of subtlety and completeness.

1. Notice awareness. Stay with that until distracted. Repeat.
2. As you notice awareness, also see its union with emptiness. Stay until distracted. Repeat.
3. Continue the second meditation until you can see awareness and emptiness with one glance. Stay until distracted. Repeat.
4. Make the third meditation your primary meditation practice. That is, do this and only this again and again for an entire meditation period.

PART IV:

COMPASSION

21. COMPASSION COMES FROM EMPTINESS

Just as a bird needs two wings to fly,
so a practitioner needs the two wings of wisdom and compassion.

—Tibetan saying

TULKU URGYEN RINPOCHE said that, because our experiences are empty and will vanish, we don't have to worry about them. The heart is freed from fixating on experience. This freedom of heart opens the doors for all the beautiful qualities of the mind to come forth. This is the basis for the carefree, joyful attitude that we find in great spiritual teachers.

This inner freedom born from emptiness unlocks compassion, the care for the suffering of all beings. When the mind is not preoccupied with self-concern, the heart is moved by the suffering we see in the lives of others. As the Buddha put it, "We shall abide with compassion for their welfare, with a mind imbued with loving-kindness."[1]

From comments like Tulku Urgyen's, it might seem as though one's insights into emptiness and the experience of freedom would lead one to nihilistically declare that "Everything is empty, so nothing matters." This, however, is a gross distortion of awakened understanding and of the Buddhist view. The awakened understanding reveals that when one knows that everything is empty, nothing can block one's sense of freedom. The arahant Adhimutta did not object when bandits planned to kill him. Sāriputta asserted that no change in the world could bring him sorrow.[2] Equanimity strengthens when we understand the implications of inner and outer emptiness. Events may no longer disturb a fully enlightened being, but it would not be correct to say that the experiences of unenlightened beings "don't matter." That would be the creed of nihilism.

Unenlightened beings are empty in the sense that there is no central self within our mind-body process. Our sense experiences are empty in that they are all fleeting and disintegrating. But because we don't yet fully understand emptiness in both these senses, we continue to grasp and therefore we continue to suffer. From beginningless time, the Buddha said, we have roamed and wandered, hindered by ignorance and fettered by craving, suffering and swelling the cemeteries.[3]

All across the planet today we see the outcome of human greed, hatred, and ignorance in the enormous suffering of the victims of war, genocide, murder, rape, poverty, racism, religious persecution, and sexual abuse. We see the unbearable suffering of animals from hunting, fishing, cruel exploitation, inhumane farming methods, and human-made climate change. As the heart awakens to the freedom from our own self-inflicted oppression, we also awaken to loving-kindness for all beings in existence. We cannot help but be moved by the incredible burden of suffering carried by so many. As I write these words, tears are coming to my eyes.

This is compassion, the trembling of the heart's natural tenderness in response to suffering. This quivering is felt keenly by an awakened being. An awakened person has surrendered the defenses that place the suffering "out there" or "somewhere else." We know there is no inside and no outside to awareness. Everything and everyone are alive within us. Having seen the emptiness of self, we know our commonality with all living beings. We all are conscious; we all feel pleasure and pain; we all are vulnerable.

If the Buddha had felt that others' experiences did not matter, he would never have devoted himself to teaching for forty-five years. His life as a teacher was not easy. His own monks disobeyed him, people argued with him heatedly, and more than one person tried to kill him. All the while, he continued to live simply as an ascetic monk. A visitor once asked the Buddha why he chose to live in the forest. By that time he was well-known and supported by kings. He could have had a pleasant life in a palace near a city with servants and fine meals. He replied that he lived in the forest because "I see a pleasant abiding for myself here and now, and I have compassion for future generations."[4] That is, by setting the example of living simply as a renunciate in the forest, he could inspire many others to live that way in the future and thus have the best conditions for awakening.

Motivated by compassion, the Buddha sacrificed his own comfort for the welfare of others. Such selfless activity has been the model in the Buddhist tradition for thousands of years now. When one sees through the false and limiting view of selfhood, the work of the path extends beyond our individual development to take in all beings everywhere who are still prone to suffering. We wish for all beings to be happy—this is the quality of friendliness and goodwill that is loving-kindness (*mettā*). We wish for all beings to be freed from their suffering—this is the quality of caring known as compassion (*karuṇā*). As we develop in insight, we need also to develop in the growth of loving-kindness and compassion, not only for ourselves and our loved ones, but for all beings. If these generous, heartfelt emotions do not grow in a practitioner, then even a "valid" insight into emptiness can lead to a disconnected kind of nihilism.

THE WISH TO BENEFIT OTHERS

When *mettā* and *karuṇā* grow alongside insight, then the understanding of emptiness leads to even greater love and compassion. Why? Because when we let go of the burdens of self and clinging, the heart relaxes deeply and our view expands. Then, when we incline the mind toward love and compassion for others, these wholesome emotions respond strongly and easily. We discover that we really do want others to experience the same freedom and happiness that we've found. This deep wish for the welfare of others can become a new motivation in our practice, even before we have fully awakened.

Suppose we develop loving-kindness and sincerely wish for all beings to be happy. And suppose we develop compassion and sincerely wish for all beings not to suffer. These are easy phrases to say but more difficult to feel! It takes practice to be able to consistently and sincerely feel these wishes for others. Now let's suppose we feel these wishes in a genuine way. We have arrived, however briefly, at the experience of boundless loving-kindness and boundless compassion. We call them "boundless" because they extend to all beings without reservation.

You might ask, "What can I do to make these wishes come true? How can I, as a practitioner of the Buddha's Dharma, best help other beings relieve their suffering and find happiness? Wouldn't the best response be to bring those beings completely out of suffering and into the most reliable kind of happiness? And if so, doesn't that imply bringing them to full awakening? How would that be possible? Won't I need to awaken in order to truly help others awaken?"

The answer suggested in some Buddhist schools to all these questions is to cultivate *bodhicitta*, "the awakening heart." *Bodhi* means awakening, or enlightenment, and *citta* means heart, or mind. *Bodhicitta* is the wish to become enlightened in order to help lead other beings out of suffering and into the greatest possible happiness, which is liberation. The awakening heart grows out of loving-kindness and compassion for all beings and carries with it the will to act for their benefit. This quality can be fostered by reflecting upon it frequently, as we do in the practices of love and compassion. Reflecting upon *bodhicitta* frequently generates the aspiration and encourages us to practice diligently in order to realize the aim of awakening. It can be helpful to recall the aspiration to awaken *bodhicitta* at the beginning of any period of practice by repeating a phrase like this:

> By the merit of my generosity and other virtuous acts,
> May I attain awakening for the benefit of all sentient beings.

The first line refers to the perfections (Pali: *pāramī*), the qualities that lead to awakening, and expresses our commitment to realize the goal ourselves. The second line expresses this aspiration as a way to benefit all beings. When *bodhicitta* grows alongside insight, it keeps us connected to others in an altruistic way and prevents the rise of nihilism or pessimism.

This altruistic motive is expressed well in a passage from Shantideva, an eighth-century Indian teacher. This verse is a personal favorite of His Holiness the Dalai Lama.

> For as long as space endures
> And for as long as living beings remain,

Until then may I too abide
To dispel the misery of this world.[5]

The Dalai Lama himself is a beautiful personification of the spirit of *bodhicitta* in his deep commitment to continue his own practice while helping relieve the suffering of others. In commenting on his own work, he said:

> Regarding service to Tibet, service to Buddhism, service to humanity . . . I have done as much as I can. Regarding my own spiritual practice, when I share my experiences with more advanced meditators— even those who have spent years in the mountains, practicing single-pointedness of mind—I don't lag too far behind.[6]

The Buddha strongly advised that we keep this dual motivation at the heart of our efforts:

> In this way, bhikkhus, you must train yourselves. Perceiving one's own benefit, one should practice tirelessly. Perceiving the benefit to others, one should practice tirelessly. Perceiving the benefit to both, one should practice tirelessly.[7]

WISDOM AND COMPASSION TOGETHER

This is the balance of compassion (or loving-kindness) and wisdom that marks a maturity of spiritual development. If there is only dry wisdom, one's own suffering may be eased but one neglects the sense of care and connection to others. It is not that one should feel guilt or shame if such neglect is taking place. There is no moral absolutism in Buddhism that says to anyone, "You must care for others or you are a bad person!" Rather, every practitioner needs to take each step on the Buddhist path freely out of their own understanding. If there is an absence of care for others, this simply points to a way in which that person has not yet fully developed. It is natural in the early stages of this path that one's attention is primarily—or even completely—on one's own suffering. But as the path develops, the practitioner's heart becomes less burdened and their outlook naturally starts to widen, taking in the suffering of others, humans and animals. If this connection is not strengthened, the practitioner will be neglecting an important part of their own being. It is for our own welfare that we develop love and compassion, and it is also for the welfare of others.

If love and compassion are strongly developed but the insight into emptiness is not, we have no foundation for equanimity. Every pain in the world lands on our heart with no way to understand it and no capacity to hold it. Our heart can feel broken every day with no hope of mending. With wisdom, we know that suffering is empty too. The insight into emptiness reveals that there is no actual being at the center of suffering. Suffering is only the friction between what is and what is wanted. As one meditator put it, "Suffering is rope burn," from holding on tightly to what must eventually be pulled from our fingers. We have seen our own suffering in this way, and so we know it is also true for others, even if they don't yet understand it. It says in the *Visuddhimagga*, "There is suffering but no one who suffers. Empty phenomena roll on."[8] If we don't understand that "no one suffers," we will be overwhelmed by each instance of suffering and will see the world as unredeemable. This excess of grief can lead to paralysis and inactivity, which benefit neither ourselves nor others. Understanding emptiness, our minds remain balanced even while we feel the suffering in the world.

Emptiness needs compassion, and compassion needs emptiness. As we saw in chapter 13, this balance is also expressed in the teachings on the divine abidings (*brahma vihāra*). There, the quality of equanimity is a necessary support for the factors of loving-kindness and compassion so that the mind doesn't tip into their near enemies, namely, attached affection or overwhelming grief.

THERE IS NO "BEING"

Awakened seeing recognizes that there is no actual "being" present anywhere, either in life or in death. Only the aggregates are born, and only the aggregates die. This kind of insight is shown clearly in a pair of dialogues with nuns at the time of the Buddha. In the first dialogue, Māra, the powerful spirit who is the embodiment of temptation and distraction, approaches the nun Vajirā in order to frighten her and make her abandon her meditation:

By whom has this being been created?
Who is the maker of this being?

Vajirā immediately understands that the question is posed by the tempter and answers:

Why now do you assume "a being"?
Māra, is that your speculative view?
This is a heap of sheer formations:
Here no being is found.
Just as, with an assemblage of parts,
The word "chariot" is used,
So, when the aggregates exist,
There is the convention, "a being."[9]

Vajirā points out that "a being" is only a conventional designation for a collection of parts. The five aggregates are what actually exist, insofar as anything can be said to exist. It is they that arise and they that cease. To think that "a being" truly exists is to confuse the conventional truth with the deeper or ultimate truth. It is this confusion that makes one prey to the conventional understanding, which is limited and leads to grief and suffering. Yet this is how most of the world lives, not understanding that there is no self at the center of the aggregates, no one who owns these assemblages, and so no "being" who is born or dies.

In the second dialogue, Māra attacks the nun Selā. The image of a puppet is sometimes used to evoke the view of a body that is pushed and pulled by the forces of ignorance and craving. Māra asks Selā:

By whom has this puppet been created?
Where is the maker of this puppet?
Where has the puppet arisen?
Where does the puppet cease?

But Selā is too wise for him. She replies:

This puppet is not made by itself,
Nor ... by another. ...
Just so the aggregates ...
And these six bases of sensory contact,
Have come to be dependent on a cause;
With the cause's breakup they will cease.[10]

Because Selā understands the empty nature of the aggregates and sense bases, she is not threatened by the thought of their dissolution. In both cases, the nuns see through him, and Māra vanishes in defeat. Death need not weigh heavily when one has clearly seen the absence of a "being" in the aggregates.

AWAKENING TO WISDOM AND COMPASSION

The promise of awakening is that when we learn to see ourselves and others from the ultimate point of view, we can be freed from confusion, grief, and suffering. We understand that there is no self within our experience, nor is there a self within others' experience. Only the aggregates arise and fall, and even they are empty phenomena. Chinese Buddhist teacher Cheng-li puts it this way: "The winds of circumstance blow across emptiness. Whom can they harm?"

All the changing circumstances of the world are felt in the empty space of consciousness. There is never a "being" who can be harmed by them. Circumstances arise and pass, and it is as if they were never there.

This ultimate way of seeing is what frees the heart from the burden of its preoccupation with self. It also frees the heart from becoming overwhelmed by the suffering of others who are still bound by the conventional view of selfhood, because one knows that there is not a self there suffering—and yet one's heart still quivers with sympathy.

We might say that seeing the ultimate truth of emptiness frees the heart, while seeing the conventional truth of beings opens the heart to compassion. The more our own heart is freed from the burden of self, the more accessible to us is compassion. The fullness of spiritual life involves the development of both these faculties together so that one does not predominate to the exclusion of the other. If seeing emptiness becomes an exclusive focus, there will not be the movement to compassion. There is then the risk of emptiness becoming a fixed view that blocks reflection on the suffering of others. As Nāgārjuna said, "Those who believe in emptiness are incorrigible."[11] If compassion becomes an exclusive focus, there will not be the inner freedom and peace needed for our own balance or for helping others.

As spiritual life matures, we are able to see conventional truth and ultimate truth at the same time. We practice this by learning to see ourselves and others in both ways, through different life situations. As understanding develops, we practice shifting back and forth between the two views so we can see freedom in one moment and compassion in the next. When our understanding is mature, we see the two truths fully integrated—as one reality with two aspects. At that time, wisdom and compassion can be fused, and we practice for our own benefit and for the benefit of others, without being overwhelmed by suffering.

Acariya Dhammapala was a classical Theravadan author of several commentaries that have survived to the present day. Little is known of his life, but it seems likely that he lived in southern India or Sri Lanka some time after the great commentator Buddhaghosa, who lived in the fifth century c.e. His best-known work is *A Treatise on the Pāramīs*, which seeks to inspire the bodhisattva ideal within the Theravada school. In this passage, Dhammapala articulates the profound integration of wisdom and compassion that motivates the bodhisattva.

> Through wisdom the bodhisattva brings himself across (the stream of becoming), through compassion he leads others across. Through wisdom the bodhisattva understands the suffering of others, through compassion she strives to alleviate their suffering. . . . Through wisdom he aspires for Nibbāna, through compassion he remains in the round of existence. . . . Through compassion the bodhisattava trembles with sympathy for all, but because her compassion is accompanied by wisdom her mind is unattached.[12]

The bodhisattva's aspirations can be summarized as follows:

> Crossed I would cross, freed I would free, tamed I would tame, calmed I would calm, comforted I would comfort, attained to

Nibbāna I would lead to Nibbāna, purified I would purify, enlightened I would enlighten![13]

Even as an awakened being works tirelessly for the liberation of others, he or she always remembers that emptiness is the true nature of oneself, others, the aggregates and sense bases, the path, and even enlightenment. One's life and work in the world are summed up in this Tibetan saying: "My dreamlike body appeared to dreamlike beings to show them the dreamlike path to dreamlike enlightenment."

As you journey along this path of awakening, I hope that your heart will never stop responding to the many forms of suffering in this world, and that you will always have faith in your ability to find inner freedom in the midst of it. If you keep emptiness at the center, it will show you the way to the greatest freedom, and that will open the doors to a heartfelt connection to all of life. When emptiness is possible, everything is possible.

ACKNOWLEDGMENTS

I'M VERY GRATEFUL to Bhikkhu Anālayo for his careful reading of the text and for his many kind comments which helped bring it into closer alignment with the perspectives of Early Buddhism, which is my home as well. The deviations that remain are my own. Bhikkhu Bodhi has been an invaluable resource through his masterful translations of the Pali discourses, which have become my primary Dharma view. The book has also benefited enormously from my very skillful editors, and I deeply thank Josh Bartok at Wisdom for his bold and wise pruning, Arnie Kotler for his crisp wordsmithing, Nancy Burnett for her structural clarity, and Catherine Madore for her final exacting read.

SOURCES AND ABBREVIATIONS

Works cited often will be abbreviated as follows.

PALI TEXTS

AN	Anguttara Nikāya
Dhp	Dhammapada
DN	Dīgha Nikāya
Iti	Itivuttaka
MN	Majjhima Nikāya
Sn	Sutta Nipāta
SN	Samyutta Nikāya
Ud	Udāna
Vsm	Visuddhimagga

SANSKRIT TEXTS

MMK   Mūlamadhyamakakārikā by Nāgārjuna

ENGLISH TRANSLATIONS

CDB   *The Connected Discourses of the Buddha: A New Translation of the Samyutta Nikāya*, translated by Bhikkhu Bodhi (Somerville, MA: Wisdom Publications, 2000)

LDB   *The Long Discourses of the Buddha: A New Translation of the Dīgha Nikāya*, translated by Maurice Walshe (Somerville, MA: Wisdom Publications, 2005)

MLDB   *The Middle Length Discourses of the Buddha: A New Translation of the Majjhima Nikāya*, translated by Bhikkhu Ñānamoli and Bhikkhu Bodhi (Somerville, MA: Wisdom Publications, 1995)

NDB   *The Numerical Discourses of the Buddha: A Translation of the Anguttara Nikāya*, translated by Bhikkhu Bodhi (Somerville, MA: Wisdom Publications, 2012)

Num   *Numerical Discourses of the Buddha: An Anthology of Suttas from the Anguttara Nikāya*, translated and edited by Nyanaponika Thera and Bhikkhu Bodhi (Walnut Creek, CA: AltaMira Press, 1999)

NOTES

INTRODUCTION

1. MMK 24.14, in Stephen Batchelor, *Verses from the Center* (New York: Riverhead Books, 2000), 124.
2. DN 33.1.10, in LDB, p. 486.
3. Public talk, Madison, Wisconsin, July 22, 2008.
4. Spirit Rock Meditation Center regularly offers online video classes in beginning meditation practice. Another good resource is the *Insight Meditation Kit* by Sharon Salzberg and Joseph Goldstein, which includes a book, CDs, and online access to an instructor.
5. Edward Conze, *A Short History of Buddhism* (London: Unwin Paperbacks, 1986), 45.

1. THE WORLD IS EMPTY OF SELF

1. Sri Nisargadatta Maharaj, *I Am That*, part 2, trans. Maurice Frydman (Bombay: Chetana, 1978), 43.
2. SN 22:99, in CDB, p. 957.
3. MN 113.21, version by author.
4. SN 35:85, in CDB, p. 1163.

5. SN 1:25, in CDB, p. 102.
6. SN 44:10, in CDB, p. 1393.

2. THE FAULTY LOGIC OF "I"

1. Shunryu Suzuki, *Zen Mind, Beginner's Mind* (New York: Weatherhill, 1973), 110.
2. J. Krishnamurti, *Freedom from the Known* (Bombay: B. I. Publications, 1982), 96.
3. MN 35.13, in MLDB, p. 325.

3. WHAT IS REAL?

1. Sri Nisargadatta Maharaj, *I Am That*, part 1, trans. by Maurice Frydman (Bombay: Chetana, 1978), 237.
2. SN 35:23, adapted from a translation in *Teachings of the Buddha*, ed. Jack Kornfield (Boston: Shambhala Publications, 1996), 41.
3. Adapted from MN 22.38, in MLDB, p. 234; and SN 22:86, in CDB, p. 938.
4. Oliver Sacks, *An Anthropologist on Mars* (New York: Vintage Books, 1996), 114.

4. THE FIVE AGGREGATES ARE NOT SELF

1. Sri Nisargadatta Maharaj, *I Am That*, part 1, 233.
2. SN 12:61, in CDB, p. 595.
3. Alice Collett and Bhikkhu Anālayo, "Bhikkhave and Bhikkhu as Gender-inclusive Terminology in Early Buddhist Texts," *Journal of Buddhist Ethics* 21 (2014): 782.
4. MN 109.15, in *MLDB*, p. 890.
5. Ajahn Chah, *Living Dhamma* (Thailand: Wat Nong Pah Pong, 1981), 88.
6. MN 109.10, in MLDB, p. 889.
7. MN 109.11, in MLDB, p. 889.
8. MN 109.16, in MLDB, p. 891.
9. SN 22:33, in CDB, p. 877.
10. Theragāthā 16:1, adapted from a translation by Bhikkhu Ñānananda, in *Nibbana: The Mind Stilled*, vol. 2 (Sri Lanka: Dharma Grantha Mudrana Bharaya, 2004), 168.

5. CREATING A SELF

1. Advice to Joseph Goldstein, 1967. Personal communication.
2. MN 18.
3. MN 18.16, in MLDB, p. 203.
4. Timothy Wilson, University of Virginia at Charlottesville, *Science* magazine, July 4, 2014. Reported in many news sources, including the *Washington Post*, July 3, 2014.

5. Sn 1103, adapted from K. R. Norman, *The Rhinoceros Horn and Other Early Buddhist Poems* (London: Pali Text Society, 1984), 178.
6. AN 3:38, in *The Life of the Buddha*, trans. Bhikkhu Ñāṇamoli (Kandy, Sri Lanka: Buddhist Publication Society, 1992), 9.
7. SN 21:2, in CDB, p. 714.
8. Yongey Mingyur Rinpoche with Helen Tworkov, *Turning Confusion into Clarity* (Boston & London: Snow Lion, 2014), 31.
9. MN 109.13, in MLDB, p. 890.
10. SN 22:89, in CDB, p. 944.
11. Jack Kornfield and Paul Breiter, *A Still Forest Pool* (Wheaton, IL: The Theosophical Publishing House, 1985), 52.

6. WHEN THE AGGREGATES FALL APART

1. Abridged from SN 12:2, in CDB, p. 534.
2. Adapted from translations by Thanissaro Bhikkhu, http://accesstoinsight.org/lib/thai/mun/ballad.html, and Khemasanto Bhikkhu, http://www.abhayagiri.org.
3. MN 10.
4. MMK 24.8, in Jay L. Garfield, *The Fundamental Wisdom of the Middle Way* (New York and Oxford: Oxford University Press, 1995), 296.
5. MMK 24.10, adapted from David J. Kalupahana, *Nāgārjuna: The Philosophy of the Middle Way* (Albany, NY: State University of New York Press, 1986), 333.

7. BEYOND SELF

1. MMK 18.4, in Batchelor, *Verses from the Center*, 114.
2. Sn 1035, adapted from various translations.
3. Wei Wu Wei, *Posthumous Pieces* (Hong Kong: Hong Kong University Press, 1968), 48.
4. AN 8:54 in NDB, p. 1196.
5. Mahasi Sayadaw, *The Progress of Insight* (Kandy, Sri Lanka: The Forest Hermitage, 1963), 14.
6. "Burnt Norton," *T. S. Eliot: Collected Poems 1909–1962* (London: Faber and Faber, 1974), 192.
7. Li Po, translated by Sam Hamill, in *Crossing the Yellow River: Three Hundred Poems from the Chinese* (Rochester, NY: BOA Editions, 2000).
8. AN 10:2, NDB, p. 1341. In other words, concentration leads to insight, to wisdom. In another passage concentration is called one of the bases of liberation (AN 5:26, in *Num*, p. 130).

9. Ud 1.10, abridged from various translations.

10. AN 1.216, in NDB, p. 110.

11. Sharon Salzberg, *Lovingkindness: The Revolutionary Art of Happiness* (Boston: Shambhala Publications, 1995).

12. "The Trip Treatment," in *The New Yorker*, Feb. 9, 2015, p. 45.

8. BEARING EMPTINESS

1. Carl Sagan, *Contact* (Logan, IA: Perfection Learning, 1997).

2. Quoted in Christina Feldman, *The Buddhist Path to Simplicity* (London: Thorsons, 2001), 60.

3. Paraphrased from J. Krishnamurti, *Commentaries on Living, First Series* (Wheaton, IL: Theosophical Publishing House, 1986), 244.

4. *The Dhammapada*, verse 290, translated by Gil Fronsdal (Boston: Shambhala Publications, 2005), 75.

5. Wall hanging, "The True Meaning of Life," http://taraimports.com.

6. Sharon Salzberg, *Faith: Trusting Your Own Deepest Experience* (New York: Riverhead Books, 2002), 12.

7. Bhikkhu Bodhi, *The Noble Eightfold Path* (Kandy, Sri Lanka: Buddhist Publication Society, 1994), 116.

9. KARMA: PATTERNS OF BECOMING

1. Question and answers with Western Buddhist teachers, Dharamsala, India, ca. 2000.

2. AN 6:63, in NDB, p. 963.

3. MN 9.4ff, in MLDB, p. 132.

4. AN 1:284, in NDB, p. 114.

5. MN 9.4, in MLDB, p. 132.

6. AN 4:62, in NDB, p. 453.

7. AN 4:62, translated by Thanissaro Bhikkhu in *Handful of Leaves*, vol. 3 (Valley Center, CA: Metta Forest Monastery, 2003), 86.

8. Dhp 1–2, adapted from translations by Narada Thera, *Dhammapada* (New Delhi: Sagar Publications, 1972), 1, 5; and Thomas Byrom, *Dhammapada: The Sayings of the Buddha* (Boston: Shambhala Publications, 1993), 1–2.

9. MN 135.4, adapted from Ven. Nyanatiloka, *Buddhist Dictionary* (Kandy, Sri Lanka: Buddhist Publication Society, 1980), 92; and MLDB, p. 1053.

10. Paraphrased from Sharon Salzberg, *Lovingkindness*, 147.

11. MN 141.

12. SN 36:21, in CDB, p. 1278.

13. MN 86, in MLDB, p. 710.

14. MN 19.6, 19.11, in MLDB, p. 208–9.

15. Adapted from several versions, e.g., Sharon Salzberg, *Lovingkindness*, 83.

16. AN 4:77.

10. WHO IS REBORN?

1. In the film *The Search for Signs of Intelligent Life in the Universe*, Jane Wagner (author), John Bailey (director) (Los Angeles: Orion Classics, 1991).

2. Stephen Batchelor, *Buddhism Without Beliefs: A Contemporary Guide to Awakening* (New York: Riverhead Books, 1997).

3. Vsm 13.13ff. The Burmese master Pa Auk Sayadaw has trained many disciples in this method.

4. Dr. Ian Stevenson, *Children Who Remember Previous Lives* (Charlottesville, VA: University of Virginia Press, 1988).

5. SN 3:20, adapted from P. A. Payutto, *Good Evil & Beyond* (Bangkok: Buddhadhamma Foundation, 1993), 104.

6. MN 60.

7. Public talk, Spirit Rock, ca. 2005.

8. SN 12:12, in CDB, p. 541.

9. MN 38.26, in MLDB, p. 358.

10. DN 15.21, in LDB, p. 226.

11. AN 3:61, in Num, p. 63; see also NDB, p. 269.

12. CDB, note 24, p. 733.

13. Chapter 6 in Peter Harvey, *The Selfless Mind: Personality, Consciousness and Nirvana in Early Buddhism* (Richmond, UK: Curzon Press, 1995).

14. SN 12:2, in CDB, p. 534.

15. Ibid.

11. THE END OF KARMA

1. Quoted in Alan Watts, *The Way of Zen* (New York: Pantheon Books, 1962), 133.

2. MN 109.14, in MLDB, p. 890.

3. Sri Nisargadatta Maharaj, *I Am That*, part 1, 263.

4. Adapted from various translations online and with thanks to Claire Gesshin Greenwood.

5. *Webster's New Collegiate Dictionary*, 8th ed. (Springfield, MA: Merriam-Webster, 1973).

6. Quoted by Suzuki Roshi in *Zen Mind, Beginner's Mind*, 75.

7. MN 98.61, in MLDB, p. 807.

8. AN 2:19, adapted from translations by Bhikkhu Bodhi, NDB, p. 150; and Nyanaponika Thera, *Anguttara Nikaya I* (Kandy, Sri Lanka: Buddhist Publication Society, 1981), 10.

9. SN 22:101, adapted from CDB, p. 960.

10. AN 7:67, adapted from Nyanaponika Thera, *Anguttara Nikaya II* (Kandy, Sri Lanka: Buddhist Publication Society, 1988), 89.

11. Sri Nisargadatta Maharaj, *I Am That*, part 2, 7.

12. Iti 60; see also AN 8:36, with *bhāvanā* understood to mean *mettā*.

13. MN 26.18, in MLDB, p. 260.

14. Dhp 154, adapted from translations by Narada Thera, *Dhammapada* (Sagar Publications, New Delhi, 1972), 140; and Thanissaro Bhikkhu, *Dhammapada* (Barre, MA: Dhamma Dana Publications, 1998), 43–44.

15. MN 4.

16. MN 4.32, in MLDB, p. 106.

17. AN 4:232, in NDB, p. 601.

18. AN 4:234.

19. AN 4:237, in NDB, p. 605.

20. MN 141 and AN 5:177.

21. Sn 744–45, adapted from translations by H. Saddhatissa, *The Sutta-Nipāta* (London: Curzon Press, 1985), 87; and Norman, *The Rhinoceros Horn*, 124.

22. *Tao Te Ching*, 2–3, trans. Stephen Mitchell (New York: Harper & Row, 1988), 2–3.

12. ABIDING IN EMPTINESS

1. T. S. Eliot, "Burnt Norton."

2. Suzuki, *Zen Mind, Beginner's Mind*, 129.

3. MN 26.34ff.

4. MN 55.7.

5. MN 121.3.

6. MN 151.2.

7. MN 121.

8. MN 121.4, in CDB, p. 965.

9. MN 121.4, in CDB, p. 966.

10. Thanissaro Bhikku, "Emptiness," http://www.accesstoinsight.org/lib/authors/thanissaro/emptiness.html.

11. MMK 18.5.

12. MN 122.6, in CDB, p. 972.

13. Luang Pu Dun, in *The Island: An Anthology of the Buddha's Teachings on Nibbāna*, ed. Ajahn Pasanno and Ajahn Amaro (Redwood Valley, CA: Abhayagiri Monastic Foundation, 2010), 118.

14. "Deforestation in Thailand," Wikipedia, http://en.wikipedia.org/wiki/Deforestation_in_Thailand.

15. The total forest cover in Thailand today is around 29 percent, but only 13 percent is from primary forests. Source: http://rainforests.mongabay.com/20thailand.htm.

16. Mun, "Ballad of Liberation from the Khandhas," adapted from a translation by Thanissaro Bhikkhu, http://www.accesstoinsight.org/lib/thai/mun/ballad.html.

17. Ibid.

18. Ibid.

19. Suzuki, *Zen Mind, Beginner's Mind*, 35.

20. Upasika Kee Nanayon, *Pure and Simple*, trans. Thanissaro Bhikkhu (Somerville, MA: Wisdom Publications, 2005), xiv.

21. Ibid., 2.

22. Ibid., 24.

23. MN 43.35, in MLDB, p. 395.

24. Kee, *Pure and Simple*, 25.

25. AN 4:199, adapted from various translations.

26. SN 1:23.

27. Bhikkhu Ñānamoli, trans., *The Path of Purification* (Kandy, Sri Lanka: Buddhist Publication Society, 1975), 1.

28. Ibid.

29. Suzuki, *Zen Mind, Beginner's Mind*, 128.

30. Anālayo, *Compassion and Emptiness in Early Buddhist Meditation* (Cambridge, UK: Windhorse Publications, 2015).

13. CESSATION AND NIBBĀNA

1. Suzuki, *Zen Mind, Beginner's Mind*, 85.

2. SN 1:1, adapted from *An Anthology from the Samyutta Nikāya: Part Two*, trans. Bhikkhu Ñānananda (Kandy, Sri Lanka: Buddhist Publication Society, 1983), 1.

3. SN 12:23, adapted from CDB, p. 556.

4. AN 7:83, adapted from NDB, p. 1100.

5. *Webster's New Collegiate Dictionary*, 8th ed.

6. Dhp 290, quoted in chapter 8 of this book.

7. MN 14.5.

8. Dhp 203.

9. AN 10:91, in NDB, p. 1461.

10. MN 64.9, adapted from MLDB, p. 540; and Bhikkhu Ñānananda, *Mind Stilled*, 1.

11. *Tao Te Ching*, verse 1, adapted from several translations.

12. MN 26.19, in MLDB, p. 260.

13. Ud 8.3.

14. MN 26.19.

15. SN 35:117, adapted from Bhikkhu Ñānananda, *The Magic of the Mind* (Kandy, Sri Lanka: Buddhist Publication Society, 1974), 77; and CDB, p. 1191.

16. *Koans of the Way of Reality*, Case 108, quoted by John Daido Loori Roshi in *Mountain Record* 21, no. 1 (Fall 2002).

17. Private conversation, May 2010.

18. Private communication, 2004.

19. Ajahn Maha Boowa, *Straight from the Heart*, trans. Thanissaro Bhikkhu (Udorn Thani, Thailand: Wat Pa Ban Taad, 1987), 121ff.

20. Ibid., 123.

21. SN 56:11, in CDB, p. 1846.

22. Robert E. Buswell, Jr., *Tracing Back the Radiance: Chinul's Korean Way of Zen* (Honolulu: University of Hawaii Press, 1991), 102.

14. A LUMP OF FOAM

1. Suzuki, *Zen Mind, Beginner's Mind*, 104.

2. *Buddhadharma*, Summer 2002.

3. "Odor," Wikipedia, http://en.wikipedia.org/wiki/Odor.

4. From NDP Group, Feb. 5, 2015, http://www.statisticbrain.com/perfume-industry-statistics.

5. From NDP Group, Feb. 5, 2015, http://www.statisticbrain.com/restaurant-industry-statistics.

6. AN 4:159.

7. SN 22:95, adapted from CDB, p. 951.

8. T. W. Rhys-Davids and William Stede, eds., *Pali-English Dictionary* (Oxford: Pali Text Society, 1998), 571. Hereafter abbreviated as *PTS Dictionary*.

9. Ibid., 304.

10. Ibid., 88.

11. AN 7:66.

12. AN 1:576–82, adapted from NDB, p. 129.

13. SN 6:6, in CDB, p. 243.

14. SN 22:97, abridged from CDB, p. 956.

15. SN 22:95, op. cit.

15. THE MAGIC SHOW

1. MN 76.7, DN 2.23, SN 24:5.

2. MN 140.13.

3. AN 3:61.

4. Bhikkhu Bodhi, MLDB, p. 47.

5. For example, DN 14.2.18, DN 15.22, SN 12:65, SN 12:67.

6. SN 12:65, in CDB, p. 602.

7. Ibid.

8. SN 12:67, in CDB, pp. 608–9.

9. DN 15.22, adapted from LDB, p. 226.

10. SN 22:95, op. cit.

11. See for example Dr. Gary Schwartz, *The Afterlife Experiments: Breakthrough Scientific Evidence of Life After Death* (New York: Atria Publishing Group, 2002).

12. AN 4:45, in NDB, p. 435. Here the cessation of the world is to be understood as a synonym for the cessation of suffering, as was the cessation of consciousness in chapter 13.

13. A. F. Price and Wong Mou-lam, trans., *The Diamond Sutra and the Sutra of Hui-Neng* (Boston: Shambhala Publications, 1990), 53.

14. Dhp 46, in Gil Fronsdal, *The Dhammapada*, 12.

15. Jean LaFond, conversation, November 1998.

16. Private communication, 2004.

16. THE MIDDLE WAY

1. Suzuki, *Zen Mind, Beginner's Mind*, 109.

2. SN 12:15, in CDB, p. 544.

3. Adapted from many translations; line numbers have been added.

4. Suzuki, *Zen Mind, Beginner's Mind*, 138.

5. MMK 18.7, translation by Stephen Batchelor, http://stephenbatchelor.org/index.php/en/verses-from-the-center.

6. Price and Wong, *The Diamond Sutra and the Sutra of Hui-Neng*, 70.

7. Adapted from several translations.

8. Adapted from Alan Watts, *The Way of Zen*, 99.

9. MMK 24.8–10, adapted from various translations.

10. MN 22.13, in MLDB, p. 228.

11. Sn 803, adapted from various translations.

12. Sn 837, adapted from H. Saddhatissa, *The Sutta-Nipāta*, 98.

13. Sn 847, in Jack Kornfield, ed., *Teachings of the Buddha* (Boston: Shambhala Publications, 1996), 117.

14. Bhikkhu Bodhi, *A Comprehensive Manual of Abhidhamma* (Seattle: BPS Pariyatti Editions, 2000), 13. This book is recommended as an introduction to the Abhidhamma and the *Patthāna*.

15. SN 12:21, in CDB, p. 552.

16. MN 28.28.

17. MMK 24.18, in Jay L. Garfield, *The Fundamental Wisdom of the Middle Way*, 304.

17. THE NATURE OF AWARENESS

1. Suzuki, *Zen Mind, Beginner's Mind*, 35.
2. Ibid.
3. Wei Wu Wei, *Posthumous Pieces*, 82.
4. Ajahn Pasanno and Ajahn Amaro, *The Island*, 195.
5. Ibid.
6. SN 35:23.
7. *Wu-men kuan*, Case 41, adapted from various translations including Stephen Batchelor, *Verses from the Center*, 26; and Alan Watts, *The Way of Zen*, 92.
8. Lama Shabkar, *Flight of the Garuda*, chap. 4, trans. Stephen Batchelor, unpublished, 1996.
9. Suzuki, *Zen Mind, Beginner's Mind*, 83.
10. MN 62.17, in MLDB, p. 530.
11. Buddhadasa Bhikkhu, *Heartwood of the Bodhi Tree: The Buddha's Teaching on Voidness* (Somerville, MA: Wisdom Publications, 1994), 33.

18. WOMB OF THE BUDDHAS

1. Lex Hixon, *Mother of the Buddhas* (Wheaton, IL: Quest Books, 1993), 198.
2. Shabkar, *Flight of the Garuda*, chap. 4.
3. AN 1:51–52, adapted from NDB, p. 97.
4. DN 11.85, adapted from LDB, p. 179.

19. SUNLIGHT IN AN EMPTY SPACE

1. Taigen Dan Leighton, *Cultivating the Empty Field* (Boston: Tuttle Publishing, 2000), 30.
2. Iti 43, *The Udāna and the Itivuttaka*, trans. John Ireland (Kandy, Sri Lanka: Buddhist Publication Society, 1997), 181.
3. Ud 8.1, ibid., 102.
4. SN 45:139, in CDB, p. 1551.
5. SN 43:19.
6. SN 43:25.
7. SN 43:1.
8. AN 3:130.
9. Buddhadasa Bhikkhu, *Heartwood of the Bodhi Tree*, 28.
10. Bhikkhu Bodhi, CDB, p. 1444.
11. Ajahn Maha Boowa, *Straight from the Heart*, 100.
12. Joseph Goldstein, *One Dharma* (New York: HarperCollins, 2002), 10.
13. SN 12:64, in CDB, p. 601.

14. Saint John of the Cross, *Dark Night of the Soul*, trans. E. Allison Peers (Grand Rapids, MI: Christian Classics Ethereal Library, 1994), 78. Thanks to Lila Kate Wheeler for this reference.

15. Ud 8.3.

16. SN 43:22.

17. SN 48:42, in *An Anthology from the Samyutta Nikāya, Part III*, trans. M. O'Connell Walshe (Kandy, Sri Lanka: Buddhist Publication Society, 1985), 77–78.

18. AN 10:58 in *The Island*, ed. Ajahn Pasanno and Ajahn Amaro, 128.

20. AWARE OF AWARENESS

1. Dudjom Lingpa, *Buddhahood without Meditation* (Junction City, CA: Padma Publishing, 1994), 151.

2. Suzuki, *Zen Mind, Beginner's Mind*, 47.

3. Ajahn Jumnien, talk at Spirit Rock, translated by Jack Kornfield, May 30, 1997.

4. Buddhadasa Bhikkhu, *Heartwood of the Bodhi Tree*, 26.

5. Dudjom Lingpa, *Buddhahood without Meditation*, 129.

6. Tulku Urgyen Rinpoche, *As It Is*, vol. 1 (Hong Kong: Rangjung Yeshe Publications, 1999), 53.

7. Douglas Harding, http://www.headless.org/on-having-no-head.htm.

8. Surya Das, *The Snow Lion's Turquoise Mane* (San Francisco: HarperSanFrancisco, 1992), 206.

9. AN 7:61, in NDB, p. 1061.

10. Dhp 122, adapted from various translations.

11. Stephen Mitchell, *The Enlightened Heart* (New York: Harper and Row, 1989), 89.

12. AN 4:21, condensed from NDB, pp. 406–7.

13. Sn 837.

21. COMPASSION COMES FROM EMPTINESS

1. MN 21.11, adapted from MLDB, p. 221.

2. SN 21:2.

3. SN 15:1.

4. MN 4.34, in MLDB, p. 107.

5. Shantideva, *A Guide to the Bodhisattva's Way of Life*, trans. Stephen Batchelor (Dharamsala, India: Library of Tibetan Works and Archives, 1979), 176.

6. His Holiness the Dalai Lama and Victor Chan, *The Wisdom of Forgiveness* (New York: Riverhead Books, 2004), 137.

7. SN 22:12, adapted from translations in *An Anthology from the Samyutta Nikāya: Part III*, trans. M. O'Connell Walshe, 20; and CDB, p. 553.

8. Vsm 16.90 and 19.20, from translations by Bhikkhu Ñāṇamoli, *The Path of Purification*, 587; and Nyanatiloka, *The Word of the Buddha* (Kandy, Sri Lanka: Buddhist Publication Society, 1967), 43.

9. SN 5:10, in CDB, p. 230.

10. SN 5:9, in CDB, pp. 228–29.

11. MMK 13.8.

12. Dhammapala, *A Treatise on the Pāramis*, in Bhikkhu Bodhi, trans., *The Discourse on the All-Embracing Net of Views* (Kandy, Sri Lanka: Buddhist Publication Society, 1978), 259.

13. Ibid., 251.

GLOSSARY
OF PALI AND SANSKRIT TERMS

Below is a list of the frequently used Pali and Sanskrit terms in this work, along with their meaning and a phonetic guide to their pronunciation. The great majority of the words are from Pali. Where a word is from the Sanskrit, it will be indicated by "Skt." before the definition is given. The pronunciation of Pali words is quite standardized, but there is more complexity than we have indicated in the simple rules below. See, for example, *Introduction to Pali* by A. K. Warder for more detail. Nonetheless, we trust that English speakers can make themselves well understood with these renditions.

Pronunciation of vowels:

a	as in "cut"
ā	as in "father"
i	as in "king"
ī	as in "keen"
u	as in "put"
ū	as in "rule"

e   as in "way," as in "bed" before a double consonant

o   as in "home," as in "got" before a double consonant

The consonants:

g   as in "get," phonetically "g"

c   as in "chat," phonetically "ch"

ñ   as in "canyon," phonetically "ny"

ṁ   as in "song," phonetically "ng"

A consonant followed by an "h" indicates a slight outbreath, as in "Thailand," not like "that." Double consonants like "dd" are both pronounced, as in "bad dog." Accents tend to go on the syllable before a double consonant or with a long vowel, but they are less stressed than in English. The cerebrals (or retroflexes) (ṭ, ṭh, ḍ, ḍh, ṇ) are spoken with the tongue on the roof of the mouth; the dentals (t, th, d, dh, n) with the tongue on the upper teeth.

ahaṁkāra: I-making; identifying the self as being something. See also *mamaṁkāra*.

anattā: Not-self. The understanding that all things are without an enduring self or essence.

arahant: In Early Buddhism, a fully enlightened being, completely free from greed, hatred, and delusion; has personally attained nibbāna.

asāra: Insubstantial, without substance.

avijjā: Ignorance, the first of the twelve links in dependent origination; a fetter not removed until full awakening.

āyatana: Base or sphere of sense experience. There are six internal bases (eye, ear, nose, tongue, body, mind) and six external bases (sight, sound, smell, taste, touch, mind object).

bhikkhu: Monk; a man who has taken full ordination in the Buddhist monastic sangha. In meditation contexts, can refer to any sincere practitioner.

bodhicitta: (Skt.) Awakening heart; literally, awake mind. The aspiration to become awakened in order to help all other sentient beings reach awakening.

brahma vihāra: Divine abiding(s). Four states to be developed in relation to oneself and other beings: *mettā, karuṇā, muditā, upekkhā* (see under individual entries).

buddha: A self-awakened being. Capitalized, refers to the historical person, Siddhattha Gotama, who awakened in our era and became the first teacher of the Dhamma.

cetanā: Volition; could also be translated as motivation or intention. The mental factor underlying *kamma* that determines the wholesome or unwholesome nature of an action.

dāna: Generosity, an act of giving.

Dhamma: (Skt.: Dharma) The teaching of the Buddha; truth, law, the way things are, nature.

dukkha: Usually translated as suffering; also includes the full range of the disagreeable experiences in life, including the unsatisfactoriness and unreliability of conditioned things.

ekaggatā: One-pointedness or unification of mind; a synonym for concentration.

jhāna: A state of strong concentration sometimes described as an absorption.

kamma: (Skt.: karma) Literally, action. In the Buddha's meaning, action with volition. Generally, the law that actions with wholesome volition have wholesome results while actions from unwholesome volitions have unwholesome results.

karuṇā: Compassion, the second of the four *brahma vihāra*.

khandha: Aggregate. The five aggregates of *rūpa, vedanā, saññā, sankhāra, viññāṇa* (see under individual entries) describe the range of human sense experience.

khanti: Patience, one of ten *pāramī* in Theravada Buddhism.

Madhyamaka: (Skt.) Mahayana school of philosophy founded by Nāgārjuna, teaching the Middle Way.

Mahayana: (Skt.) Literally, great vehicle. The Buddhist schools that emerged around 100 B.C.E. based on the Perfection of Wisdom and other texts. These schools continued to evolve through the Yogācāra and today form the basis for most Northern Buddhist schools in Tibet, China, Japan, and Korea.

mamaṁkāra: My-making; identifying the self as owning something. See also *ahaṁkāra*.

māna: Conceit, the tendency to take oneself to be something; also the tendency to compare oneself as being greater than, equal to, or less than another.

maññanā: The activity of conceiving of a self.

mano: Mind, as a sense organ; mind organ. The sense base that cognizes mind objects.

māyā: (Skt.) Illusion. The belief that the world of the senses is solid and substantial.

mettā: Loving-kindness, or good will. The first of the four *brahma vihāra* (see entry, above).

muditā: Sympathetic or appreciative joy. The third of the four *brahma vihāra* (see entry, above).

nāmarūpa: Name-and-form. The combination of the body with five mental factors (contact, feeling, perception, volition, attention) necessary for naming or discriminating objects.

ñāṇa: Knowledge; specifically in Buddhism, knowledge gained from an insight into the nature of things.

nekkhamma: Renunciation, one of ten *pāramī* in Theravada Buddhism.

nibbāna: (Skt.: nirvana) Refers to both the unconditioned element and also the liberated state of mind of an arahant. The goal of Early Buddhist practice is the realization of nibbāna, which brings an unshakable peace.

nibbidā: Disenchantment; loss of fascination with sense objects.

nimitta: Sign; an individual characteristic of an existent thing.

nirodha: Cessation, ending, stopping; often said of the ending of craving.

pabhasarram: Radiance or luminosity; a sign of the purified mind.

papañca: Conceptual proliferations; thoughts that swirl away uncontrolled and out of touch with the reality of the present moment.

pāramitā: (Skt.) Perfection. In Mahāyāna Buddhism, the six qualities that must be developed in order to become a buddha: generosity, virtue, patience, energy, concentration, and wisdom.

pāramī: Perfection. In Theravada Buddhism, the ten qualities that must be developed in order to become a buddha: generosity, virtue, renunciation, wisdom, energy, patience, truthfulness, determination, loving-kindness, and equanimity.

paṭicca samuppāda: Dependent arising, the principle that all conditioned things arise based on prior causes and conditions. Also dependent origination, the description of twelve causal links from ignorance to suffering, including the chain contact-feeling-craving-clinging.

phassa: Contact through one of the six senses. The meeting of a sense object, sense organ, and sense consciousness.

prajñāpāramitā: (Skt.) Literally, perfection of wisdom. Capitalized, refers to the body of Mahayana Buddhist literature having to do with the identity of emptiness and form.

puñña: Merit, or wholesome action.

ritta: Void, being devoid of, empty.

rūpa: Material form. As the first aggregate, includes the body, the five physical sense organs and objects, and all physical matter.

saddhā: Faith. Could also be translated as confidence or trust.

sakkāyadiṭṭhi: Personality view; believing oneself to be or to own something.

samādhi: Concentration, collectedness, composure, unification of mind.

samatha: Tranquility, serenity. A type of mindfulness practice, distinguished from *vipassanā* (see entry, below).

samsara: Literally, "wandering on." Denotes the cyclic nature of conditioned existence for sentient beings, with birth followed by death, followed by another birth.

saṁvṛiti : (Skt.) Conventional, when spoken of the two kinds of truth. Literally, all-concealing.

Sangha: Traditionally, the community of monastics or practitioners who are partly or fully awakened; modern: community of committed practitioners.

sankhāra: Volitional formations, or formations. As the fourth aggregate, refers to all mental factors, states of mind, moods, emotions, and thoughts. In other contexts, *sankhāra* means conditioned phenomena.

saññā: Perception. The act of recognizing or categorizing an object at one of the sense doors. One of the five *khandha* (see entry above).

sati: Mindfulness, the seventh factor of the eightfold noble path.

sīla: Ethical conduct, virtue, morality. Conduct aligned with certain ethical precepts.

sotāpanna: Stream-enterer, one who has reached the first stage of awakening and uprooted the first three fetters by directly realizing the unconditioned, nibbāna.

sukha: Happiness, with a connotation of contentment and ease.

suñña: (Skt.: shūnya) Empty. Lacking self or substance.

suññatā: (Skt.: shūnyatā) Emptiness. Attribute of something that is empty. Also a meditative state characterized by simplicity of perception; a meditative state that does not add to reality.

sutra: (Skt.) Literally, thread; in Mahayana Buddhism, it refers to a canonical text, usually in Sanskrit.

sutta: Literally, thread; in the Pali Canon, one of the discourses spoken by the historical Buddha.

taṇhā: Craving. In the four noble truths, the cause of suffering. Manifests as greed, aversion, and delusion.

tathatā: Suchness. The unique and individual expression of an existent thing.

Tathāgata: Synonym for the Buddha; the term Gotama Buddha often used to refer to himself. Literally, either "the one thus come" or "the one thus gone."

tathāgata garbha: (Skt.) Literally, womb (or embryo) of the tathāgatas; commonly translated as buddha nature.

Theravada: Literally, way of the elders. One of the eighteen schools of Early Buddhism; the only one alive today and the only one with a complete canon. Adjective: Theravadan (about the school) or Theravadin (a follower of the school).

tuccha: Hollow, empty, vain.

upādāna: Clinging or grasping. The ninth link in the twelvefold chain of dependent origination, following craving.

upekkhā: Equanimity. A balance of mind free from greed and aversion. The last of the four *brahma vihāra* and one of the ten *pāramī* (see entries above).

vedanā: Feeling, or feeling tone. The quality in each sense contact of being pleasant, unpleasant, or neither-pleasant-nor-unpleasant.

vimutti: Liberation, release.

viññāṇa: Consciousness. Primarily refers to the six types of sense consciousness, but is occasionally used for the broader field of conscious experience.

vipassanā: Insight. An outcome of mindfulness practice, distinguished from *samatha*. Sometimes used as a general term for styles of insight meditation.

virāga: Dispassion; literally, without lust. Also connotes fading away.

yathābhūta ñāṇadassana: Knowing and seeing things as they are.

Yogācāra: (Skt.) Literally, the practice of yoga. A later Mahayana school characterized by an emphasis on the primacy of mind, thus sometimes called the Cittamatra, or Mind-Only, school.

INDEX

wandering of, 56
See also awareness; interest . . .
autopsies: observing, 76–78
avenues of insights into not-self, 85–97
See also calm/stillness; enlightenment;
   impermanence; spaciousness; unification
   of mind
avenues of learning/understanding/wisdom,
   6–7, 31, 50
aversion, 66
See also greed, aversion/hatred, and
   delusion
awakening: to wisdom and compassion,
   264–66
See also enlightenment
awareness, 211–53
   of awareness. *See* meditation on awareness
   definition, 213, 218
   discovery of, 212
   emptiness of. *See under* emptiness
   enlightenment and, 169–70
   as the field of consciousness, 212–13, 218
   as knowing/cognizance, 213, 214, 215–16,
      219, 220, 227
   looking toward, 246–47
   meditation on. *See* meditation on
      awareness
   and nibbāna, 237
   radiance/luminosity, 220, 226, 227, 228, 236
   trust in, 150, 159, 171
   vast, 96
   See also attention; consciousness;
      experience
ax handle metaphor, 137

B
Ba Khin, U, 182–83
Bāhiya, the Buddha's instruction to, 93–94,
   215

"Ballad of Liberation from the Aggregates"
   (Mun), 75, 152–53
base of nothingness, 4
bearing the truth of emptiness:
   fear of emptiness, 62, 100–1
   losing old ideas of/goals for oneself, 101–3
   qualities for, 104–6
belief in a self, 14, 55, 61–62, 97
   argument for, 109
   See also ideas of a self; sense of self/"I"
Berra, Yogi, 137
big mind, 213–14
Big Sky Mind. *See under* meditations
birth:
   consciousness and, 188
   of the self, 69–70, 83
birth and death, 75, 127
   See also life and death
blamelessness, bliss of, 112, 161
blaming others for their suffering, 117–18
blind man story, 34
bliss of blamelessness, 112, 161
Bodhi, Bhikkhu, 106, 128, 180, 207
bodhi verse (Huineng), 203
bodhicitta, 260
Bodhidharma, 217
bodhisattva, 265–66
the body:
   and consciousness, 78–79
   and experience, 29
   "I" as (taken to be), 19–20, 25, 42–43, 49
   mindfulness of, 181–83
   as nature, 42–43
   and personality, 74–75, 109
body scan. *See under* meditations
book cover metaphor, 191–92
Boorstein, Sylvia, 120
boundary between self and the world, 95–96
boundlessness of consciousness, 227, 228
brahma vihāras, 94

of oneness, 132. *See also* insights into
  phenomena
sensory. *See* sense experience
See also awareness; the present moment

F

fading away of craving, 162–63, 223
faith, 103, 105–6, 160
  leap of for abiding in emptiness, 159
  source of, 123
falling apart of the aggregates, 73–82
fear:
  of death, 22
  of emptiness, 62, 100–1
  reality vs., 149–50
fearlessness of Adhimutta, 51–52
feeling (feeling tone), 32–33, 36–37, 59, 61,
  65, 70
  emptiness, 184
  meditation on (exercise), 38–39
feelings. *See* emotions
finding the source of suffering, 31
finding the true meaning of life, 102
first stage of enlightenment (stream-entry),
  50, 96–97, 171, 194–95
five aggregates. *See* the aggregates
flawed assumptions re self/"I," 22–25, 25
  See also "continuity" of self . . .
flowers of Māra, cutting off the, 193
forbearance (patience), 104–5
forest practice, 148–49, 152, 154, 258–59
to forget everything, 157
to forget the self, 132
forgetting not-self, 97
form (material form), 32, 36
formations. *See* volitional formations
four imponderables, 122
four noble truths:
  Ajahn Dun's formulation, 151–52
  as concepts, 205–7

third noble truth, 145. *See also* cessation
freedom, 75, 92–93, 97, 106, 223–24, 226–27
  compassion and loving-kindness as from,
    257–60, 262, 266
  See also enlightenment (awakening/
    liberation)
Freud, Sigmund, 100
a friend's story and reality, 80–81
fundamental and conventional views, 80–82
Fundamental Verses on the Middle Way
  (Nāgārjuna), 192–93, 198–99
future and past, 78–79

G

gap between death and rebirth, 129
gap in experience, 168
generosity, 139
giving no attention to signs, 150–54
goals. *See* purpose
Goenka, S. N., 182–83
Goldstein, Joseph, 214–15, 220, 235
good conduct. *See* ethical conduct
Goodman, Trudy, 136
grace, 167
grasping, 66–67, 68, 206, 223, 226–27, 258
  See also clinging/holding on; selfing
greed, 66
  in modern culture, 13
greed, aversion/hatred, and delusion, 66, 68,
    135, 142, 154, 195, 228, 243
  abandoning, 193
  end of, 165
  opposites, 111
  withering of, 163
ground of consciousness, 192
guilt for our own suffering, 117

H

habits, 121–22, 134–35
  changing, 135–36, 136–37

happiness (*sukha*), 47
  karma and, 112–14, 116
  kinds/forms, 161–62
Harding, Douglas: *On Having No Head*,
  246–47
harming others, 13–14, 120–21
hate, 155
  See also greed, aversion/hatred, and
    delusion
hearing (the Dharma), 6, 88–90
Heart Sutra, 187, 199–202, 205, 206–7
Hebb, Donald, 122
helping others, 102, 119–20, 259, 260–61,
  265–66
holding on. *See* clinging...
Honeyball discourse, 58–61
Hongren, 202–4
Hongzhi, 233
Huineng, 202–4
Huike, 217
human condition, 70

I

"I, me, mine," 27
  as conventional, 14–15, 21–22, 42, 45
  duality of "me" and "not me"/self and
    other, 41, 42, 227, 228
  flawed assumptions re, 22–25, 25. *See also*
    "continuity" of self...
  meanings of, 19–21, 23, 25
  as not among the aggregates, 41–42
  my story (I-story), 61–62
  my story and my reality, 81–82
  See also personality; self; sense of self/"I"
I-making, 68–69
  See also selfing
I-story, 61–62
ideas of a self, 14
  losing old ones, 101–2
  See also belief in a self; sense of self/"I"

identification of self. *See* self-identification
ignorance. *See* delusion
illusion, a world of, 191–92
impermanence (change), 4, 46, 70
  benefit, 183
  as constant, 181, 201
  nothing fixed, 133, 138, 206–7, 218
  seeing, 30–31, 53, 85–86
imponderables, four, 122
"independence" of self/"I," 23, 25
"independence" of things, 176
indifference to others, 163, 257–58
inquiry, 211–12
  into emptiness, 8
  questions for, 215–16, 246, 247
insight (meditative insight), 7, 79
  into the law of karma, the Buddha's,
    140–41
  searching and, 217–18
  See also insights into emptiness; insights
    into not-self; insights into phenomena;
    seeing; wisdom
insight meditation, 7, 225
  body scanning, 23
  instructions in, 56
  See also meditation
insights into emptiness: compassion and
    loving-kindness as from, 257–60, 262,
    266
  See also insights into not-self; insights into
    phenomena
insights into not-self, 50, 83–85, 89–90, 97,
  194
  avenues of, 85–97. *See also* calm/stillness;
    enlightenment; impermanence; spacious-
    ness; unification of mind
  as unsettling, 99–100, 103
insights into phenomena, 194, 195
instructions:
  the Buddha's to Bāhiya, 93–94, 215

objects. *See* mind objects; sense objects

the observer: "I" as (taken to be), 20–21, 23, 25, 49

observing autopsies, 76–78

obsession with self, 14

old habits, letting go of, 101–3

On Having No Head (Harding), 246–47

One Dharma (Goldstein), 235

one-pointedness, 9, 91

oneness experience, 132

  See also insights into phenomena

openness. *See* emptiness

origin of suffering, 31, 62, 64, 150

origin of the world, 192

  See also dependent origination

"other" (otherness), 42

others:

  blaming for their suffering, 117–18

  duality of self and other/"me" and "not me," 41, 42, 227, 228

  harming, 13–14, 120–21

  helping, 102, 119–21, 259, 260–61, 265–66

  indifference to, 163, 257–58

  veneration for sages, 251

  wish to benefit, 259–60

the owner (of the body/things/emotions/mind states):

  "I" as (taken to be), 20, 25, 47, 49

  "I" as not (taken to be), 47–48

P

Pali Canon, 8

Pali terms, 9–10

  for emptiness, 180

  for mind, 216–17

Pandita Sayadaw, U, 245

paradox in emptiness, 199–201

paradox of the two truths, 202–4

passive voice instructions, 214–15

past and future, 78–79

past lives: the Buddha's remembering of, 140–41

the path (Buddhist/eightfold path), 5, 116, 197, 228, 250

  the eight factors, 143–44; right effort practices, 116

  "not tarrying and not hurrying," 159

  wholesome actions/karma as, 115–17, 135

  work of, 102, 259

Path of Purification. See Visuddhimagga

patience, 104–5

Patrul Rinpoche, 249

Patthāna, 207–8

paying attention, 211

  to sensations, 29, 56, 178–79, 182–83

  to thoughts and emotions, 29–30, 56–57

  See also investigation; noticing

peace (of mind), 147, 161–62, 169, 195

  See also equanimity

perception (recognition), 33–37, 59, 61, 89

  emptiness, 149, 184

  as just noticing, 3–4

  picking up, 152–53

  simplifying, 148–49

the perfections, 129, 260

Perls, Fritz, 30

"permanence" of things, 175–76, 198

  See also "continuity" of self . . .

a person as described by the Buddha, 27–28

  See also personality

personal responsibility, 113–14, 117

personality, 35, 74, 75, 110–11, 121–22

  the body and, 74–75, 109. *See also under* consciousness

  "continuity," 22, 25, 86, 109, 115, 127, 131

  self-image, 109–10, 134

  See also character; "I, me, mine"

personality view, 48–50, 97, 134

phenomena, 175–208

emptiness/insubstantiality, 3, 6, 175–85,
187–88, 194, 195, 208, 244
insights into, 194, 195
investigation of, 175–85, 187–95. *See also*
noticing; paying attention
nibbāna as the context for, 239–40
seeing. *See* seeing
See also material form; mind objects; sense
objects; things
picking up perception, 152–53
plantain tree image, 184
pleasures, sense, 161–62
power of mindfulness and wisdom, 136
power of new intentions/volitions, 137–39
practice:
basic elements, 6–7
the Buddha's instruction to Bāhiya, 93–94, 215
constancy, 219
effort, 116, 144, 251
forest practice, 148–49, 152, 154, 258–59
noting practice, 245
purpose/goal, 46–47, 57, 64, 135, 139
tireless, 261
Prajñāpāramitā Sutra, 223
presence, 3–4, 223
the present moment, 78–79, 91
interest in experience in, 88, 91, 223
living in, 5
stream metaphor, 133
See also experience
progress in meditation, 56
proliferation of thoughts, 60–61
creation of self by, 61–62
default-mode network, 95
emptiness and, 149
punishment: karma misunderstood as, 118
pure space of knowing: resting attention in,
242–45, 248–49
purification of the mind, 116, 144
purpose (goals):

losing old goals for oneself, 102–3
of spiritual life/meditation/practice,
46–47, 57, 64, 135, 139

Q

questioning the logic of "I," 21–22
questions:
answering, 204
for inquiry, 215–16, 246, 247

R

radiance/luminosity of awareness/the mind,
220, 226–28, 236
Rahula, 219
rainbow image, 192
reality:
concepts and, 201
convention and, 78–79, 82; reflections on,
79–82
vs. fear, 149–50
story and, 80–82
taking refuge in, 244–45, 249
See also the Dharma; truth
rebirth, 125–30
recognition: of the unity of emptiness and
cognizance, 225, 229
See also perception
reflection (on the Dharma), 6–7
refuge in reality, taking, 244–45, 249
relationships, 119–21
renunciation, 102, 151, 159–60
See also letting go
repetitive patterns in the brain, 122
responsibility, personal, 113–14, 117
responsiveness (of mind), 223–25, 229
resting attention in the pure space of knowing, 242–44, 244–45, 248–49
resting mentally/inwardly, 147, 151
results: intentions and, 111–12
See also karma

reverence for the Dhamma, 251
right action ... right view (eightfold path factors), 143–44
   practices for right effort, 116
root. *See* origin
rope metaphor, 137
rudder of intention, 139, 159

S

Saccaka, the Buddha vs., 24
Sacks, Oliver, 34
the sacred in everyday life, 239–40
Sagan, Carl, 99
sages, veneration for, 251
Salzberg, Sharon, 94
samādhi. *See* concentration
samsara, 130
   Lake Samsara, 137–38
   "masters of samsara," 139
   nostalgia for, 102
Sanskrit terms, 9–10
Sāriputta, 63, 148, 189, 233, 257–58
Sayadaw, Mahasi, 85, 168, 235, 245
Sayadaw, U Pandita, 245
schools of Buddhism, 6, 8, 204
searching: and insight, 217–18
   See also finding ...
seeing (sight):
   building sight, 89
   form and, 32
   as it actually is, 50–52
   without a seer/sense of "I," 88–90
   with wisdom, 50–52, 68–69
   See also insight; seeing ...
seeing arising and passing, 85–86, 208
seeing delusion more clearly, 103
seeing emptiness, 4–5
seeing impermanence/change, 30–31, 53, 85–86
seeing karma at work, 119–23

seeing things as they are, 30–31, 50–52, 91, 93–94, 96, 148–49, 160
seeing the two truths, 264–65
seeing the unity of emptiness and awareness/cognizance, 247–48
Selā: Māra and, 263–64
self (the self), 13–171
   the aggregates as not, 41–53
   belief in. *See* belief in a self
   birth of, 69–70, 83
   boundary between the world and, 95–96
   compassion for yourself, 104
   creation. *See* creating/creation of self
   deconstruction of, 73–82. *See also* the aggregates as not, *above*
   duality of self and other/"me" and "not me," 41, 42, 227, 228
   emptiness, 3, 5–6, 14, 41, 73, 194
   flawed assumptions about, 22–25. *See also* "continuity" of self ...
   to forget the self, 132
   ideas of. *See* ideas of a self
   identification of. *See* self-identification
   losing old ideas of/goals for, 101–3
   misunderstanding of, 14, 16
   as not in acts of intention/volition, 114–15
   obsession with, 14
   a person as described by the Buddha, 27–28. *See also* personality
   sense of. *See* sense of self/"I"
   views of, 48; personality view, 48–50, 97, 134
   See also "I, me, mine"; not-self; personality; selfing
self-acceptance, 110
self-centeredness:
   in modern culture, 13
   and suffering, 13–15
   See also selfing

self-identification, 19–26, 133–35
  with the aggregates, 42–46
  See also under "I, me, mine"
self-image, 109–10, 134
selfing, 68–70, 150
  slowing and stopping, 83–98, 103
  and suffering, 70
  See also clinging/holding on; grasping;
    self-centeredness
sensations:
  meditation on (exercise), 26
  paying attention to, 29, 56, 178–79, 182–83
  See also sense contact; sense experience
sense bases (organs and objects), 29
  in meditation, 29–30
  and suffering, 31
  See also sense objects; sense organs
sense consciousness, 64, 166–70, 213, 217,
    227–28, 234, 236–37, 243
  See also sense experience
sense contact (contact), 33, 58–59, 61, 64, 70,
    92, 96
  quality. *See* feeling (feeling tone)
  as unsatisfying, 164
sense experience:
  the body and, 29
  coming back to, 56(2)
  letting go, 151
  loss of interest in, 161–62, 166
  as momentary, 181, 201
  pleasures, 161–62
  thinning out of, 96
  See also sense contact
sense objects, 28
  emptiness, 175–83, 187–88
  naming/categorizing, 34–35, 176
  sense organs and, 29, 64. *See also* sense
    bases
sense of self/"I," 55, 87, 92
  returning of, 97

seeing/hearing without, 88–90
  weakening of, 86–87
  See also belief in a self; "I, me, mine"; ideas
    of a self
sense organs, 28
  and sense objects, 29, 64. *See also* sense bases
sense pleasures, 161–62
  See also sense experience
senses: emptiness, 175–83, 187–88
  See also sense bases (organs and objects)
serving others. *See* helping others
Shabkar, Lama, 217–18, 224
Shantideva, 260–61
Shenxiu, 203
Shorter Discourse on Emptiness (the Buddha),
    148–49, 150
sickness: the Buddha on, 63
sight. *See* seeing
signlessness of consciousness, 227–28
signs: giving no attention to, 150–54
sila. *See* ethical conduct
Silesius, Angelus, 251
simplifying perception, 148–49
"singleness" of self/"I," 24–25
sister's death, 74–75
six sense bases. *See* sense bases
smells: noticing, 177–78
social convention of "I"/"me," 14–15, 21–22,
    42, 45
sounds:
  meditation on (exercise), 38
  noticing, 38, 95, 176–77
source. *See* origin
space:
  meditation as, 219
  sunlight in space images, 236–38
spaciousness, 96
speech:
  right speech, 143
  unwholesome, 112

proliferation of. *See* proliferation of
thoughts
See also concepts; thinking
three aggregates. *See* the aggregates
three avenues of learning/understanding/
wisdom, 6–7, 31, 50
three bases of meritorious actions, 139, 142
three characteristics, 235
threefold nature. *See* buddha nature
Tibetan sayings, 257, 266
Tomlin, Lily, 125
totality of things, 28, 176
See also the aggregates
touch: noticing, 178–79
transcendent dependent origination, chain
of, 160–65
transcending suffering, 160–64
A Treatise on the Pārāmis (Dhammapala),
265–66
the triple gem, 105
Trungpa Rinpoche, Chögyam, 101, 102
trust in emptiness/awareness, 150, 159, 171, 225
trusting wholesome intentions/volitions,
145–46
truth:
discovering, 100–1
finding the true meaning of life, 102
of not-self, 138
seeing. *See* seeing
See also the Dharma; four noble truths;
reality; two truths
Tsoknyi Rinpoche, 139, 195, 205–6
two truths, 202, 205
paradox of, 202–4
seeing, 264–65

U

ultimate truth, 202
and conventional truth, 203–5
seeing, 264–65

The Unbearable Lightness of Being, 100
understanding (learning):
helpfulness, 205–6
of not-self/emptiness, 55, 97
three avenues of, 6–7, 31, 50
See also knowing; misunderstandings;
wisdom
unentangled knowing, 154–57
unification of mind, 87–96
See also concentration; investigation;
loving-kindness
unified mind. *See* concentration
unity of emptiness and awareness/cogni-
zance, 223–25
Goldstein's struggle with, 235
meditation on (exercise), 230–31
recognition of, 225, 229
seeing, 247–48
thought experiment on, 236–37
the universe: morality as embedded in, 123
unwholesome actions, 112, 126
unwholesome intentions/volitions, 111–12,
119
Urgyen, Tulku, Rinpoche, 245, 248, 257

V

Vajirā: Māra and, 262–63
vast awareness, 96
veneration for sages, 251
"Verses on Liberation . . .". *See* "Ballad of
Liberation . . ."
views:
conventional and fundamental, 80–82
right view, 143
of the self, 48; personality view, 48–50,
97, 134
speculative views on karma, 111
wrong/misguided views, 65
viññāṇa, 217
See also consciousness

virtue, 139
    See also morality
Visuddhimagga (Buddhaghosa), 27, 85, 100, 126, 156, 168, 262
volition. *See* intention/volition
volitional formations (formations), 35–36, 184
    new ones, 137–38
    personality as, 35, 74, 75, 110–11, 121–22
    See also thinking

W

wandering of attention, 56
wealth and sense pleasures, 162
Wei Wu Wei, 84, 214
"What am I?," 246
"What is, is . . . ," 149
Wheel of Existence, 64
"Who am I?," 247
"Who is looking?," 247
wholesome actions/karma, 112, 126–27
    as our protection, 130
    as the path, 115–17, 135
    three bases of meritorious actions, 139, 142
wholesome intentions/volitions, 111–12, 119
    trusting, 145–46
wholesome states of mind, 116
will. *See* intention/volition
wisdom, 83, 85, 97
    and compassion, 261–62; awakening to, 264–66

eightfold path factors, 143
nondoing wisdom, 145
power, 136
seeing with, 50–52, 68–69
three avenues of, 6–7, 31, 50
See also knowing; understanding
wish to benefit others, 259–60
witnessing death, 73–78
Wittgenstein, Ludwig, 21
womb of the tathāgatas/buddhas. *See* tathāgata garbha
work of the path, 102, 259
the world:
    as an appearance in consciousness/mind, 191–92
    boundary between self and, 95–96
    emptiness, 14
    morality as embedded in the universe, 123
    origin and cessation, 192. *See also* dependent origination
    See also phenomena
wrong views (misguided views), 65

Y

Yogācāra school, 6

Z

Zen schools, 204
Zenrin Kushu, 131

ABOUT THE AUTHOR

GUY ARMSTRONG has been leading insight meditation retreats since 1984 in the United States, Europe, and Australia. His training included living as a monk for a year in the Thai forest lineage. Guy is a guiding teacher of the Insight Meditation Society and a member of the Spirit Rock Teachers Council. He lives in Woodacre, California.

ALSO AVAILABLE FROM WISDOM PUBLICATIONS

A Heart Full of Peace
Joseph Goldstein
Foreword by H. H. the Dalai Lama

"In this short but substantive volume, Joseph Goldstein, who lectures and leads retreats around the world, presents his thoughts on the practice of compassion, love, kindness, restraint, a skillful mind, and a peaceful heart as an antidote to the materialism of our age."—*Spirituality & Practice*

Wisdom Wide and Deep
A Practical Handbook for Mastering Jhāna and Vipassanā
Shaila Catherine
Foreword by Pa-Auk Sayadaw

"If you are interested in Dharma study, then Shaila's book belongs in your library."—Phillip Moffitt, author of *Dancing with Life*

Know Where You're Going
A Complete Buddhist Guide to Meditation, Faith, and Everyday Transcendence
Ayya Khema

"In this practical volume, Ayya Khema presents a complete meditation course and outlines the benefits accruing to those who do regular practice: letting go, equanimity, and courtesy toward all sentient beings. Throughout are sprinkled a variety of metta meditations of loving-kindness."—*Spirituality & Practice*

Manual of Insight
Mahāsi Sayadaw
Forewords by Joseph Goldstein and Daniel Goleman

"The teachings of Mahasi Sayadaw formed the essential context in which I learned, practiced, and studied meditation. That context is beautifully expressed in this book. I believe, as a Western laywoman who has been able to access the liberating teachings of the Buddha in a direct and pure form, I owe an inexpressible debt to Mahasi Sayadaw's scholarship, understanding, and courage of transmission. It is a great gift to have this translation available."—Sharon Salzberg, author of *Lovingkindness*

Mindfulness with Breathing
A Manual for Serious Beginners
Ajahn Buddhadasa Bhikkhu
Translated by Santikaro Bhikkhu

"A precious yogic manual."—Larry Rosenberg, author of *Breath by Breath*

Essence of the Heart Sutra
The Dalai Lama's Heart of Wisdom Teachings
His Holiness the Dalai Lama
Translated and Edited by Geshe Thupten Jinpa

"Lovingly and wisely edited by Jinpa, the bulk of the book is consumed with a fairly meaty exploration of the Heart of Wisdom sutra, a classical Mahayana text, and as such will be useful to established practitioners as well as neophytes."—*Publishers Weekly*

Emptiness
The Foundation of Buddhist Thought, Volume 5
Geshe Tashi Tsering
Gordon McDougall
Foreword by Lama Zopa Rinpoche

"Geshe Tashi's systematic approach to Buddhist thought allows readers to gradually but surely enhance their knowledge of Buddhism without feeling overwhelmed."—*Eastern Horizon*

About Wisdom Publications

Wisdom Publications is the leading publisher of classic and contemporary Buddhist books and practical works on mindfulness. To learn more about us or to explore our other books, please visit our website at wisdompubs.org or contact us at the address below.

> Wisdom Publications
> 199 Elm Street
> Somerville, MA 02144 USA

We are a 501(c)(3) organization, and donations in support of our mission are tax deductible.

Wisdom Publications is affiliated with the Foundation for the Preservation of the Mahayana Tradition (FPMT).